BAD SEX

Library of Gender and Popular Culture

From Mad Men to gaming culture, performance art to steampunk fashion, the presentation and representation of gender continues to saturate popular media. This series seeks to explore the intersection of gender and popular culture, engaging with a variety of texts – drawn primarily from Art, Fashion, TV, Cinema, Cultural Studies and Media Studies – as a way of considering various models for understanding the complementary relationship between 'gender identities' and 'popular culture'. By considering race, ethnicity, class and sexual identities across a range of cultural forms, each book in the series adopts a critical stance towards issues surrounding the development of gender identities and popular and mass cultural 'products'.

For further information or enquiries, please contact the library series editors:
Claire Nally: claire.nally@northumbria.ac.uk
Angela Smith: angela.smith@sunderland.ac.uk

Published and forthcoming titles:

The Aesthetics of Camp: Post-Queer Gender and Popular Culture
By Anna Malinowska

Ageing Femininity on Screen: The Older Woman in Contemporary Cinema
By Niall Richardson

All-American TV Crime Drama: Feminism and Identity Politics in Law and Order: Special Victims Unit
By Sujata Moorti and Lisa Cuklanz

Are You Not Entertained?: Mapping the Gladiator across Visual Media
By Lindsay Steenberg

Bad Girls, Dirty Bodies: Sex, Performance and Safe Femininity
By Gemma Commane

Conflicting Masculinities: Men in Television Period Drama
By Katherine Byrne, Julie Anne Taddeo and James Leggott (Eds)

Fat on Film: Gender, Race and Body Size in Contemporary Hollywood Cinema
By Barbara Plotz

Fathers on Film: Paternity and Masculinity in 1990s Hollywood
By Katie Barnett

Film Bodies: Queer Feminist Encounters with Gender and Sexuality in Cinema
By Katharina Lindner

From the Margins to the Mainstream: Women On and Off Screen in Television and Film
By Marianne Kac-Vergne and Julie Assouly (Eds)

Gay Pornography: Representations of Sexuality and Masculinity
By John Mercer

Gender and Austerity in Popular Culture: Femininity, Masculinity and Recession in Film and Television
By Helen Davies and Claire O'Callaghan (Eds)

Gender and Early Television: Mapping Women's Role in Emerging US and British Media, 1850–1950
By Sarah Arnold

Gender and Genre in 1990s Hollywood: Challenging Definitions of Sex, Women, and Femininity
By Patricia Di Risio

The Gendered Motorcycle: Representations in Society, Media and Popular Culture
By Esperanza Miyake

Girls Like This, Boys Like That: The Reproduction of Gender in Contemporary Youth Cultures
By Victoria Cann

'Guilty Pleasures': European Audiences and Contemporary Hollywood Romantic Comedy
By Alice Guilluy

The Gypsy Woman: Representations in Literature and Visual Culture
By Jodie Matthews

Male and Female Violence in Popular Media
By Elisa Giomi and Sveva Magaraggia

Masculinity in Contemporary Science Fiction Cinema: Cyborgs, Troopers and Other Men of the Future
By Marianne Kac-Vergne

Pop & Postfeminism: Female Dandyism in Popular Music
By Nathalie Weidhase

Positive Images: Gay Men and HIV/AIDS in the Culture of 'Post-Crisis'
By Dion Kagan

Postfeminism and Contemporary Vampire Romance
By Lea Gerhards

Queer Horror Film and Television: Sexuality and Masculinity at the Margins
By Darren Elliott-Smith

Queer Sexualities in Early Film: Cinema and Male-Male Intimacy
By Shane Brown

Screening Queer Memory: LGBTQ Pasts in Contemporary Film and Television
By Anamarija Horvat

Stand-up Comedy and Contemporary Feminisms: Sexism, Stereotypes and Structural Inequalities
By Ellie Tomsett

Steampunk: Gender and the NeoVictorian
By Claire Nally

Television Comedy and Femininity: Queering Gender
By Rosie White

Tweenhood: Femininity and Celebrity in Tween Popular Culture
By Melanie Kennedy

Women Who Kill: Gender and Sexuality in Film and Series of the PostFeminist Era
By David Roche and Cristelle Maury (Eds)

Wonder Woman: Feminism, Culture and the Body
By Joan Ormrod

Young Women, Girls and Postfeminism in Contemporary British Film
By Sarah Hill

BAD SEX

Sexuality, Gender and Affect in Contemporary TV

By Jacqueline Gibbs, Billy Holzberg and Aura Lehtonen

BLOOMSBURY ACADEMIC
LONDON • NEW YORK • OXFORD • NEW DELHI • SYDNEY

BLOOMSBURY ACADEMIC
Bloomsbury Publishing Plc
50 Bedford Square, London, WC1B 3DP, UK
1385 Broadway, New York, NY 10018, USA
29 Earlsfort Terrace, Dublin 2, Ireland

BLOOMSBURY, BLOOMSBURY ACADEMIC and the Diana logo are trademarks of Bloomsbury Publishing Plc

First published in Great Britain 2025

Cover design: Ben Anslow
Cover image © Elena Durey

A catalogue record for this book is available from the British Library.

ISBN: HB: 978-1-3504-1852-3
PB:978-1-3504-1856-1
ePDF: 978-1-3504-1854-7
eBook: 978-1-3504-1853-0

Series: Library of Gender and Popular Culture

Typeset by Deanta Global Publishing Services, Chennai, India
Printed and bound in Great Britain

To find out more about our authors and books visit www.bloomsbury.com and sign up for our newsletters.

CONTENTS

FIGURES

ACKNOWLEDGEMENTS

First of all, we would like to thank the series editors of the *Library of Gender and Popular Culture*, Claire Nally and Angela Smith, for their interest in and support for including this book on bad sex as part of the series. We are grateful to Veidehi Hans, who has been a fantastic editor throughout the process, and the wider publishing team at Bloomsbury for committing to making the book available to wider audiences. Thank you also to the anonymous reviewers who provided invaluable and generous feedback on the proposal and manuscript.

We are lucky to work within teams of dedicated colleagues and friends supporting us to do interdisciplinary research in queer feminist studies at King's College London; City, University of London; and the University of Greenwich. Thanks also to our colleagues and friends at our former departments who continue to influence our thinking: in particular the Department of Gender Studies at LSE and Middlesex University. We also want to thank the audience and our co-presenters at the Lesbian Lives Conference 2024 in Brighton for your enthusiastic feedback and critique of our writing in progress.

This book has been a refreshing exercise in collective research and writing, inspired by conversations amongst us, as well as our wider queer and intellectual networks of support. Thank you to the many friends, lovers and colleagues who have provided crucial insight, reflection and critique throughout the different stages of writing on bad sex. Thank you in particular to Annette Behrens, Yi and Ho Ting C, Dalia Fleming, Frances G, Dan Glass, Merle Groneweg, Jamie Hakim, Rebekka Hammelsbeck, Sarah Lamble, Kate McNicholas Smith, Tomás Ojeda, Tsari Paxton, Amy Perlin, Mitch Pfeifer, Lydia R, Priya Raghavan, Howie Rechavia-Taylor, Alex Roxton, Seb S, Jazmyn Sadri and Brell Wilson for your time, enthusiasm and care in reading draft chapters and/or discussing the wider ideas of the book. We are indebted to many of you not just for your willingness to watch, analyse and talk about sex on TV with us but also for providing the day-to-day care, community and friendship which allowed us to complete this book.

This book has been inspired by the passionate and insightful community of television, sexuality, gender and media scholars, but also the online reviewers, podcasters, recappers, tweeters, redditors, wiki-contributors and comment writers who build and sustain the online 'kitchen table' of collective TV viewing and analysis. We hope our book adds something to these conversations!

An earlier version of the first chapter, 'Bad Straight Sex and Heteropessimism in *Fleabag*', initially appeared in *Feminist Media Studies* as Holzberg, B and Lehtonen, A (2021), 'The Affective Life of Heterosexuality: Heteropessimism and Postfeminism in *Fleabag*'. *Feminist Media Studies*, 22(8): 1902–17.

SERIES EDITORS' INTRODUCTION

Many of the books in this Library challenge us to look at visual texts that could make us feel uncomfortable, or which deal with otherwise taboo topics. *Bad Sex: Sexuality, Gender and Affect in Contemporary TV* is one such book. Jacqueline Gibbs, Billy Holzberg, and Aura Lehtonen draw on a wide range of Anglophone TV texts from the 2010s onwards to explore how the concept of bad sex has been used for entertainment.

Other books in the series have explored the concept of bad sex in the course of wider discussions, such as John Mercer's *Gay Pornography* (2017), Katharina Lindner's *Film Bodies* (2018), Darren Elliott-Smith's *Queer Horror* (2016) and Gemma Commane's *Bad Girls, Dirty Bodies* (2021). In choosing to focus on television representations since 2010, Gibbs, Holzberg and Lehtonen have echoed the concerns of other contributors to the library who seek to explore postfeminist sensibilities. If we look at Catherine McDermott's *Feel-Bad Postfeminism* (2022), for example, which covers some of the same texts as Bad Sex, we can see how a disillusionment with the promises and supposed freedoms of postfeminism came about following the global financial crash of 2007–2008 and led to a form of 'messy feminism'. In fact, this disillusionment is a factor in the development of Fourth Wave Feminism, a point confirmed in Bad Sex through the choice of texts such as *I May Destroy You*. By adopting a neoliberal lens to their context, Gibbs, Holzberg and Lehtonen are able to provide another layer of attention in their exploration of this shifting terrain of contemporary sexual politics. Technological advances around this time also have an impact on the way gender and sexuality is presented to us, as the online streaming era brings with it markets for previously minoritized subjects, and there has been the concomitant rise in online platforms and social media where fans have discussed and critiqued TV programmes and so influenced future productions. Online chatter, of course, often deals with issues of sex and gender, and provides a space to discuss topics that were previously taboo.

The concept of bad sex is one that Gibbs, Holzberg, and Lehtonen define as 'awkward, complex and disappointing', as well as being outside the normatively heterosexual, monogamous, and reproductive. They argue that this is as a result of a shift towards greater diversity in the production side of TV. Various publications in the library show this has been a long struggle: Marianne Kac-Vergne and Julie Assouly's edited collection, *From the Margins to the Mainstream: Women in Film and Television* (2022), and Sarah Arnold's *Gender and Early Television: Mapping Women's Roles in Emerging US and British Media, 1850-1950* (2022) each demonstrates, in different ways, the journey to wider gendered representation in the TV industry. .

This complex negotiation of power inequalities also includes violence and abuse. This is the territory of another definition of bad sex that Gibbs, Holzberg and Lehtonen's book covers. The use of rape as entertainment was made very clear in Sarah Projansky's seminal study, *Watching Rape: Film and Television in Postfeminist Culture* (2001), where she undermined the complicit view that feminism had achieved equality for women and that inequality could still be seen very clearly in depictions of rape and sexual assault in film and television.

The idea of bad sex as a complex site of unfulfilled promised, awkward feelings and a complex negotiation of power inequalities can also be seen to be played for entertainment. As the authors point out, many of the texts they discuss could be termed 'dramedy', where bad sex and drama is mixed with comedy. Such texts provide a space for diversity, with sexual, gender, age, and racial diversity being prominent in many of these. As such, the links with some of the books in this library mentioned earlier are relevant. However, the focus on viewing such texts through the lens of bad sex is this current book's strength. As they point out, the bad sex from the point of view of a straight cis male in this wide range of programmes is largely absent.

As many books in this library testify, subcultures and previously hidden cultures continue to influence popular culture in intriguing ways.

Claire Nally and Angela Smith

INTRODUCTION
BAD SEX ON THE SMALL SCREEN

Introduction

Everyone seems to be having bad sex. *Time Magazine* wonders 'why everyone is having bad sex (especially young people)' (Yagoda 2023), Katherine Angel in *The Guardian* proposes that 'we need to take bad sex more seriously' (2021b), and questions about bad sex abound on Reddit threads and 'Agony Aunt' style newspaper columns (see e.g. Wiseman 2022). The observation that we live in times of bad sex is peculiar, given that this is also a time in which we are supposedly sexually more liberated than ever, in which sex-positive feminist and queer movements have won crucial victories, and in which sex is omnipresent. Why, then, has sex gone bad? This book suggests that these developments – the queer and feminist struggles for sexual freedom and diversity, and the rise of bad sex – are not contrary to but rather related to and constitutive of each other. At a time when the glossy norms of 'good' straight sex are broken open, and queer, feminist, trans, Black, racialized, and disabled perspectives enter the scene of sex, sex becomes the dilemma it arguably always has been: a site of both pleasure and domination where power dynamics and differences get negotiated, reproduced, and challenged. Bad sex, then, is not so much a complaint or a simple description, but a powerful lens to analyse and understand the contemporary cultural and political landscape of sex and sexuality.

This book develops a critical analysis of bad sex through an examination of contemporary English-language television. Arguably, nowhere has the move to bad sex – awkward, complex, and disappointing – been as pronounced and productive as in diversified representations of sex on the small screen. Fleabag is speaking directly to you while having uncomfortable anal intercourse (*Fleabag* 2016, 2019); Adam from *Sex Education* (2019–23) is pretending to orgasm; and Ash in *It's a Sin* (2021) is condescendingly declining sex with an inexperienced, unshowered Richie. From the straight girls of *Euphoria* (2019–) to the queers of *Feel Good* (2020–21) and *Please Like Me* (2013–16), everyone on our screens seems to also be having bad sex. In their representations of sex as messy, awkward, and disappointing, these shows have become part of a cultural politics that is hotly debated off-screen, acting as key sites through which the latest dynamics of sexual and gendered diversity are negotiated under the contemporary conditions of neoliberalism and growing inequality. What makes these more recent representations of sex and sexuality on TV so interesting is how they chart a new representational landscape of sex that diverts from earlier representations, where sex was usually either dangerous and taboo, or liberatory and glamorous. In particular, they break with the can-do sexual politics of prior shows like *Sex and the City* (1998–2004), *The L Word* (2004–9) and *Queer as Folk* (1999–2000; 2000–5), where sex tended to feature as part of neoliberal, mostly white and middle-class, stories of individual achievement.

Instead, many of the representations we examine in this book dwell on everything in sex that is awkward, unsatisfying, and uncomfortable, and that (even when enjoyable) often fails to live up to its expectations. The storylines and characters examined here frequently ask us to question the very idea of what makes sex good or bad, or what makes an encounter sex in the first place. In developing the titular concept of bad sex, then, this book begins from the premise that the last decade has brought with it more nuanced and diverse representations of sex on screen that in many ways are more interesting and compelling than their predecessors. The diversification of how sex and sexuality are represented is driven by growing diversification on the production side, as women, trans and non-binary, Black and racialized, working-class, and disabled TV professionals carve space in a traditionally white, middle-class, cis male-dominated industry.

As a result of these shifts, the sex depicted in many of these more recent minoritarian representations is *bad* in the double sense of being non-normative and transgressive, as well as awkward or unsatisfactory. It is not just *bad* in the sense of Gayle Rubin's (1984) schema in that it does not conform to normative expectations – heterosexual, monogamous, reproductive – but also in the sense that it is often experienced as bad – awkward, difficult or regrettable – by those having it. In fact, we argue that it is precisely because a greater diversity of people are having sex on TV today that there is now more room to explore all the ways in which sex isn't working for everyone. In other words, sex and intimacy often fail to live up to their affective and political potential, particularly for minoritized subjects, since sex and sexuality remain a dense focal point through which racial, gendered, and sexual inequalities are reproduced.

Through a focus on English-speaking TV shows from the last decade, this book analyses sex as a complex site of unfulfilled promises, awkward feelings, and the negotiation of power inequalities – as an often-disappointing or even outright *bad* object of attachment. We argue that these contemporary representations reveal the affective and political potential of sex in a different guise – not only in scenes of straightforward sexual enjoyment or pleasure, but crucially in those of discomfort, awkwardness and boredom and, in some cases, even violence and abuse. In fact, shows like *I May Destroy You* (2020), which we explore in the book, deal explicitly with non-consensual encounters, sexual violence, and rape; and thus, the question of what separates *just* bad sex from sexual misconduct, rape, and violence haunts our framing of bad sex. The question of what makes sex bad, and, moreover, when it ceases to be understandable as sex, is central to this book precisely because this same question has animated many of the shows under discussion here, along with the broader public discourse on the problematic of bad sex vis-à-vis sexual violence over the last decade. In Bad Sex, we unpack the boundaries of bad sex and explore where such representations sit within the broader structures of sexist, racist, transphobic, ableist, and homophobic violence and injustice explored in these shows.

This does not mean that the shows, and so this book, do not also deal with sex that might be more straightforwardly understood as *good* – fun, easy, pleasurable, or even liberatory. While such representations are clearly present in some of the shows we discuss, we find that often even the good sex fails to live up to its expectations, particularly when it is had by people whose lives are otherwise not going all that well. In such cases, we suggest that radical depictions of good or transgressive sex can also act as an ambivalent promise – unable to actually bring about self-realization, well-being, and social change, despite all the hope we might attach to them. In a context of increasing inequality, environmental collapse and the rise of right-wing authoritarianisms, sex remains a dense focal point of psychic and affective attachments, often unable to hold the emotional weight it is invested with. Thus, we argue that even where sex might be portrayed as increasingly diverse and liberatory for some in the contemporary media landscape, it is often also portrayed as failing to live up to its affective and political potential. In this way, our discussion builds on work that asks what the political potential of sexual and gendered desires is in broader neoliberal contexts of increasing precarity and inequality (Berlant 2011; Illouz 2012; Lehtonen 2023).[1] How do we make sense of the proliferation of bad sex on TV, in relation to the material, racialized, gendered, and classed inequalities generated by prominent neoliberal politics and growing right-wing authoritarianisms – as well as their growing contestations around and through various social justice framings?

In this, we are not the first to identify the move towards the *bad* in contemporary sexual representation, or even to zone in on the concept of bad sex more generally. References to bad sex are replete not only in discourses of sexual violence in the wake of MeToo, which we will discuss in more detail below, but increasingly also in contemporary feminist podcasting and writing about sex (Aronowitz 2022; Cookney 2022; Scott 2019; Seresin 2019), tongue-in-cheek literary analysis (The Guardian 2019) and academic writing on the future of sex and sexuality (Angel 2021a; Srinivasan 2022; Ward 2020). The omnipresence of bad sex also drives a plethora of contemporary think pieces on topics ranging from female voluntary celibacy (Hagen 2024; Saner 2023) and the 'dangers' and promises of gay dating apps (Chen 2023), to Gen Z's distaste for sex scenes (Burton 2023) and changing sexual habits (Willingham 2022) – perhaps suggesting a more recent, detectable shift towards the *de*sexualization of representation, which we will return to in our conclusion. While diverse in their motivations, political inclinations and solutions for a 'better' sexual future, this discourse shares a recognition that sex in the 2010s and beyond can no longer be assumed to be a straightforward 'good' – desired, largely enjoyable, and uncomplicated. It also suggests that if such a sentiment is observable, it is worthy of investigation.

In turning to the depiction of bad sex in contemporary TV, we extend this frame and explore the affective and political potential that representations of bad sex might have in a context where inequality and precarity are deepening, on the one hand, and where sexual rights are imagined to have been substantially achieved, on the other. What affective and political horizons remain open in this highly precarious, but oversexed, neoliberal world? And importantly, how might such horizons be cultivated not just on our TV screens, but in our broader cultures and politics, too? In analysing these questions, Bad Sex builds on and contributes to intersectional queer and feminist work in cultural studies, in particular studies on the changing politics of representation in contemporary screen cultures (Bradbury-Rance 2019; Gill 2008; McNicholas Smith 2020; McRobbie 2004; Sobande 2019a); affect studies and work on public feelings (Ahmed 2010; Berlant 2011; Cvetkovich 2012; Hemmings 2011); as well as contemporary debates about the future of sex (Angel 2021a; Hakim 2019a; Srinivasan 2022; Ward 2020).

If everyone we see on the small screen is having (bad) sex, this is neither a judgement nor simply an observation. Rather, in this book we suggest that bad sex is a key frame for exploring the complex issues of inequality, thwarted political hope, and sustained resistance that are made tangible in (often dismissed) forms of televisual representation.

When sex was still good

If much of the sex we see on our screens is bad, then where did the good sex go? Many readers will remember that representing sex on TV is actually comparatively new, and it used to be (or so we thought) positive, sexy, fun, and fulfilling. Indeed, the new representational landscape we chart as bad sex in this book is a break from the 1990s and 2000s, when sex appeared more explicitly on television for the first time. When in the late 1990s *Sex and the City* depicted the active sex and dining lives of four single, upper-middle-class, white women in New York City, it transgressed televisual boundaries by including storylines about anal sex, vibrators, porn, and bisexuality. For Carrie Bradshaw and her friends, sex was part of a neoliberal narrative of individual success and empowerment – easily available, usually enjoyable, and often something to celebrate. Similarly, in *Queer as Folk*, a group of young gay men partied past the politics of UK homophobia and the aftermath of the AIDS crisis onto Manchester's Canal Street (and later Pittsburgh in the US), enjoying the pleasures and adventures that white, middle-class gay culture had to offer. In *The L Word* a group of feminine, well-heeled, and mostly wealthy lesbians hooked up in West Hollywood's contemporary art galleries, swimming pools, and tennis clubs, where a working-class or butch lesbian was rarely in sight. Pioneering televisual sexual representation by depicting strap-on sex, oral sex between women, lesbian fertility treatments, and threesomes, the show anticipated comparisons to *Sex and the City* through its tongue-in-cheek tagline: 'Same sex, different city'.

This was the era that Angela McRobbie (2004) and Rosalind Gill (2008) famously discuss in terms of its postfeminist sensibility, with its de-emphasis on political practice and 'focus on individualism, choice and empowerment' (Gill 2007: 147) instead. Indeed, *Sex and the City* portrayed cis women's sex positivity as largely disentangled from feminist debates, reframing sexual experimentation as part of individual, consumerist success and fun, while *The L Word* and *Queer as Folk* presented gay and lesbian sex as frequent and almost always affirming – particularly when isolated from the broader queer and LGBT politics of the late 1990s. Seemingly unencumbered by the raging sex wars, economic booms and busts, the AIDS crisis and homophobic politics of the 1980s and 1990s, the characters in *Sex and the City, The L Word*, and *Queer as Folk* had and enjoyed sex often, and rarely discussed any of its social and political implications. In this way, the sex on our screens in the late 1990s and early 2000s was not just new and transgressive, but also overwhelmingly and straightforwardly *good*.[2]

But if the turn of the millennium was marked by a postfeminist sex positivity, as an offshoot of neoliberal and consumerist 'can-do' culture, it was the 2010s that saw the emergence of what Meredith Nash and Ruby Grant (2015) call a 'post?-feminist' sensibility. As a predecessor to the sexual, affective, and political dynamics of many of the shows we discuss in this book, Lena Dunham's *Girls* (2012–17) told the stories of four women struggling through their twenties. These 'girls' were as securely positioned in their middle-classness and whiteness as the protagonists of *Sex and the City*, but written to be more average, more broke and more angsty than them. Through the affect of 'cringe' and an undertone of irony, viewers witnessed characters achieving almost nothing in their romantic and professional lives that they had been told they were entitled to, while having mostly average, awkward sex, shot in low light and unflattering poses (Gill 2017a; Havas and Sulimma 2020). Where postfeminism had been marked by televisual representation that underlined the promises of neoliberalism, in the context of the global financial crisis, the entrenchment of social inequalities and the erosion of middle-class entitlements, *Girls* was celebrated for its authenticity in depicting the legacy of an era defined by disappointment, apathy, and irony. While the show came to be increasingly critiqued for its racial and class myopias (Blay 2017; Holmes 2022), it is hard to ignore *Girls* as a forerunner of a new televisual genre that we capture here through the concept of bad sex.

The rise of bad sex

Indeed, five years before MeToo would renew a public discourse about consent, sexual politics, and sexual violence, viewers of *Girls* engaged in heated discussion of the limits of bad sex. While the show had been heralded for its 'more nuanced representation' (Nash and Grant 2015: 983) of young women's sexuality on screen, the season 2 episode 'On All Fours' featured main love interest Adam dominantly instructing his

Figure 0.1 Natalia avoids Adam's eyes after the controversial scene in *Girls*. *Girls* © Apatow Productions/HBO 2012–17.

new girlfriend Natalia through a sexual encounter that she was visibly distressed by. Sitting up in the messy, low-lit bedroom, Natalia avoids Adam's eyes and tells him: 'I don't think I like it like that . . . I, like, really didn't like that' (Figure 0.1). Earlier, it had been the confident and sexually liberated Natalia who had guided Adam through sex using the practice of 'enthusiastic consent' – which Angel (2021a) considers the new expectation placed on straight women's speech during and about sex as the guarantor that it will stay *good*. In the reviews and online discussion that followed, Adam and Natalia's sexual encounter, with its chilling undertones of misogynistic revenge and objectification, was controversially labelled as 'grey rape' (Lyons 2013).

With the benefit of ten years, the coarseness of the phrase 'grey rape' to describe an encounter that clearly broke previously discussed understandings of pleasure, consent, and trust feels somewhat uncomfortable.[3] But it is interesting precisely because the scene prompted particularly younger, straight, white, cis women to share and discuss their uncomfortable and uncertain, and at times horrible, experiences of sex (or the ambivalent feelings they had after it) – in other words, it made into a topic of public discourse and deliberation just how often sex really was *bad*. This conversation was almost exclusively channelled through a growing base of online recaps, Twitter and Reddit discussions, and the comment sections of online reviews, as well as, we imagine, myriad offline conversations in the pub or around the kitchen table – rather than taking place in esteemed academic publications or in traditional news media (at least initially). So how is it that a televisual dramedy, which seemed to revel in its ambivalent relationship to both liberal feminist and postfeminist progress narratives, one known for dealing in 'an endless negotiation of objectification and subjectification' (Nash and Grant 2015: 985), became such a poignant example of this one kind of sexual experience? While today *Girls* comes across as a representative of a more common television genre representing the sex lives of particularly located (white, cis, straight and middle-class) millennials, why was it *television* that made possible this collective conversation about the unpleasant realities of sex under neoliberalism, negotiated particularly by young women?

Certainly, *Girls* was not the first television show to depict such a scenario: both television and cinema are replete with scenes of violating sex. However, like a 2015 episode (and the later debate about the writer) of *Master of None* (2015–21), these televisual moments seemed to capture something about a shifting public sentiment around gender and sexuality. While these discourses drew on decades of feminist, anti-racist and queer thinking, theorizing, and activism, in this moment they exerted particular pressure on *cultural* representations and spaces of cultural production as interlocutors in this re-energized (and heavily contested) sexual politics (see e.g. Lennon and Alsop 2020). Indeed, in contrast to both the sensationalized, yet routine, sexual violence of procedural police dramas, and the liberatory and enjoyable sex of cable programming of the 1990s and 2000s, the early 2010s seemed to mark the beginning of a more complicated representational landscape, where the ugly, mundane, average, boring, uncomfortable and disappointing (and yes, sometimes violent) were increasingly centred as the key modes and moods of sexual storytelling in Anglo-American television. This landscape constitutes the beginnings of what we frame as bad sex television in this book – now increasingly capturing the triple meaning of the term bad sex: first, non-normative; second, awkward and uncomfortable; and third, often see-sawing back and forth across the boundary between sexual violence and 'just' bad sex.[4]

Since *Girls*, this genre of bad sex TV has arguably only grown in the context of more intersectional sexual and gendered politics, and the ever-expanding neoliberal crisis politics of the 2010s. While remaining ambiguous and multifaceted in terms of their representations of bad sex, increasingly these programmes centre minoritized subjects,women, queer, trans and disabled people as their flawed antiheroes, managing uninspirational (sex) lives in mostly bad and disappointing times. Many of these shows are semi-autobiographical and/or focus on first-person narration in portraying lost and insecure millennials trying to navigate the promises and disappointments, the allures and dangers of sex. Many fall into the genre of 'dramedy', combining elements of traditional dramas, while also providing comedic relief (Havas and Sulimma 2020; Leyda and Negra 2023). This includes stories by and about straight women (*Better Things*; *Catastrophe*; *Chewing Gum*; *Fleabag*; *I May Destroy You*; *Insecure*; *Shrill*; *Starstruck*; *This Way Up*); bisexual women (*Broad City*; *The Bisexual*); lesbians, queer women and trans and non-binary queers (*Feel Good*; *I Love Dick*; *Sort Of*; *Transparent*; *Twenties*; *Vida*; *Work in Progress*); and gay men (*Banana*; *Cucumber*; *Juice*, *Please Like Me*; *Special*). Other more recent shows focus on how a generation of even younger, often Gen Z teenagers navigate the new landscape of bad sex amidst expectations of a supposedly liberated sexuality (*Euphoria*; *Everything Now*; *Gossip Girl*; *Heartbreak High*; *Sex Education*). These shows work in tandem and intersect with (often queer, feminist and trans focused) programmes that look back to the past by either imagining a time in which life was hard but sex was still good (*A League of Their Own*; *Glow*; *It's a Sin*; *Pose*), or by reimagining the classic good sex shows of the early 2000s through a more intersectional lens (*And Just Like That . . .*; *Queer as Folk*; *The L Word: Generation Q*; *Will & Grace*).[5]

While the shows we classify here under the umbrella of bad sex are diverse and not always neatly categorizable through this frame, what they share is complex and honest depictions of sex as a site of simultaneous attachment and disappointment, pleasure and pain, and negotiation and struggle. Many of them feature or even centre queer storylines, and include racialized, disabled, and other marginalized characters who have previously rarely had the chance to have sex on screen. Given the focus on bad sex, it is not surprising that exclusively straight cis male perspectives are largely absent from these shows. Indeed, while television has often featured straight men struggling to *secure* sex and relationships (*How I Met Your Mother; Peep Show*; *The Big Bang Theory*; *The Inbetweeners*), the actual sex they have is rarely a site of interest in these examples, mostly assumed to be good (for them) when achieved. Instead, the shows we focus on centre marginalized, often precarious, millennial and Gen Z characters who, in neoliberal worlds of decline and crisis, try (and mostly fail) to find some meaning and comfort in sex and intimacy. They use irony, humour, cringe, and emotional flatness to represent sex as disappointing, difficult, and weird – *especially* when they manage to have it. Despite these precarities, however, many of the characters we examine sustain their attachments to structures of privilege, from whiteness to middle-classness, perhaps allowing them to dwell in the bad feelings of bad sex with little risk – as we explore in many of the chapters to come.

Thus, here we argue that, despite – or maybe because of – their pessimistic focus on bad sex, shows like *Fleabag, Work in Progress* (2019, 2021), *Feel Good, Special* (2019, 2021) and *Please Like Me* not only include stories revealing about the disappointing boredom of normative sex and heterosexual monogamy but also portray the excitement and pleasure of different, often queer, relationships and forms of intimacy. *Pose* (2018–21) and *It's a Sin* reimagine queer and trans people having sex in the shadow of political and social repression during the AIDS crisis, while through *Sex Education, I May Destroy You*, and *Euphoria* we explore discussions around consent and pleasure in the face of sexual violence, online harassment, and racial fetishization. Many of these shows also allow us to delve into questions of neurodiversity, disability, and mental health struggles, and how they inform and intersect with the pressures and disappointments of bad sex. In an era where diverse representations remain the exception rather than the norm, we take TV cultures as a key site for rethinking the narrative and representational repertoires of sex and sexuality. In this, we insist that televisual representations of bad sex not just contribute to but often instigate broader debates about what good sex is, or might be, particularly for marginalized subjects.

Sex on the small screen

Given the real events and anxieties that have prompted this shifting terrain of contemporary sexual politics, it might seem strange to suggest we might learn something important from fictional television for our understanding of bad sex. Why not focus on newspaper think pieces? Demographic trends or empirical data about changing sexual behaviours? Or the more 'respectable' spaces of cultural analysis – literature and cinema? But it is no accident that our analysis is focused on the televisual rather than the sociological, the empirical, the literary, or the cinematic. Indeed, in contrast to earlier understandings of television as the place of low-brow, non-cinematic, consumer broadcasting – 'the idiot box' – we are hardly the first to suggest TV's increasing (or perhaps 'golden') value and currency in contemporary popular culture, cultural production, and cultural criticism (St James 2013). Following the work of queer scholars like Jack Halberstam (2020) and José Esteban Muńoz (1996), we suggest that it is in the often-devalued and more ephemeral forms of cultural production, such as TV, that queer storylines and counterhegemonic representations of sex can be found and celebrated.

As both a 'technology and a tool of cultural storytelling' (Lotz 2014: 3), TV's place as a cultural mediator has sharpened in the post-network era of the 2010s, now less focused on meeting fast-paced production deadlines and large primetime viewership numbers through single release platforms. Mike Van Esler (2020) argues that recognition of television began in the 1990s with the development of long-form narrative programming, such as *The Sopranos* (1999–2007), and later *Mad Men* (2007–15), *Breaking Bad* (2008–13), *The Wire* (2002–8) and others. Here, the spread of cable networks across the United States allowed for the production of new 'niche' series (albeit US-centric, as well as mostly white, straight, cis male focused), credited for their cinematography, storytelling, and character development – previously particular to indie or arthouse cinema (Lotz 2014; Lyons and Tzioumakis 2023; St James 2013). Just as cable television allowed writers and producers some freedom in representation, alongside shifts and developments in narrative, episodic, and cinematographic form, it became more common to see sex and sexuality, nudity, and graphic violence depicted on our television screens. Even as the sex lives of the much celebrated, complex antiheroes of *The Sopranos* or *Mad Men* were articulated through normative (or in fact, hegemonic) gender, familial, and racial frames, cable television certainly allowed for more sex to appear on screen.

By the 2010s, the development of online streaming services further challenged the dominance of both free-to-air and cable networks in terms of viewership, production, and categorization. The wider availability of the internet drove the global dissemination of nationally produced television, with streaming platforms such as YouTube, Amazon, Netflix, and Hulu providing predominantly US-focused television productions to global audiences. Netflix (with an estimated global audience of 237 million by 2025 (Lee et al. 2021)) has posed a somewhat ambiguous challenge to both traditional TV production and the metrics of 'good' TV (Ford 2019). With the development of 'alt-genre' or 'microtags' capable of recording and marketing to specific groups' genre interests and viewing practices, and the capacity to produce or purchase programming in globally diverse locations, the production of shows once considered too niche or unconventional for mainstream or cable audiences has grown (Ford 2019; Van Esler 2020). Alongside these shifts in production, marketing, and dissemination, the 2010s also brought shifts in TV viewership, tastes, and behaviours. As Amanda Lotz argues, the weekly office 'water cooler' discussion following the 'society-wide viewing of particular programmes is now an uncommon experience' (2014: 5), with binge watching instead becoming the norm particularly for younger audiences' engagement with TV (Steiner and Xu 2020). These changes in audience behaviour and consumption mean that many platforms now release episodic series in one go, and it is not unusual for programmes to be defined by their 'bingeability'. The traditional cliffhanger structure of episodic TV increasingly loses its resonance amongst a knowing audience who might wait only seconds, not days, to consume the next episode.

The new markets of TV have meant that new spaces for formerly minoritized subjects have been created. As part of these shifting demands on viewership and commercial production, women, queer, trans and non-binary, Black and minoritized, working-class and disabled writers, directors, producers, and cast members have grabbed some space within a traditionally white and middle-class, cis male-dominated television industry (Griffin 2023; Oppliger 2022). As a result, representations have at least somewhat diversified, with streaming platforms in particular tending to include higher proportions of queer, trans and racialized characters (Żerebecki et al. 2021). It is thus in recognition of this changing television production landscape, which brings with it a diversified but ambiguous fictional representation of sex, intimacy and sexuality, that this book is positioned within. Furthermore, new, often queer and/or feminist, spaces for television criticism have also arisen (Campbells and Colman 2019; Ford 2019; Williams and Gonlin 2017). While television studies in the 1990s and 2000s started to take an interest in television as a cultural product, it has continued to attract less attention than cinema within academic analysis, particularly where its conventions are not considered traditionally or adequately 'cinematic' (Allen and Hill 2004; Ford 2019; Mittell and Thompson 2020). Instead, arguably some of the most detailed and interesting recent cultural analysis of (sex on) TV has been provided by fans, internet bloggers, and journalists, where the aforementioned shifts in production and casting are being matched by the building of diverse online communities where TV is discussed, dissected, and critiqued.

Within these growing spaces, television has clearly replaced literature and film as the focal site of public cultural critique and discussion – especially when it comes to questions of sex.

Kitchen table methodology

In Bad Sex, we take televisual representation seriously as a cultural site worthy of investigation for its representation and negotiation of the contemporary politics of sex, sexuality, and gender, precisely because of the shifts we have highlighted above. In this, we join forces with emerging scholarship on new TV cultures (see e.g. Benson-Allott 2020; Byrd 2019; Havas and Sulimma 2020; Lane 2019; Leyda and Negra 2023; Sobande 2019a), as well as audience platforms for television critique and discussion that have developed alongside the above shifts in production dynamics. We are inspired by the incisive TV analysis produced by podcasters, bloggers, journalists, and diverse online communities, who chronicle television, and the pleasures of discussing sex on screen, with far more investment than traditional critics and sites of institutional recognition. Episode deconstructions or 'recaps' on websites such as *Den of Geek*, *The A.V. Club*, *Vulture*, and *Autostraddle* exist as an established genre of TV review (Mittell and Thompson 2020), and audiences now commonly engage in collective, 'live' episode deconstruction on Reddit and Twitter (Williams and Gonlin 2017).

Accordingly, many of the series that feature in our analysis have been lauded by fans on social media and in popular reviews for bringing something new or transgressive to conversations around sex and sexuality. Our focus is often on shows that have generated considerable debate and discussion, such as *I May Destroy You*, *Fleabag*, *Euphoria*, *Sex Education*, *It's a Sin* and *Pose*, as well as shows that have perhaps received less attention but nonetheless reveal important aspects of the contemporary cultural politics of sex and sexuality, such as *Feel Good*, *Special*, *Work in Progress*, and *Please Like Me*. In each chapter, we zoom in on one to three main shows, allowing us to explore key themes in the representation and discussion of sex on screen – although often similar themes are also evident in other shows we do not explore. We also contextualize the shows within the broader televisual, political, and representational landscape, and, in some instances, explicitly bring in their public reception.

It is likely that readers of this book will also note some conspicuous absences. Like the lists of 'recommended viewing' that typify television cultures today, some 'big name' shows of the last decade that deal with sex, gender or sexual politics (*Broad City*; *I Love Dick*; *Insecure*; *Normal People*; *Orange Is the New Black*; *Transparent)* do not feature much in the following chapters, just as some less-discussed programmes (*Feel Good*; *Special*; *Work in Progress*) are centred. Many of the shows we discuss here were hotly contested on related terms to those we discuss through the lens of bad sex, or moved into public discourse for their powerful implications for broader sexual and gender politics. Others may have been watched, streamed in a day, forgotten or axed – maybe barely making it to public or private discourse. Indeed, when speaking to others about this book, recommendations of what should be in it proliferated. Certainly, we have also struggled with what to include, or what best captures something about the sexual politics of the present. While some of our (and others') genuine favourites missed out, at the same time our selection is also inevitably shaped by our social and cultural locations as white queer millennials living and working in the UK – and the myopias necessarily resulting from these locations. Thus, we hope that our approach to collective writing and viewing television provides a significant intervention into the exploration of sex, gender, and affect in contemporary TV – rather than a conclusive summary of it. Likewise, we hope it contributes to an already-active and fascinating space of online recapping, analysis, and discussion of contemporary TV cultures. It may even be of interest to those who write television itself.

As three queer millennial writers and teachers in gender and sexuality studies, television has consistently remained a focal point of our personal and academic conversations across the years. Whether meeting between the three of us, or with other queer friends and colleagues, discussion and exploration of TV often operates as an entry point into wider discussions about sex and its personal and political ramifications. This is not surprising, given that we are part of a generation raised amongst emerging technologies, growing up in an era saturated with English-language soap operas, dramas, and comedies – projected into our homes whether we understood them or not, or at least available in the video store in the years before we could illegally download them. More importantly, we grew up in an era also characterized by television's 'first' queers gradually appearing on screen (*Ellen*; *Friends*; *Will & Grace*). All of this taught us early on to look earnestly *at* as well as *to* television – maybe there could be something for us there, too. Growing up in Australia, Germany, and Finland during the era of good sex television, we were only pre-teens imagining what adulthood would look like when Samantha, Carrie, Miranda and Charlotte were first traipsing the streets of New York, only learning what it might look and feel like to be queer when Shane and Bette seduced lesbians in Los Angeles. None of us even lived in the UK then, to be able to imagine walking amongst the gay men of Canal Street one day. But at the same time, despite our (mostly) non-Anglo-American locations, we all remember clearly how we nevertheless felt we had been there with them, and found ways to watch these shows, often secretly, in simultaneous shame and excitement, as ways into our own queer becoming.

Indeed, this book emerges from a decade of conversations analysing, desiring, hating, and loving television as a collective affective experience and a dense site of sexual meaning: Sharing grief for teen years lived without Eric of *Sex Education* or Jules of *Euphoria* as on-screen friends. Texting ecstatically when we read that *The L Word* is coming back, and arguing over whether Carrie and Miranda's new adventures in *And Just Like That . . .* (2021–) live up to our prior attachments and expectations (they do not!). In these ways, our book starts from the kitchen table discussion of television.[6] Here we are deliberately borrowing from the queer concept of kitchen table polyamory, where the 'kitchen table' serves as a metaphor for the idea that contentious and complex dynamics of sexuality, sex, and intimacy can be discussed and unpacked *collectively*, perhaps while sharing a meal with partners, lovers, and significant others (see e.g. Schippers 2019). The idea behind kitchen table polyamory reflects queer practices of communality, where – particularly in the context of broader social misrecognition – coming together with intention can be a way of fostering collective care, resistance to norms of gender and sexuality and alternatives to the perceived dullness of monogamous coupledom. It suggests not only that the challenges and complications of life (romantic, sexual, and otherwise) should be *on the table* to discuss but also that the isolated to and fro of monogamous coupling and the heteronormative family might not offer enough collective space to quell the emotional blows of contemporary romance, sexual expectation, segregated nuclear family life, and neoliberal precarity, for most people.[7]

So, just as we argue that new, active television cultures have emerged to dissect the ins and outs of sex on TV, our book emerges from the belief that television remains better understood as a collective experience – even in the time of online viewership. Thus, rather than treating the shows we analyse here as objects to be consumed and reviewed from the couch alone, our writing process in this book has modelled the modes and forms of consumption that shape TV cultures today – where viewers sit around an often-online kitchen table to dissect, make sense of and navigate all the complicated and diverse things television can mean for them. Similarly, both before and during (and most likely, after!) the writing process for this book, we have often gathered around a metaphorical kitchen table to talk not just about the latest episodes of a show in terms of their content but also about how we feel about them, whether they reflect our own (sexual) experiences, and whether they tell us something interesting about contemporary sexual politics and cultures – with the table shifting variously from a restaurant table, the pub or a WhatsApp group, to a hurried huddle on the street after seeing a film or show together.

We, thus, view the collective practices of blogging, tweeting, commenting, meme creation and frustration over spoilers that typify contemporary TV cultures as an interesting point of intervention in themselves. In writing this book, we have tried to model such a process in our methodology by collectively watching (and usually rewatching) every one of these programmes, shaping the chapters through a process of discussion and shared observation. In practical terms, our method includes taking notes while watching, debating, social media scrolling, rewatching, making connections to other shows we have seen, chit-chatting, sharing many feelings, and arguing – altogether developing something that feels to us a collective process akin to contemporary television consumption, where both viewership of sex on TV and discussions about it happen around the metaphorical kitchen table.

Beyond queer critique

It is further important to note that our readings of these shows do not intend to be primarily or exclusively critical. While critique is a common methodological approach in feminist and queer media studies, and one that we certainly adopt, much of our writing traces our affective attachments, pleasures or ambivalences towards these programmes – the '*and also did you notice*'s, the '*what if*s and '*oh, I must have missed that bit*'s of collective consumption and engagement. In our queer readings of these shows, we focus particularly on the *affective* dynamics of the shows' representations. This involves asking questions such as: How did we, as viewers and consumers of television, *feel* when we watched these shows, or indeed when we talked about them afterwards? How do others (critics, bloggers, other academics) describe their feelings and emotional attachments to the shows, or their characters? How do the characters themselves feel about what is happening to them? Do the shows have an overarching, detectable mood or tone? In asking these types of questions, we are deliberately moving beyond the discursive or textual; while often the narratives, storylines and textuality of these shows also have something interesting to say about contemporary sexual politics, frequently it is in the affective/emotional attachments they cultivate that the most interesting sexual meanings can be found. Importantly then, 'affect' denotes not just individual but also *collective* feelings and attachments.

Accordingly, we are here interested in understanding what forms of collective attachment, excitement and hope, as well as disappointment and hopelessness, these shows engender and make possible in relation to sex – and relatedly, what forms of sexual politics might be enabled (or not) by these attachments. Across this book we suggest that much of the significance of sexual representation in contemporary television is to be found in the wider *affective* attachments and meanings made tangible by these sexual representations – attachments that are often more interesting and productive than the amount, screen time or exact style of good or bad sex on screen. Our methodology and reading practice then focus on identifying what, following Raymond Williams, we might call the wider 'structures of feeling' in relation to sex: a kind of feeling and thinking which is lived, experienced, and talked about 'before it can become fully articulate and defined' (1977: 131). Differently to Williams' emphasis on class and primary focus on the realist novel, we turn to TV to understand emergent forms of sexual politics in the last decade – cultural meanings and affective attachments that are often still 'embryonic' in Williams' terms, but which might give us crucial insights into the negotiation of new, maybe even 'better', sexual futures.

This methodology differs crucially from more classical cultural critique tending to focus on the uncovering of hidden ideologies or power relations below the surface of representation. Jafari Allen (2022), writing on Black queer cultures, has movingly demonstrated the limits of understanding cultural forms through a solely critical stance and disengagement from the life worlds of research. Criticality, after all, is, as Rita Felski (2015) argues, often seen as a 'better' stance to take, if wishing to present oneself as an objective analyst of popular culture. In contrast, being emotionally attached, loving something, caring deeply for something and not being that interested in something are not typically the approaches taken in academic writing about popular cultural forms and representations. As such, it is important for us to claim outright that some of the shows we analyse in these chapters are intensely beloved by us – while others are liked or enjoyed, some disliked or endured, and yet others receive a symbolic shrug, and not much else. The pleasures of watching TV might not always align with on-screen pleasures either – as the book's focus on bad sex suggests. As viewers, we might feel uncertain or alienated, or even disgusted by something that the characters themselves experience as deeply pleasurable or fun; or conversely, we might experience pleasure while watching characters being miserable or having sex that is awkward or 'bad'.

In these ways, our analysis often begins from a complex place of loving or caring attachment to representations that inevitably fail to represent what we hoped, but at the same time engender a deep desire to *talk* about what we just watched. This is particularly the case when we have an ambivalent disappointment with shows that (from a standpoint of criticality) should have felt just right. Such a focus on affect and collectivity is important precisely because it is feelings – love, excitement, disgust, anger, frustration or disappointment – that provide clues as to why fictional television has become such an important interlocutor within the aforementioned politics of sex, gender, and sexuality in the neoliberal present (Berlant 2011; Cvetcovich 2012). If it is the sentiment towards (bad) sex that has shifted, what is it about these fictional representations that enables, or captures, this shift in the structures of feeling? And what does that structure of feeling tell us about the kind of sex that we long for, hope for, in the present?

There is also a temporal dimension to our reading practice, given the collective acknowledgement of *better*-imagined childhoods and youths that the television of today might have provided us with, and the importance television sustains to feeling our way through the political present. In comparison to today's more diversified representations of sex and sexuality, we had to look pretty far, or between the lines, to find representations we *desired* in the era of good sex on the small screen. We now laugh at pretending not to have seen that there was one gay or lesbian kiss on TV in high school; yet we still narrate our personal stories of 'coming out' alongside the trials of *The L Word* or *Queer as Folk*. No doubt, many readers have had to (and continue having to) imagine much harder than we did to mould themselves into the limited, often white and middle-class, archetypes that the television of the 1990s, 2000s and 2010s presented to us. Indeed, we know that television can never carry (and could never have carried) the weight of being both looked *at* and *to* – for meaning, comfort, pleasure, and hope; for queer role models, sex education, and political inspiration.

But, in the European and Australian contexts we grew up with their still limited public and political acknowledgements of queerness, it is perhaps understandable that television was and continues to be where we rest some of that hope.

And we are certainly not the only ones. When talking about this book to friends and colleagues, a common response has been: '*Oh, I wish I had these representations as a teenager*'. The comment presumes two collective agreements: first, that particularly for queer and other minoritized viewers, representations of sexuality on TV are now *better*; and second, that, particularly when it comes to sex and sexuality, television is the space where we can *learn* something about what we might desire, and how to talk about all the difficult places that desire might take us. Bad Sex is driven by interrogating the underlying premises of these assumptions. First, what makes representations of sex and sexuality now 'better' than they were before? While we are undoubtedly in an era of more diverse and complex representations of sex and sexuality, as we suggest throughout this introduction and the chapters that follow, at the same time representations of sex and sexuality over the last decade are much more likely to be of sex that is *bad*. That is, they tend to deal with sex that isn't good, fulfilling or liberatory for anyone, or sex that lingers on the fringes of what makes it sex, what makes it enjoyable and who should have a 'right' to it. Second, the book asks what it is we imagine we learn, collectively, from television, or in other words, what the affective and political teachings of contemporary sex on television might be. Thus, we suggest that we might look *to* television for what it tells us, about ourselves, about sex, about the possibilities of the political present.

In the following chapters, we explore the idea that representations of sex on TV are now better, or have progressed, as they allow us to learn more about the complicated truths and painful realities of sexuality and sex in our lives. That is, in learning that sex can be both liberatory and painful, enjoyable and awkward, we are exposed to pedagogic and affective frames that guide us to talk about and experience the *good*, *bad*, and *good enough* sex, and the many, co-constituted forms of pleasure and power that come to bear on it. And yet, like the implicit curriculum of high school, the lessons we learn from TV are not always straightforward. Many of us remember the message of the homophobic bully in the playground or an awkward sexual encounter with far more resonance than we do the teachings of the official sex and relationship education curriculum. So, in the chapters that follow, we explore what might be understood as the explicit, official curriculum of contemporary television – in its seemingly improved representational diversity – as well as its implicit, affective teachings – which may or may not be that different to the past. Often, we argue that representations of bad sex and sexuality on TV tell us more about the possibilities, nostalgic attachments, and limitations of contemporary political and sexual imaginaries than they do about how to have sex or what the sexual subjects of today should *do*. Thus, we adopt the analytic of bad sex to illuminate the political potential that sexually diverse or non-normative representations might have, in a context of imaginations of already-achieved sexual and gender equality, and simultaneously growing inequality and precarity. By watching, analysing, sometimes critiquing, but always feeling something about the bad sex of our contemporary televisual era, we hope to get closer to what good sex looks like tomorrow, for everyone.

Structure and key arguments of the book

The first three chapters of Bad Sex focus on, at times semi-autobiographical, dramedy shows that emphasize first-person narration to highlight the promises and disappointments that seem to characterize contemporary millennial life. These shows act as exemplars of the bad sex frame, whereby lost and somewhat precarious, but usually white and middle-class, characters struggle to navigate both sex and their wider lives – and sex itself is often experienced as flat, awkward, cringeworthy, or at the very least disappointing. In Chapter 1, representations of bad straight sex in *Fleabag* act as the lens through which we investigate contemporary cultures of heterosexuality. Our queer reading of the show suggests that its focus on bad sex with shitty men needs to be understood as part of a wider heteropessimist sensibility, which critiques the neoliberal, gendered constraints of heteronormativity – yet at the same time creates a renewed investment in them.

Given that Fleabag's (failed) attempts to detach from heterosexual fantasies of the 'good life' serve mostly to highlight how heteronormativity continues to be reproduced in contemporary imaginaries of sex and sexuality, in Chapter 2 we wonder if lesbian and bisexual cis women, or trans and non-binary people, can escape the confines of heteronormativity and do it better. Here we examine the exploration of good, exciting, fun, and experimental queer sex in *Feel Good* and *Work in Progress*, against the backdrop of often painful and uncomfortable stories of chronic mental health conditions and drug dependency. While queer sex for these characters acts as an exciting way of escaping sadness (at least temporarily), at the same time it often remains otherwise untethered from personal happiness, social change and broader sexual politics.

So what about gay men? In Chapter 3, we consider how characters like *Please Like Me*'s Josh and *Special*'s Ryan trouble common representations of gay men as both sexually and professionally successful – often portrayed as the virile and proud champions of new liberated sexual cultures. Like the straight women, lesbians, and trans and non-binary people of the previous two chapters, gay men in these shows are not okay – and the sex isn't always either. Yet, by letting go of the imperative of great sex, both characters find ways to navigate cultures of hetero- and homonormative ableism to find what we call 'good enough sex' – sex that, all things considered, is nurturing, connecting, and joyful. In this way, the two shows invite us to see both the potential and the limitations of dwelling in queer and crip shame around bad sex. So taken altogether, the first three chapters explore the affective attachments and political potentials generated by and within the bad sex frame – what other sexual futures and pleasures could emerge for these unhappy characters, whether straight or queer, beyond their knowing dissatisfaction with disappointing sex? Is pleasurable sex enough, given the otherwise isolated lives many of the characters live, pressured by the neoliberal imperatives of individualized success and self-improvement?

If sex in the present tends to be presented as awkward or difficult, then how do contemporary shows imagine (or reimagine) the sex of the past? The next two chapters offer not just better sex but also often more collective and diverse forms of survival, coaxing us to attach nostalgically to the good sex of the past. Here we suggest that these representations of a time when sex was still *good* tell us more about our own disappointments with the contemporary cultural landscape of bad sex than about the actual sex or sexual politics of the past. In Chapter 4, we examine how the much-celebrated shows *Pose* and *It's a Sin* present the 1980s and 1990s as a time when sex was a site of transformative intimacy, community, and survival, representing sexual and intimate histories which have been largely unreflected in and unsanctioned by dominant televisual frames. These shows take place against the backdrop of the AIDS epidemic, and offer up queer joy, pleasure, and community as a resistant force against the hostile world that saw the characters' (sex) lives as perverse, dangerous, and full of loss.

The last few years have seen nostalgia not only for the representations of good sex in the past but also for the more optimistic shows of the late 1990s and early 2000s. In Chapter 5, we explore *And Just Like That . . .*, *The L Word: Generation Q*, (2019–23) and *Queer as Folk* (2022) as updated versions of foundational postfeminist and post-queer liberatory shows where sex was still *good* – as well as overwhelmingly white, middle-class, and gender normative. The three reboots negotiate their relationships to today's diversified sexual, gender, and queer politics in different ways, with some seeking explicit recuperation, while others try to simply forget the mistakes of the original. Regardless though, here we wonder what is behind the impulse to return to programmes that reflected limited, often exclusionary, sexual politics? Why go back to an ex we now know wasn't that great for us – even if the sex was good? In Chapter 5, we argue that these reimaginings indicate an attachment to the more straightforward (and more homogenous) class, gendered, and racial politics of the era of good sex that they at the same time mark as over; while in Chapter 4, we suggest that the reimagining of a better past (queerer, more joyful, more collective, and with more sex) perhaps tells us more about what we feel we are missing in the present. Given the proliferating scene of bad sex and the broader (political and intimate) difficulties and disappointments of today, it seems to be easier to find good sex and queer community in the past.

If bad sex is the dominant lens of televisual representation of sex in the present, and if in these times good sex can only really exist in a reimagined past, then what are the future possibilities for good, or at least better, sex? Our final two chapters foreground two very different modes of learning to do sex differently in the future. In Chapter 6, we explore how *I May Destroy You* invokes contradiction, humour, and narrative disjointedness to radically but delicately reframe common representations of sexual violence, challenging the essentialized victim/perpetrator binary through intersectional explorations of violence (and responses to it). In this chapter, we explore the implications and possibilities these new representations of sexual violence and trauma carry in the post-MeToo era, questioning if and how common, limited frames of victimization, violence and trauma can be challenged and pressured by more recent cultural forms that portray and enact a more complex, intersectional politics against sexual violence. The last substantial chapter of Bad Sex, Chapter 7, then asks what has really changed in the representation of sex and sexuality as we enter the mid-2020s, given that representations of bad straight sex, stereotypical depictions of sexual violence, and unhappy queer characters continue to proliferate. Here we consider how representations of anxious and uncertain teenage sexuality in *Sex Education* provide some of the more hopeful recent representations of sexual politics – both straight and queer – contrasting this with the popular and glossy, yet also deeply painful and often violent, representation of teen sexuality in *Euphoria*. Through examining these two shows' depictions of teenage sexuality, our final chapter asks what possible affective attachments and pedagogies exist for unlearning bad sex in the future.

All that sex on TV, but what have we really learned? Finally, in the conclusion to the book, we consider what the future of sex on TV might look like, given more recent shifts towards not representing sex at all. Through asking if one solution to the problem of bad sex could be disengaging from sex, we question the political and intimate implications of the turn towards 'no sex'.

Chapter 1

BAD STRAIGHT SEX AND HETEROPESSIMISM IN *FLEABAG*

Introduction

In the introduction to Bad Sex, we considered the televisual cultures of the 1990s and early 2000s as presenting the promise of sexual liberation for some normative, neoliberal subjects – that we explored through the frame of good sex. For characters in shows like *Sex and the City* (1998–2004) and *Queer as Folk* (1999–2000), sexuality was a site of possibility and consumption – and sex was had often and casually on the route towards individualizing self-fulfilment. Yet, while mostly remembered for its explicit representations of female sexuality and the significance of female friendship, by the end of *Sex and the City*, all four characters were in long-term, monogamous heterosexual relationships, reaping heteronormativity's rewards—even if some of the hetero-optimism of the original show is tempered in the 2021 reboot, which we discuss in Chapter 5. Cut to fifteen years later, when Asa Seresin identifies the 'palpable' emergence of 'heteropessimism', consisting of 'performative disaffiliations with heterosexuality, usually expressed in the form of regret, embarrassment, or hopelessness about straight experience' (2019). Aligning with the disappointments of bad sex we have emphasized in our introduction, Seresin notes that while heteropessimism has a long history, it is 'particularly palpable in the present' (2019). A whole genre of cultural production lamenting the sorry state of heterosexuality has emerged across the UK and the US in recent years. Opinion pieces have appeared in popular media outlets from *Buzzfeed* – where Shannon Keating describes 2019 as a 'tough year for heterosexuality' (2019b) – to *The New York Times*, where Stephanie Coontz pointedly asks, 'how to make your marriage gayer?' (2020). Although expressions of heteropessimism provide commonplace cultural references for both men and women, it is particularly women's dissatisfaction with heterosexuality – and heterosexual men – that has gained the most cultural and scholarly traction (see e.g. Angel 2021a; Srinivasan 2022; Ward 2020).

A particularly salient televisual example of heteropessimism is *Fleabag* (2016, 2019) – an 'original bad-girl comedy' (Nussbaum 2016) about the life of a young, white, cis, middle-class single woman in London that earned star and creator Phoebe Waller-Bridge a series of accolades from BAFTAs to Emmys and Golden Globes. Premiering on BBC 3 in 2016, the two seasons of the show generated significant public and scholarly commentary with scholars like Rosalind Gill (2017b) identifying the series as a key cultural object for thinking through contemporary attachments to, as well as detachments from, feminism. Popular readings of the show have tended to situate it within the spate of recent 'dramedy' TV series that centralize complex female 'antiheroes' – from *Girls* and *Broad City* in the US, to *Chewing Gum* and *The Bisexual* in the UK (see e.g. Gill 2017a; Havas and Sulimma 2020; Woods 2019). In contrast, in this chapter we use *Fleabag* to investigate how the women-centred dramedies of the 2010s have commonly deployed a knowing, seemingly feminist-informed, detachment from the good sex of the *Sex and the City* era, where outward expressions of anti-aspirationalism and sexual abjection introduce what, in this book, we call the frame of bad sex. In clever, funny, and sometimes shocking ways, *Fleabag* and other 'precarious-girl comedies' break down many of the strict expectations of contemporary neoliberal femininity by associating their protagonists with failure, cringe, and the messy, embodied experience of female sexuality instead. With its 'endless alienation a source of humor' (Wanzo 2016: 29; see also Woods 2019), *Fleabag* is not only lacking hope about the possibilities of good sex but also resigned to the bad sex of the neoliberal present.

Yet we argue that, in its refusal of alternative feminist and queer possibilities, *Fleabag* sustains an affective attachment to the promises of heterosexual desire, despite much narrative evidence of the likelihood it will continue to disappoint. In this chapter, we thus take a slightly different angle to commentators who have examined *Fleabag* in opposition to the representations of femininity and feminism in the earlier generation of women-centred postfeminist TV shows like *Sex and the City* (Gill 2017b; Havas and Sulimma 2020; Nussbaum 2016; Woods 2019). Rather, we bring a focus on bad sex to bear on the series' representations, to situate it within the cultural moment of heteropessimism, and to ask whether this moment allows other imaginaries of sexual futures to emerge, beyond a knowing dissatisfaction. Our analysis aligns with Seresin's argument that heteropessimism has 'perversely . . . created a renewed investment in the consistency of heterosexuality, a reinscription of heterosexuality's tired features, even as this investment takes the disguised form of negative feeling' (2019). In other words, its affective structure is akin to a shoulder shrug, which, in line with the postfeminist televisual cultures of the late 1990s and early 2000s, fails to present much alternative to the gendered and sexual confines of bad sex.

Bad straight sex

Fleabag's popularity is not surprising, given the intelligent ways in which the show breaks with traditional gender roles and normative expectations of female sexuality, avoiding tropes of feminine innocence and passive sexual desire from the first scene onwards. We meet the main character, Fleabag, opening the door to a man she has called over to have sex with. Looking into the camera, she addresses the viewer directly, commenting that once they are in the bedroom 'after some very standard bouncing, he is edging towards your asshole' and that she lets him as 'he's come all the way here'. Upon waking, the man tells her how special the night has been for him, as it has been the first time he has had anal sex, and kisses her on the forehead. Fleabag seems sceptical of his earnest affection and, turning towards the camera, comments that all she wonders about is: 'do I have a massive arsehole?' In this scene, we encounter the core features that have made the show such a success: Fleabag is crass and unladylike, sceptical of romance and affection, and instead indulges in casual sex with many different men, relishing biting irony and grinding self-doubt.

For most of the first season, we follow Fleabag in her hunt for casual sex. We see her taking her dates to sex shops and seducing her lawyer, a stranger on a bus, and later on even a celibate Catholic priest. All the men Fleabag meets are presented through stereotypical and often vulgar nicknames such as 'Hot Misogynist', 'Arsehole Guy' and 'Bus Rodent'. Bus Rodent (referred to as such for his large front teeth) proves to be not only bad at sex but also emotionally inept and unable to follow her jokes. Fleabag's beautiful lover in the leather jacket, Arsehole Guy, is portrayed as vain and self-involved. What these characters share is a failure to understand or care about Fleabag's inner world. They are also presented as wilfully clueless optimists in the face of the gendered pressures of heterosexual dating – in sharp contrast to Fleabag's witty, pessimistic critique. At least initially, then, the show's general heteropessimist sensibility 'that has a heavy focus on men as the root of the problem' (Seresin 2019) makes perfect sense, given the many disappointing men the show introduces Fleabag (and us) to. Here *Fleabag* wittily illustrates, as Jane Ward notes, that 'straight life is characterised by the inescapable influence of sexism and toxic masculinity, both of which are either praised or passively tolerated in straight spaces' (2020: 8). It is also filled with *knowing* engagements with disappointing, bad sex.

When Fleabag finds herself in a relationship – such as with Harry, a childlike 'nice guy' who keeps returning to her for his toy dinosaur collection – she remains emotionally distant and reverses classical gender roles. While Harry cries after watching *Cats* and cleans her house every time they break up, Fleabag leads him on and masturbates to videos of Barack Obama while he sleeps. When Harry eventually breaks up with her for good, he remains coded feminine/emasculated during the scene by wearing a post-shower towel on his head. It is these sexual transgressions and subversions of traditional gender roles that carry the main feminist potential of the series. Fleabag is not a passive romantic waiting for her Prince Charming, but an imperfect, even selfish, young woman confused about her own desires, yet willing to explore and follow them. As such, female sexual desire in *Fleabag* is portrayed as awkward, difficult, and at times deeply painful – befitting the frame of bad sex. Different from characters such as Samantha Jones or Carrie Bradshaw in *Sex and the City*, Fleabag does not celebrate her sexual desire as part of a larger narrative of individual achievement and neoliberal success (Chen 2013). Instead, the sex she has with selfish men – who rave about her small breasts or try to engage in said anal sex without communicating with her first – is represented as mostly weird and uncomfortable. Such sex scenes that are 'not stylish, nor beautifully-lit, nor artfully filmed' (2017a: 235), as Rosalind Gill notes in relation to *Girls* (2012–17), align more closely with the representative and aesthetic grammar of 'cringe' than that of sexual pleasure or liberation (Havas and Sulimma 2020; Trimmel 2018).

In the second episode of the series, Fleabag confesses that she is addicted to 'the performance of [sex]. The awkwardness of it. The drama of it. The moment you realise someone wants your body', and then adds: 'Not so much the feeling of it'. Her emotionally detached hunt for sex is nearly compulsive, with at times disturbing consequences for her everyday life. When applying for a loan, Fleabag lifts her sweater to reveal nothing but a bra underneath – although it is not clear whether accidentally – not only causing her to lose the loan but also leading the loan manager to ask her to leave. Throughout the

Figure 1.1 *Fleabag* breaks the fourth wall to express her surprise and discomfort during sex with 'Rodent guy'. *Fleabag* © Two Brothers Pictures/ BBC 2016–19.

show, Fleabag continues to joke about rape and make inappropriate comments about her and others' sex lives. When having sex with Bus Rodent, crouched awkwardly over the counter of her café, Fleabag is clearly uncomfortable and comments that it is 'surprisingly bony . . . like having sex with a protractor' (Figure 1.1). In such scenes, Fleabag does not shy away from negative feelings or experiences – if anything, as Faye Woods argues, she 'revels in shame, desire, disgust, pain and joy' (2019: 196) and portrays sex to be 'at times abject, rather than erotic' (2019: 205). As such, *Fleabag*'s sexual representations align with series like *Girls* and *Broad City* (2014–19), which have similarly been celebrated for charting a more vulnerable, complex, and at times abject depiction of female sexuality and the bad sex (disappointing, average or boring) it often involves.

The main character's compulsive search for (bad) sex might be seen as part of the show's wider anti-aspirationalism, which Gillian Silverman and Sarah Hagelin (2018) point out as a key feature of this new wave of female-led television. Born into a white, middle-class family, Fleabag seems to have few career aspirations. She is content with running a small café whose only remarkable features are its guinea pig decorations and 'chatty Wednesdays' attended by lonely locals looking for someone to talk to. Different to *Girls*, where the main character Hannah fails to attain but still desires the glamorous life of a writer like Carrie Bradshaw, career aspirations are not part of the affective grammar of *Fleabag*. This is most evident in the contrast that the series builds between Fleabag and her sister Claire – a successful businesswoman – who is so concerned with appearing successful that she even organizes her own surprise birthday party. As Orlaith Darling argues, it is specifically in the contrast between Fleabag and her sister that the show 'exposes the shortcomings of neoliberal value systems' (2020: 1) of self-reliance, aspirationalism, and gendered hypervigilance. Claire is portrayed as the archetypical neoliberal feminist who prides herself on 'having it all' – a family and a stellar career as the two goals of neoliberal feminist achievement (Rottenberg 2014). Yet, her life is portrayed as bitter and heartless through the running joke that her 'cold heart' would be much happier in Finland, in contrast to Fleabag's messy, uncontrolled, but undeniably more fun existence. At one point in the series, Fleabag, accidentally, yet highly symbolically, even smashes the 'Women in Business' award that Claire is about to present.

Fleabag's anti-aspirationalism comes across most clearly in her rejection of normative heterosexual marriage and family life. All the heterosexual relationships around her are depicted as nightmares: Claire is in an abusive relationship with an undeserving man who drinks too much, makes sexist jokes, and tries to kiss her sister at her 'surprise' birthday party. Fleabag's father is in a codependent relationship with a controlling artist – the Godmother – who pushed her way into his life after Fleabag's mother died. And Fleabag's chances of finding Mr Big seem equally bleak, as all the men she dates turn out to be either selfish, clueless, or both. As viewers, we are invited to join in with the critique of these relationships, as well as the heterosexual desires that underpin them, through the show's emblematic breaking of the fourth wall – to witness 'the entrapment, the disappointment, the antagonism, the boredom, the unwanted sex, the toxic masculinity, and the countless daily injustices endured by straight women' (Ward 2020: 4). In turning to the camera and speaking directly to the audience, Fleabag invites us to share her judgements of heterosexual dating, perhaps exemplifying Ward's argument that 'from a queer point of view, one of the defining features of straight culture is complaint' (2020: 128). When having sex with the Arsehole Guy, for instance, she comments that he is losing his erection because he is falling in love, joking about the pathetic ways in which emotional attachment breaks the performance of virile masculinity. As in Michaela Coel's *Chewing Gum* (2015, 2017) (discussed further below), we, as viewers, are Fleabag's confidantes and intimate accomplices in her biting attacks on straight, white men and heterosexual middle-class life (Brown 2013; Havas and Sulimma 2020; Woods 2019).

While the direct address allows Fleabag to escape reality, as well as to tell us that she *knows* this is bad sex, real solace from the demands of neoliberal, heterosexual dating life is only found in rare moments of female bonding. While Fleabag's relationship with her sister is tumultuous and competitive, they bond in their grief over their mother's death and their dislike for the Godmother, whom they attempt to sabotage by repeatedly stealing her favourite art piece. They cuddle up together after a failed meditation retreat, and Fleabag protects her sister when she has a miscarriage. Yet, the most affectively charged scenes of intimacy are found in the flashbacks with Fleabag's best friend Boo, whose death stands as the pivotal event of the first season that leads Fleabag to seek endless (hetero)sexual distraction. The biting irony and passive aggression that infuses the rest of the series fades in these moments, as we witness Fleabag and Boo laughing, cuddling, and being frank with each other. In these scenes, Fleabag lets her guard down, and, most importantly, the direct address and breaking of the fourth wall disappears. Fleabag does not need to distance herself through an external audience, as she already has an accomplice to confide in right in front of her: Boo.

In *Fleabag*, we get a sophisticated critique of heteronormativity and the cruel demands that it places not only on queer and trans people but also on young straight cis women. Attaching little hope to careers, straight men or heteronormative relationships, Fleabag seems to break with the neoliberal feminist fantasy of a 'good life' found in the double achievement of a high-achieving career and a successful family life (Rottenberg 2014). In this way, *Fleabag* appears to illustrate Lauren Berlant's argument that what they call the 'good life' in fact turns out to be 'for so many a bad life that wears out the subjects who nonetheless, and at the same time, find their conditions of possibility within it' (2011: 27) – thus continuously attaching to the fantasy of it. This feminist antihero is as difficult and self-involved as she is witty and sharp in her dissection of the stale gendered and sexual normativities reproduced through this fantasy. Affective attachment is, in turn, redirected to the intimacy found in strong female bonds – whether these are with Fleabag's sister, her deceased mother or, most importantly, her best friend Boo.

Doing it anyway

At first glance, Fleabag seems to refuse neoliberal aspirationalism, along with the depressing confines of heteronormativity that come with it, similarly to many other protagonists in the 'precarious-girl' genre – a term coined by Rebecca Wanzo to describe shows in the new millennium characterized by 'the nexus of abjection and precarity' (2016: 29). However, while it is clear that career aspirationalism and normative heterosexuality are not working for Fleabag, it is less clear to what extent she still *wants* them to work for her. Although Fleabag is initially struggling to hold onto the café she opened with her friend Boo before her death, in the second season the café is thriving. It is unclear exactly how Fleabag managed to turn the café into a success, but this certainly fits the narrative of the second series where Fleabag is 'doing well' – as if purely by virtue of her being in a better headspace customers have started flowing into her café. This small but not insignificant detail in the series' overarching narrative is just one of the ways in which *Fleabag* remains an undeniably white and middle-class narrative about anti-aspirationalism, for her anti-aspirationalism is only possible because of the various connections she has to structures of privilege. Thus, while in many ways Fleabag matches Wanzo's 'precarious-girl' descriptor, it is important to note that her precarity is first and foremost emotional, not financial.

Fleabag's staunchly middle-class depiction of precarity mirrors but also clearly differs from other precarious-girl comedies like *Insecure* (2016–21) and *Chewing Gum*.[1] Through its main character Tracey Gordon – a young Black woman living on a council estate in London – *Chewing Gum* embraces the precarious girl format to dissect the racialized and classed exclusions that accompany contemporary gender and sexual normativities (Sobande 2019a). For example, when Tracey breaks the fourth wall, it is often less to reassure us of her knowing awareness of the compromises involved in a contemporary pursuit for sexual liberation, but more to comically emphasize her misplaced optimism that it can be achieved. Lying on an unglamorous single bed as her new boyfriend plays Nintendo, Tracey enthusiastically proclaims: 'He doesn't care about anything! I mean, I've got a man who don't even want to leave the house!' Like Fleabag, Tracey sometimes interrupts bad sexual and social experiences to make frank and cutting comments, in contrast to her outward 'awkward physicality' and nervous 'chattering' (Woods 2019: 197). But at other times, such as when she tries to drunkenly seduce her boyfriend in the bathroom of their homelessness accommodation, or when she bombs a job trial offered by her upwardly mobile schoolmate before naively exclaiming that she 'smashed it', Tracy's distance from (and thus critique of) the white, middle-class ease of Fleabag is the source of much of the show's cringe and humour. It also signals a different kind of engagement with the site of (always already) bad sex in *Fleabag*.

In this way, Fleabag matches Rebecca Liu's description of the 'archetypical Young Millennial Woman – pretty, white, middle-class, cisgender, and tortured enough to be interesting but not enough to be repulsive. Often described as "relatable," she is, in actuality, not' (2019). The show frequently mixes cringe aesthetics with representations of conventional feminine beauty and white middle-class respectability (see e.g. Skeggs 1997); in other words, even when Fleabag farts, drinks, jokes about rape, and in other ways challenges normative gender expectations, she looks gorgeous while doing it – and thus remains within the bounds of respectable femininity and desirability. This is in contrast to the representation of Tracey's often quite simple sexual desires (i.e. to have sex for the first time) not only as awkward and cringeworthy but also as naive, misplaced, and even excessive. Whereas Fleabag actively pursues bad sex and almost always finds her desires reciprocated by the men around her (who themselves are having good sex), Tracey's attempts to mirror frames of sexual desirability and lose her virginity are at least initially interpreted by others as dangerously lustful, confusing, and uncomfortable, or even ludicrously racially fetishized in one encounter – when sex is bad, Tracey is often presented by others as the problem.

Thus, while Wanzo argues that 'in the woman-centered sitcom, abjection has been an important affective mode, disrupting the genre's narrative tendency to support a domestic status quo or move women toward marriage and greater professional fulfillment' (2016: 33), she also notes the 'racial and class-based differences in the embrace of not only this twenty-first-century form of comedy but also in modes of self-fashioning in neoliberal times' (2016: 30). For Wanzo (see also Ringrose and Walkerdine 2008), race and class make a difference to how, and to what extent, abjection can feature as part of a character's path towards freedom from the normative expectations of heterosexual femininity. Characters such as Fleabag and Hannah from *Girls* (the topic of Wanzo's analysis) can so easily associate themselves with abjection through their open engagements with and discussions of sex, dirt, and bodily fluids precisely because white, middle-class femininity has historically been associated with purity, and not the abject. As such, Fleabag's light-hearted toying with abject narratives and imagery may undermine and hide the harmful or violent consequences that norms of white middle-class femininity and respectability have for working-class, queer, and trans women of colour – many of which *Chewing Gum* comically exposes.

Relatedly, although the fantasy of heterosexual romance and white, middle-class coupledom is carefully broken down in *Fleabag*, in many ways attachments to them remain. These continued attachments are most notable in Fleabag's relationship with the Priest in the second, generally more optimistic, season. The Priest is a welcome break from the other men in the show – his emotional maturity appears in stark contrast to Fleabag's previous sexual partners. He is the first man Fleabag engages with who shows a genuine interest in her, and it is also with him that her facade of sarcastic detachment starts to crack (if never to the same extent as with Boo). He notices her disassociating while she makes remarks through the fourth wall: 'What is that? . . . That thing that you're doing? It's like you disappear', and she accidentally directs a comment intended at the viewer to him instead ('the arms, the neck'). Fleabag and the Priest seem to experience genuine emotional intimacy, and in the final episode of the series they confess their love to each other. Despite all the ways in which conventional romance has been shown to be futile, stupid, and even dangerous throughout the series, the desire for it reappears in the narrative of the Priest. Most importantly, with the Priest, sex could be good for Fleabag.

Reading the Priest's storyline this way helps at least partially explain what Louis Staples in *The Independent* calls an 'online thirst-fest' (2019a) over the character – perhaps later echoed in similar online responses to the brooding but kind Connell in *Normal People* (2020), or the shy but lovely Colin in *It's a Sin* (2021), discussed further in Chapter 4. The frenzy over the attractive yet unattainable character of the Priest crystallized in particular around a scene in the second season, where Fleabag goes to the church to meet him. The sexual tension is palpable, as the Priest quips to Fleabag: 'Fuck you calling me "father" like it doesn't turn you on just to say it.' He invites her to the confessional booth ('I know what to do with you'), where Fleabag lists her various 'sins' from stealing and lying to extramarital sex. Eventually the jokey tone turns more serious, and after some hesitation, she reveals some of her genuine feelings:

> I want someone to tell me what to wear in the morning . . . I want someone to tell me what to eat, what to like, what to hate, what to rage about, what to listen to, what band to like, what to buy tickets

> for, what to joke about, what not to joke about. I want someone to tell me what to believe in, who to vote for, and who to love, and how to tell them. I just think I want someone to tell me how to live my life, Father, because so far I think I've been getting it wrong.

She says she is scared, and after a pause the Priest replies, 'kneel', and then proceeds to open the curtain of the confessional and kiss her.

One way of reading this scene is through the fantasy of normative heterosexuality. In her most vulnerable moment, Fleabag begs for someone to tell her what to do, and the Priest's command for her to kneel turns what is perhaps originally a broader expression of her lack of direction in life into a sexual desire. Her request is for the Priest to take control of the situation, so as to be liberated from the ways in which 'women's speech about their desire is both demanded and idealized, touted as a marker of progressive politics' (Angel 2021a: 16), or perhaps more generally from the excessive freedoms and choices associated with being a white, middle-class woman in the twenty-first century. This scene thus reflects the common dilemma of femininity Meg-John Barker articulates (in relation to the *Fifty Shades of Grey* films) as 'the desire to be desired and pleasure in pleasing another, and the yearning to remain childlike and not agentic/responsible' (2013: 900), or Ward's suggestion that straight women and men share 'romantic and erotic attachments to an unequal gender binary' (2020: 22). In this sense it is apt the scene takes place in a confessional, as Fleabag confesses to both the Priest and the viewers that all she actually wants is for someone else to be in (patriarchal) control. Here, we are reading the scene as not a queer moment like some commentators have (see e.g. Keating 2019a), but as a yearning for the comfort of conventional and normative heterosexuality, with all of its patriarchal connotations.

Fleabag's relationship with the Priest, however, is suggestive of a desire for heteronormativity only insofar as it is unattainable. An actual relationship between the two is near impossible, and definitively revealed as such in the series' final episode, when the Priest admits that he chooses his love for God over his love for her. While Fleabag's desire for normative coupledom with the Priest remains unfulfilled, it is precisely because of this impossibility that the fantasy of conventional romance can be kept alive. The reality of heterosexual coupledom is deferred, displaced onto an imaginary future, which is perhaps also the reason behind the Priest's seemingly near-universal desirability amongst viewers. Because both Fleabag and the viewer know that the relationship will never be actualized, we can fill it with our own imaginaries instead. Similar dynamics were arguably reproduced in the consumption-driven desire for *Normal People*'s Connell: rather than focusing on finding one's own Connell, the viral 'thirst fest' around the character crystallized around owning the simple gold necklace he wears throughout the series.

This reading is confirmed in the series by Fleabag's sister Claire. When Fleabag tells her that she has 'found someone' and that 'he's a priest', she responds: 'It's just, you're a genius. You're my fucking hero' – as if to signal that she understands it is better to fall in love with the idea of a man, rather than an actual man. If 'disappointment is not how it feels when the object of your attachment fails to give you what you want; rather, disappointment is how it feels when *you* fail to detach yourself from the disappointing object' (2019: 64, emphasis original), as Andrea Long Chu argues, the Priest is the perfect heteropessimist object of desire – he can never disappoint because he is always already unattainable. Fleabag's desire for the unattainable Priest, thus, in some ways mends or bypasses the commonly encountered endless but ineffective efforts that many straight women put into repairing shitty straight men (Ward 2020).

In the final episode, Fleabag's father is about to marry the Godmother. The scenes at the wedding present a further shift in Fleabag's attitudes towards romantic relationships: she first supports her sister in following her perfect match, Klare, to the airport, choosing a romcom-like possibility over her disappointing marriage, and then calms her father when he has last minute nerves (despite perceiving his marriage as constraining to him). Her father reciprocates by saying of his future wife: 'Look I know she's not . . . everyone's cup of tea [they both laugh]. And neither are you, darling' – suggesting to Fleabag that she also has a chance of finding someone who will accept her, despite her unlikeability. Thus, at the end of the series, conventional heterosexual coupledom reappears as the inevitable goal, undermining some of the earlier more critical sensibilities. The final scene sees Fleabag walk away after saying goodbye to the Priest, and as the camera starts following her, she turns around, smiles and shakes her head, and then waves at us. Fleabag's goodbye to the viewer suggests she no longer needs the sarcastic, detached disassociation that the breaking of the fourth wall has provided her throughout the series – between abjection and aspirationalism, Fleabag chooses heteronormative aspirationalism and the quest for good sex, after all.

Repudiation of queer alternatives

But is Fleabag a straight woman? So far in this chapter we have assumed so, despite plenty of evidence to the contrary. In the very first episode of the series, Fleabag tries to pick up a woman: when she sees a very drunken woman fall down at the bus stop, Fleabag helps her into a cab and then asks, 'Do you want to come home with me?', to which the woman replies, 'What?! No way! You naughty boy'. Another encounter takes place in the second season, between Fleabag and Belinda, who has received the 'Women in Business' award presented by Claire's company. Fleabag runs after Belinda in the rain to retrieve the Godmother's statue that she has been mistakenly given as the award and later makes a pass at her – only to be rejected.

Given Fleabag's explicit attempts to sleep with women, it is somewhat surprising that much of the commentary on the show has missed her flirtations with lesbianism or bisexuality, labelling her as straight instead. As well as the explicit encounters mentioned above, lesbian references are scattered throughout the series: Fleabag makes a lesbian joke to her sister ('Do you know what the lesbian app for Grindr is called? – Twatnav'), the Godmother introduces the Priest with 'You know the most fascinating thing about Father here, is that his mother was originally a LESBI' before the scene cuts off, and when arriving at a silent retreat Fleabag suggests to her sister that they will probably be read as a lesbian couple. While some of these encounters perhaps have more to do with Fleabag's desire to shock and tantalize, lesbianism seems to *haunt* the series and its representations of femininity and feminism (Eloit and Hemmings 2019). What is curious about her attempts to sleep with women, however, is that Fleabag is coded masculine in them. She is the pursuer/aggressor, actively seeking to pick up women, and in both of the examples above she is also mistaken for a man: the drunken woman calls her a 'naughty boy', and Belinda initially runs away from her, assuming she is a man aiming to attack her on the street.

The gender-reversed nature of these encounters is also mirrored in Fleabag's relationship with Harry, which we presented as a potential subversion of traditional gender roles earlier in this chapter. When Fleabag and the Priest bump into Harry at a church fête in the second season, it is revealed that Harry has a new partner and a child. Harry talks about how difficult the birth was and how his body feels different now, to which Fleabag jokingly responds, 'it sounds like you have postnatal depression'. Harry replies: 'I do, yeah, but we're working through it.' The Priest then asks if Harry and Fleabag know each other, and after some awkwardness Harry replies: 'Er, yeah. I used to be her girlfriend.'

And yet, despite the seemingly non-heterosexual or gender-reversed *content* of these narratives, they remain very similar in *tone* – and particularly in *affective* tone – to the other relationships depicted. Fleabag's (half-hearted) attempts at sleeping with women are not met with any enthusiasm, just like her attempts at sleeping with men all result in disappointment (even when they result in multiple orgasms, as in her dalliance with her lawyer, the Hot Misogynist). She responds to both with the same cynical and sarcastic distance, and the affective register of the encounters remains one of flat detachment – *it doesn't matter who you sleep with*, the show seems to want to tell us, because it will all be just as disappointing in the end. The women and feminine men Fleabag tries to sleep with turn out to be objects just as disappointing as the macho men, because, as Chu reminds us, it is not the object itself that is disappointing but rather 'your own optimism: your continued belief in the world's being enough for the desires that tether you to it, all evidence to the contrary' (2019: 64). Thus, heteropessimism might be better described as *cruel* hetero-*optimism* – to borrow from Berlant's (2011) 'cruel optimism', which describes the condition of maintaining an optimistic attachment to objects that are actually obstacles to one's flourishing. For Berlant, 'the fantasy life of normativity' (2011: 167) is precisely such an object, and correspondingly, despite all evidence to the contrary, the heteropessimist continues to optimistically tether her desires to a world and to relationships ill-equipped to meet them.

The argument of this chapter should consequently not be (mis)read as: Fleabag's life would be so much better if she was as a lesbian (even though it might). Rather, we are identifying a particular heteropessimist sensibility that critiques the gendered constraints of the institution of heterosexuality while simultaneously embracing them – albeit with flat and cynical detachment. Even in the show's most transgressive moments, Fleabag remains affectively and self-consciously aligned with patriarchal and heteronormative power relations. Real female sexual pleasure remains not only forestalled but also unimaginable in a society guided by the gendered scripts of heteronormativity, the show seems to suggest, while also offering us little respite from these scripts – or indeed remedy to them. Fleabag's self-referential gestures of heteropessimist lament might be understood as the latest form of a postfeminist sensibility (Gill 2017a). Such a sensibility throws the subject back onto itself and proclaims that, while we can point at the gendered confines and discontents of heteronormativity, ultimately there is little we can do to change them. As such it replaces an earlier, more optimistic, paradigm of postfeminism focused on individual success, resilience and a positive mental attitude (Gill 2017b; Scharff 2016) with a more pessimistic attachment that critiques yet remains enamoured with the affective pull of heteronormativity. Although bad sex continues to be disappointing for Fleabag because in the context of heteronormativity it can only ever be so, she continues to seek sex which she never imagines will be good. As we have suggested earlier, this contrasts with *Chewing Gum*'s Tracey, who has bad sex but is usually optimistic about it – if it doesn't work out today, maybe tomorrow it will be better.

Understanding heteropessimism as a (classed, gendered, and racialized) postfeminist sensibility also helps explain the show's highly anxious relationship to feminism. Fleabag's sister's neoliberal feminist credentials of having 'two degrees, a husband, and a Burberry coat' are ridiculed as much as the Godmother's embrace of an earlier version of liberation feminism. Announcing her 'Sexhibition', the Godmother mirrors Fleabag's desire to tantalize, proudly exclaiming: 'I've taken a photo of my naked body every year for the past thirty years . . . I think it's important for women of all ages to see how my body has changed, over the years. I think they have to have a healthy perspective on my body. Don't they?' Shown to privilege self-congratulatory postures of (white, middle-class) feminist achievement over actual solidarity with the other women in her life, the Godmother's feminism is presented as just as cunning and manipulative as Claire's is cold and heartless. In *Fleabag*, then, an identification with feminism is sought, while examples of concrete feminist politics are repudiated – marked as outdated, cynical or laughable. After meditating in silence in a Quaker meeting, Fleabag stands up to declare, 'I sometimes worry that I wouldn't be such a feminist if I had bigger tits', and when a speaker at a feminist conference (rhetorically) asks who would swap ten years of their life for the 'perfect body', only Fleabag and her sister raise their hands. These scenes offer both comedy and relief, as they pull us out of earnest discussions of who deserves to call themselves a 'real' feminist, yet also create clear affective distance to (presumably humourless) feminist politics. Further though, they also present a version of feminism attached primarily to questions of body image and career aspirations – issues that arguably typify white, middle-class feminism in particular. Thus, it is not just any feminism Fleabag (and many of the other antiheroes of precarious-girl comedies) rejects, but perhaps more accurately this particular type and lineage of individualized, white, and middle-class feminism.

Afraid of being labelled a 'bad feminist' herself (BBC 2019), Waller-Bridge's biting commentary on the difficulties of living a feminist life has been celebrated by commentators, with one arguing that it 'empowers all of us guilty feminists, who, for years, have felt the need to apologise for breaking the rules of game' (Mulholland 2019). Yet, while it marks a shift from earlier postfeminist sensibilities in which young women tended to repudiate the label of feminism while embracing neoliberal values of independence and individual success (Scharff 2016), Fleabag's anxious desire for feminism is marked by an ongoing sense of shame and guilt. These anxious attachments might be explained through the heteropessimist paradox: while figures like Fleabag can identify the problems of heteronormativity, they remain unwilling (or rather unable) to step outside of its gendered and sexual confines.

As suggested earlier, the only alternatives to the heteropessimist feelings of guilt, shame, and disappointment in *Fleabag* appear in moments of female bonding, in particular in the flashback scenes with Boo. In contrast to the rest of the show, in these scenes, shot with a soft lens and in the warm light often seen in intimate love scenes, Fleabag lets her guard down and we witness intimacy, vulnerability, and companionship. After her mother dies, Fleabag cries out, 'I don't know what to do with all the love I have for her', to which Boo replies, 'I'll take it, you've gotta give it to me'. In a queer reading, we might understand Fleabag and Boo's relationship as part of what Adrienne Rich (1980) described as the 'lesbian continuum': a bond of intimacy between women unsanctioned by heteronormative social standards. From this perspective, the show is a narrative of loss and grief over an intimate relationship of trust and hopefulness. This narrative, however, seems to get troubled by the big reveal at the end of the first season when it is suggested that Boo (accidentally?) took her own life because Fleabag slept with her boyfriend. Here, the terms of the breaking of the fourth wall shift from maintaining affective intimacy to exposing a 'failure of insight' (Brown 2013: 122). 'The power dynamics of her direct address shift as [Fleabag's] control over our relationship is shattered' (Woods 2019: 209), and we, as the audience, are asked to re-evaluate our interpretation and understanding of her. Rather than as an exploration of grief and the pain of losing her best friend, the show suggests it should be read as a story of guilt, remorse, and self-hatred – or even as a pathological narrative about the compulsive and destructive sexuality that both caused and emerges as a result of that guilt.

In a queer reading, then, both the character and the audience might be said to become prey to what Judith Butler (1995) calls 'gender melancholia'. Butler describes gender melancholia as the inability to mourn same-sex love-objects in a heteronormative society that makes it impossible for the lost object to have ever been recognized as a love-object in the first place. For Butler, it is not that homosexual love is transferred onto a substitute (opposite-sex) figure, or even abandoned – rather, it is a '*preemption* of the possibility of homosexual attachment, a certain foreclosure of possibility that produces a domain of homosexuality understood as unlivable passion and ungrievable loss' (1995: 168, emphasis original). Of course Fleabag *does* grieve – loudly, improperly, pathologically – throughout the show, but we also detect a melancholic attachment to 'what exceeds, what is unrecognised, what is lost' (Eloit and Hemmings 2019: 353). In this reading, Fleabag cannot properly mourn Boo because to do so would mean needing to have already admitted that she once loved (or desired) her. This melancholic attachment is further heightened by Fleabag's social environment in which her grief is belittled and her inability to continue life as usual is pathologized – leaving her without socially sanctioned avenues for mourning her friend, confidante, and lover.

That Fleabag's attempts to sleep with women (and men) seem to evoke a *gendered* anxiety, and not just an anxiety about sexuality, as recounted above, supports such a reading. In Butler's argument, 'the fear of homosexual desire in a woman may induce a panic that she is losing her femininity' (1995: 168) because a feminine gender is formed precisely through the incorporation of the already-excluded potential feminine love-object – or in other words, the formation of femininity depends on the repudiation of homosexuality. Within this logic, 'the "truest" lesbian melancholic is the strictly straight woman' (Butler 1995: 177). Fleabag, along with the heteropessimist woman, might therefore be read as such a straight lesbian melancholic – stuck in gender melancholia and unable to mourn her lost love-object, all that she is left with, and leaves us with, is a pessimistic reattachment to heterosexuality as not just an object choice, but also a social institution, cultural imposition and affective structure. Perhaps for Fleabag, like Ward argues is the case for many straight people, heterosexuality is 'inseparable from a desire for gender and/or sexual respectability and cultural legibility' (2020: 157).

Seresin (2019) frames heteropessimism as a *performative* disaffiliation: despite all of our unhappiness with it, heterosexuality remains both inevitable and a strictly individual, rather than a structural or collective, problem. Our reading of *Fleabag* shows how such heteropessimism unavoidably operates through not only an aspirational reattachment to white, middle-class heteronormativity but also the repudiation of any viable feminist and queer alternatives. As a response to the gendered confines of heteronormativity, *Fleabag's* heteropessimist sensibility leaves both its protagonist and its viewers with little more than biting, yet self-referential, irony and sarcasm – a knowing acknowledgement of bad sex. The problem with such a postfeminist sensibility is that it is ultimately an 'anesthetic feeling, a feeling that aims to protect against overintensity of feeling and an attachment that can survive detachment from the particularity of its objects' (Berlant and Edelman 2014: 17). What *Fleabag* and its incredible success show us is that while such an anaesthetic might help us live through the constraints and disappointments of heterosexual life, yet it also forecloses any alternatives that might move us beyond its confines – that is, imaginaries of what better or good sex might look like.

In this chapter, we have explored the heteropessimist attachment to bad sex – a mode of attachment that offers a way to live through the disappointments and stalled hopes amidst the gendered pressures of neoliberalism, but little remedy to them. While *Fleabag* crystallizes this heteropessimist sentiment, it is part of a larger cultural formation that can be observed not only in many other female-led dramedy TV series like *Girls* and *Broad City* but also in proliferating online and offline discussions and pop cultural products about the difficulties of having sex as a young, straight woman. As such, we want to suggest that heteropessimism and the attachment to bad sex mark a new postfeminist sensibility, operating within a pessimistic yet strictly heterosexual imaginary that forecloses any more radical alternatives to the gendered, classed, and racialised confines of heteronormativity. Through a disavowal of the potential of non-heterosexual objects of intimacy, love and desire, the show ultimately regurgitates a cruel reattachment to the promises of bad sex under heterosexuality that, despite all its faults, retains its place as the only available horizon of possibility.

These forms of reattachment are a particularly pernicious expression of cruel optimism (clinging to disappointing objects despite their non-viability) as much as they are compulsory – no matter how much we want Fleabag/the heteropessimist woman to want *something else* (Boo), she cannot not want *the same* (the Priest). Like Ward, in this chapter, then, we have reversed the direction of the 'ally relationship', becoming 'concerned allies to the straights in our families and communities, especially the women who may be experiencing more gendered suffering than we are, and without the hot sex, queer humor, and political solidarity to which many of us queers have access' (2020: 7). But do queers today really do it so much better? In the following two chapters, we investigate whether the queer characters in *Feel Good* (2020–21), *Work in Progress* (2019, 2021), *Please Like Me* (2013–16) and *Special* (2019, 2021) indeed manage to escape the bad sex of straight culture and find good or even better sex.

Chapter 2

GOOD SEX AS QUEER/LESBIAN ESCAPE IN *FEEL GOOD* AND *WORK IN PROGRESS*

Introduction

In the previous chapter, we suggested that in shows like *Fleabag* (2016, 2019) straight sex is presented – at least for young, white, middle-class, cis women – through the lens of heteropessimism: as a fantasy ultimately doomed to fail. Sex here is disappointing and awkward, unable to fulfil the affective and ideological demands it is invested with. Given that in this genre it is 'shitty men' and the confines of heterosexual romance that make a fulfilling sexual and romantic life impossible, a logical escape from this heteropessimist dilemma might be queer and lesbian sex. After all, as we have suggested in the previous chapter, it is in the friendship with Boo that Fleabag finds moments of real intimacy, trust and fulfilment. While this friendship is not understood as a lesbian relationship as such, we argued that it still hints at the lesbian continuum of desire and relationality that could help women escape the cruel demands and disappointments of heterosexuality.

And indeed, in the more overtly queer TV shows *Feel Good* (2020–21) and *Work in Progress* (2019, 2021) that feature the queer lives of predominantly white cis women, trans men, and non-binary people, the site of good feelings is sex. In their everyday lives, the main characters of both shows, Mae and Abby, share a deep sadness and struggle with serious mental health conditions. While the non-binary bisexual comedian Mae in *Feel Good* struggles with drug dependency and PTSD, they have instant sexual chemistry and exploration with their female lover, George. The couple buys sex toys together, laughing and figuring out how to please each other proactively and humorously: 'you just want to get pushed around like a slutty bag of beans.' They talk openly about gender roles and mock stereotypical assumptions about lesbian and queer sex: 'I would never emotionally connect with you.' Similarly, in *Work in Progress*, Abby, a self-described queer dyke, suffers from obsessive compulsive disorder, has been single for many years and is using a packet of organic almonds to count down the days until she kills herself. Yet, when she meets the younger trans man Chris, he unashamedly tells her what he likes to do in bed in front of an Uber driver. After they have sex for the first time (in the dark, Abby insists), we see the usually curmudgeonly Abby walk the streets in a joyful daze, talking to strangers, patting dogs and displaying injuries which suggest an increasingly daring sex life. She later asserts: 'Things are good – what could go wrong?'

This representation of fulfilling queer sex clearly diverts from earlier hegemonic representations, particularly of lesbian sex, where queer desire is commonly either erased, domesticated or a hypersexualized spectacle performed for the straight male gaze (see e.g. Bradbury-Rance 2019; McNicholas Smith 2020). In comparison, the representation of good sex in these contemporary shows is outspokenly queer, erotic, playful, and full of intimacy. Here, sex constitutes a space of exploration and enjoyment that, at least for a moment, offers relief from the characters' mental health struggles and the clinical promises of wellness and self-improvement they have thus far engaged in. In the context of sex, Mae believes they can forget their emotional precarity and struggles with addiction, and Abby finds moments of respite from her anxieties with middle-aged, middle-class disappointment. While neither character ultimately finds solace in their romantic relationships, at least initially they attach enthusiastically to the promise of good sex as a way of feeling better.

The idea of lesbian and queer sex and relationships as an escape from the pains of heteropatriarchal relations and societal structures is, of course, not new. Monique Wittig (1992) famously positions lesbianism itself as an escape from *gendered* heteropatriarchal logics, and theorists like Audre Lorde (1984) and Adrienne Rich (1980) regard the exploration of queer sex, intimacy, and eroticism as a way to find new avenues not just for more pleasure but also for different forms of sociality and politics. While certain strands of lesbian escapism/separatism have rightfully been cast away as outdated in their potential essentialism and enshrining of a naturalized sex/gender binary (Rudy 2001; Smith and Smith 1981), scholars like Jane Ward argue that 'lesbian feminist critiques of heterosexuality . . . have renewed relevance and urgency' (2020: 4). For Ward, to ignore lesbian feminist arguments is to 'keep our focus on queer misery, and . . . fail to name the contradictions and miseries of straight culture', which queer women particularly tend to be 'wildly grateful to have escaped' (2020: 4). In a similar vein, for both of our key characters queerness and queer sex hold promise as an escape from the confines of heterosexual life, providing both structural and emotional avenues of transformation.

In this chapter, we explore the ongoing affective promise of queer escape in *Feel Good* and *Work in Progress*. We grapple with the paradox that despite enjoying sex as a site of positive affect and relationality, the central characters of the shows ultimately remain deeply unhappy. Rather than a simple narrative of queer escape, then, these shows offer a complex depiction of the (im)possibility that queer sexual and romantic intimacies can protect against the blows of homo/transphobia, illness, trauma, and neoliberal capitalism. Indeed, in a world where white middle-class normativity, individual achievement, and privatized responsibility for one's own well-being continue to be the norm, sexual escape can easily become a purely private affair rather than a collective project. Struggling to fulfil their (and our) queer utopian desires for collective worlds free of gendered and sexualized oppression, the main characters seek respite in the private sphere – ultimately reinvesting in the individualized, domesticated, gendered, classed and racialized notions of care and support that continue to fail them. Thus, the chapter charts the shows' depictions of good sex, exploring how joyful, pleasurable, and erotic sex allows for an escape from the disappointments of heterosexuality explored in the previous chapter. But it also investigates the characters' ongoing attachments to often unhelpful (and uncaring) solutions to their sadness, given the few queer or collective forms of support available to them in the neoliberal worlds they inhabit. Might an escape to queerer, more collective forms of care *and* desire be available for these sexually fulfilled yet unhappy queers?

Good sex as queer escape

The opening episodes of *Work in Progress* and *Feel Good* both emphasize sexual discovery and transformation. Queer sexual relationships are presented – at least initially – as something that can drastically change the protagonists' lives. In contrast to the heteropessimist frame we analysed in the previous chapter, where sex is presented not only as disappointing but also as separate from experiences of real emotion and intimacy, the sex that Mae and George, and Abby and Chris engage in is presented as joyful, erotic, pleasurable, and intimate. Unlike the disappointing cis straight men and non-consensual practices that typify recent explorations of straight sex on TV (including in *Fleabag*), *Work in Progress* and *Feel Good* present sexual lives as frequently funny, kinky and emotionally meaningful, and sex as something that challenges, surprises and emboldens its participants – initially at least, the kind of sex that, as viewers and as participants, we could only experience as *good*.

In *Feel Good*, George and Mae go back to George's immediately on the evening they meet, and from here we see a sunlit montage of many days of sex, play, and overnighters before Mae quickly moves in. Mae and George have instant sexual chemistry, and they do not struggle to communicate through and about their sexuality – George talks dirty to Mae in the voice of Susan Sarandon, George buys a strap-on, and they have sex in shopping centre changing rooms, cars, and hospital closets. This clearly contrasts with the representation of straight sex we discussed in the previous chapter, and when George later tries dating Elliot, self-identified as a 'bi, poly, cis man', she finds herself similarly sexually unfulfilled, as he complains that her interest in pornography reflects 'problematic power dynamics' which she must 'unlearn' for them to 'connect' during sex. Allowing her to step out of her heteropessimist disappointment with 'shitty men', reflected also in the normative relationships of her friends and family, George finds solace in the exploration, subversion, and silliness of sex with Mae, best exemplified by the warmly lit scenes of role-play scenarios that we are invited to joyfully witness in the series: Brooklyn plumber and housewife, king and courtier, doctor and an unconventionally cured headache (Figure 2.1).

As such, *Feel Good* is one of the few genuinely unexpected, funny, explorative, and sexy demonstrations of queer sex and sexuality on TV, aligning with Katherine Angel's discussion of the joys of sex 'in discovering new, different ways to be touched: in being vulnerable to the unknown' (2021a: 114). For their part as the writer, Martin has said that the aim of these scenes was to challenge typical representations of 'weird unrealistic [queer] sex', presenting 'different sex' to that previously seen (Salam 2021). *Feel Good*'s sex scenes creatively challenge both historic tropes of queer and particularly lesbian 'bed death', and pornified representations of lesbian sex as a highly feminized, bodily spectacle performed for objectifiable male pleasure (e.g. *Basic Instinct, Blue is the Warmest Colour*). Differently to *Fleabag* or *Chewing Gum* (2015–17) where heterosexual sex is frequently narrated through a flattening fourth wall to convey disappointment, and to share an intimate bond with the audience rather than the sexual partner, in *Feel Good*, George and Mae look only at each other, and as viewers we are privy to (but not invited into) the often complex sexual intimacy they share. Here, queer sex is kinky, explicit, messy, sometimes unglamorous and uneasy, sometimes private, sometimes public – but nearly always a site of complex desire, intimacy, and continued negotiation.

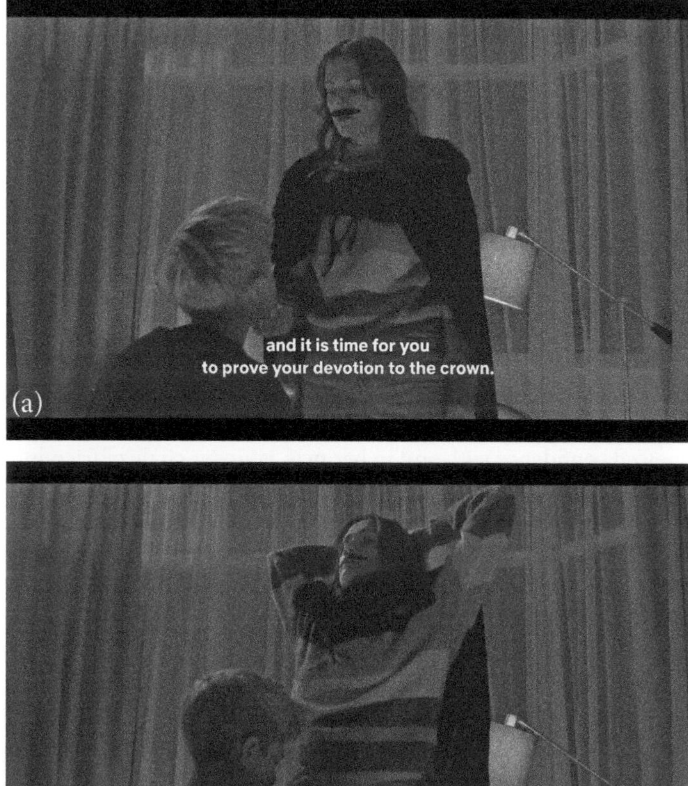

Figure 2.1 (a, b) As part of a playful montage signalling days of role-play, joyous and silly sex, Mae performs oral sex on the King (George). *Feel Good* © Objective Fiction/Channel 4 2020–21.

In *Work in Progress*, we get a similarly joyful representation of queer sex structured around an intergenerational relationship. The main characters Abby and Chris are presented as belonging to two different queer generations: Chris is a Gen Z trans man who understands few of Abby's late 1990s references, and Abby feels like 'Mitt Romney Junior' amongst Chris' effortless discussion of pronouns, top surgery, and sexuality. But Abby's rigidity, resentment, and social caution are quickly eroded by Chris' sexual and social openness and ease. While in flashbacks we see Abby fumble through hook-ups with her previous partners, the sexually and gender-explorative Chris happily tells Abby what he likes to do in bed and nonchalantly but ethically responds to Abby's sexual shame about having herpes. Abby's life appears to become more open and pleasurable as their relationship progresses. While we hear but do not see Abby's pleasure – they have sex in the dark, denying the audience access to the *visuals* of sex between them (Figure 2.2) – we come to understand her sexual reawakening through relational representations of her life with Chris, exemplifying Angel's argument that 'to be met in one's desire, and to be surprised in one's desire, is an exercise in mutual trust and negotiation of fear' (2021a: 116). Chris includes Abby in his diverse queer social world, while Abby grows more confident about expressing experiences of sexual shame and moves with a renewed confidence with and in her new, younger circle of friends.

Differently to many other shows that have explored intergenerational queer relationships (particularly when involving an older lesbian) and trans/lesbian relationships as sites of sexual and social *problems* (e.g. *Transparent*; *The L Word*), *Work in Progress* stands out for its initially hopeful representation of cross-generational and cross-gender queer sociality and sexuality. Here, intergenerational queer sex is a site of

Figure 2.2 In a visual departure from glossy and pornified representations of lesbian and queer sex, Abby and Chris turn the lights off. Chris jokes to Abby that this makes it 'hard to film', suggesting that their good sex would still be worthy of recording. *Work in Progress* © Tessa Films/Showtime 2019–21.

pleasure, learning, complexity, and compassion. Rather than the older partner pursuing the younger one, both are integrating into each other's lives – indeed, often it is Abby who learns from the younger Chris, who, as Sarah Kessler (2021) notes, quietly accommodates Abby's frequent solipsism. Such experiences are represented neither as necessarily a queer progress narrative where Abby's generation reflects only transphobia and essentialism nor as a 'forgetting' of the pains of earlier lesbian experience as is sometimes suggested within transphobic lesbian loss discourses (see e.g. Eloit and Hemmings 2019; Hemmings 2011). In this way, Abby's gentle introduction to new and transformative queer experiences via her relationship with Chris (both in sex and more broadly) might also be understood as somewhat of a recuperation of notions of queer/lesbian escape or separatism.

In this context, it is essential to note that only one of the characters explored in this chapter seems to explicitly align with a lesbian identity – Abby who labels herself a 'queer dyke'. Mae's gender and sexual identification shifts across the series and they later come to identify comically as an 'Adam Driver or a Ryan Gosling', and eventually as a non-binary bisexual. George identifies as a bisexual cis woman, and Chris is a pansexual trans man. Our reframing of the citational history of lesbian separatist discourses as queer/lesbian *escape* here thus deliberately challenges essentialized framings of the lesbian as fundamentally a fixed gendered and sexual subject. As Judith Butler suggests, it can be 'permanently unclear what precisely that sign [lesbian] signifies' (1993: 308) because 'its *specificity* can only be demarcated by exclusions that return to disrupt its claim to coherence' (1993: 309, emphasis original). In other words, 'lesbian' as an identity marker is always at least to some degree out of one's own control, and thus 'overdetermined by heterosexuality' (Case 1996: 14), or in Ward's terms, 'straightness shapes everything, precisely by narrowing the field of what is conceivable or limiting the imagination' (2020: 142). Indeed, heteropatriarchy impacts and involves subjects who do and don't themselves attach to gendered expressions of womanhood or lesbianism, therefore also speaking to the vexed history of lesbian representation that has overwhelmingly sought to ignore butch and/or gender-transgressive women, non-binary, and trans people. For Abby and Chris, and Mae and George, regardless of their personal relationships to specific sexuality or gender labels, queer sex certainly holds affective promise as an escape from heteronormative misery. This typifies precisely the kind of 'profound forms of queer joy' (2020: 5) and 'queer relief not to be straight' (2020: 2) that Ward argues are central to the experiences of queer and trans people other than cis gay men – as for the latter, queerness may indeed indicate a more straightforward *loss* of social and cultural power.

In both shows, we get a representation of good queer sex as the driver of the narrative. Sex is where the potential solution to both Mae's and Abby's illnesses and bad feelings lies. It is the force that connects them to their partners, allows them to be vulnerable, and experiment with other modes of being. In some ways, both characters are connecting with what Audre Lorde refers to as the 'erotic' as 'a well of replenishing and provocative force' (1984: 54), a source of joy and connection that allows the characters to, at least momentarily, step out of their misery. For Lorde, however, the potential of the erotic lies in the fact that once 'in touch with the erotic, [we] become less willing to accept powerlessness, or those other supplied states of being which are not native to [us], such as resignation, despair, self-effacement, depression, self-denial' (1984: 58). For Lorde, sex and the erotic are conceptualized as the means through which to tackle the wider personal and social problems engendered by white heteropatriarchy. In this way, the erotic acts as a source of power and information – not so much as an escape. The question for us then becomes, what happens to the erotic if it gets positioned as a straightforward end goal, an escape *from* the social and political worlds we live in, rather than a space from which to struggle for and imagine wider political alternatives?

Miserable lives

Both shows under discussion here present the new, good sex that the characters enjoy as the primary, if not only, respite from their otherwise unhappy lives. When we first meet Abby in *Work in Progress*, she is a 45-year-old white queer dyke who is unappreciated in her mid-level office job, and unproudly calls herself fat. She has battled severe OCD since childhood, compulsively tracking her daily existence in hundreds of hoarded notebooks, and ruminating on minor events until she is unable to physically take care of herself. She has spent her adult life unable to escape the shame of the gender-based homophobia she experiences, best exemplified by her inability or refusal to let go of a homo/transphobic character on *Saturday Night Live*, who she was taunted by in the 1990s. While Chris makes Abby feel attractive, sexually desired, and cared for from the first time they meet, Abby then confesses to him that she has sincere plans to die. Thus, while presenting Abby with some respite from her stuck existence, and the potential for a queerer, more joyous life, this frank discussion of her intended suicide also signals the dramatic unevenness of care and concern that will come to typify their emotional relationship, if not their sexual one.

Differently, while Mae appears to be doing better than Abby at first, they relapse into drug dependency early on in their relationship with George. As early as the first episode, Mae is avoiding their Narcotics Anonymous meetings – while they *had* a drug problem, they now *have* George – thus positioning their new sexual/relationship life as a cure for (or escape from) addiction and unhappiness that will, however, prove elusive throughout the two seasons. When Mae eventually tells George about their drug problem, George is unable to reciprocate the honesty and retreats into the sexual: 'Why don't you just go down on me?' Throughout the series, George and Mae remain largely unable to discuss their emotional needs and histories, as they go on to have sex in more exciting, riskier ways and places, and their sexual relationship becomes a distraction from other forms of intimacy. By season 2, Mae is suffering from worsening PTSD as the result of teenage sexual abuse, experiencing disassociation, flashbacks and panic attacks, and sabotaging George's attempts to seek external sources of support. They eventually check themselves out of a rehab clinic to hang out with their former abuser.

Both Abby and Mae's unhappiness needs to be considered in relation to their social locations. While in tone and aesthetic *Work in Progress* and *Feel Good* could be framed as queer versions of Rebecca Wanzo's (2016) 'precarious-girl' or 'cringe' millennial comedies, as we discussed with *Fleabag* in the previous chapter, neither Abby nor Mae quite fits the description. Abby, for one, is not a millennial, and neither of them are aimless twenty-somethings, nor 'girls'. Rather, they both initially come across as quite curious, generous, warm, and even ambitious, but are frequently thwarted by chronic mental and social distress – what Drew Burnett Gregory (2020b) calls the sense of being 'too much' for those around them. Moreover, neither Mae nor Abby's unhappiness is fundamentally explained via their sexuality or gender identity, which would position queerness as an inevitable *cause* of unhappiness – thus importantly challenging the well-trodden 'bury your gays' representational trope (Ahmed 2010; Waggoner 2018). Instead, Mae and Abby's sadnesses have names – drug dependency, PTSD, OCD – and queer sex, in this sense, becomes the *one good thing* in lives that are otherwise often very difficult. Both characters also face versions of homophobia, transphobia, and sexism throughout the series, experiences that are entwined with and explored alongside often very nuanced representations of complex mental health conditions and sexual trauma.

At the same time, oversimplified understandings of queer suffering can also be complicated by the notable material and racial privileges present in both shows. While it tends to be straight and cis characters (Mae's parents, George's friends, Abby's colleagues) who embody gender, sexuality, and mental health-related ignorance in the series, it is slowly revealed in *Feel Good* that Mae's parents are Oxford-educated, live in a grand house in Toronto and have made substantial efforts to care for Mae. Abby's family home, family events, and flashbacks to her childhood reflect similar forms of white, middle-class economic and cultural capital. Further, despite the often-severe state of her mental health, Abby is well liked by colleagues and, by the end of season 1, is promoted. Mae is similarly often recognized and respected by their careerist colleagues – although this representation is certainly complicated by some of the colleagues' sexual harassment and encouragement of Mae's drug dependency.

Like in *Fleabag* and many other 'precarious' comedies, here material privileges are commented on, often by the leads themselves, but the ways in which racial and class privilege structures the characters' experiences (and the show's narratives) tend to be less examined. For example, although it is unclear if they really have a criminal record due to drug dealing, Mae is able to work in a country they weren't born in, and although they appear to struggle day-to-day for income, when they relapse, they immediately find support in a seemingly under-occupied, privately funded, scenic Canadian dependency clinic. By season 2, *Work in Progress* considers the impact of wealth and racial privilege on Abby's experiences of chronic mental suffering somewhat reflexively, by acknowledging that when she needed care, she received it. Indeed, both characters' access to care and maintenance of employment across the series is notable in how much it deviates from the significant consequences of dwindling public provision and disparities in care under neoliberalism, faced particularly by non-wealthy sufferers. These rather ambiguous explorations of privilege are further emphasized in both shows by the overwhelming presence of whiteness itself. Both feature many people of colour in secondary roles, but these characters tend to primarily offer a listening ear, advice, and care to the leads when their partners are unable to – or act as romantic and sexual distractions, such as to Mae and George when they temporarily try to extricate themselves from each other.[1]

While we have argued earlier that queer sex in these shows is presented as 'good' in ways that challenge the heteropessimism of their straight televisual equivalents, they also, many other ways, reproduce similar dynamics. As Kessler (2021) argues, *Work in Progress* tends to emphasize the trauma and struggle of the characters, while acknowledgement of racial and classed locations is performed through others' ignorance. Indeed, *Work in Progress* and *Feel Good* both reflect similar racial and class privileges central to some iterations of the 'precarious-girl' genre, and the queers in these shows similarly struggle to form meaningful connections outside of sex. Both Mae and Abby are emotionally isolated by mental health issues and a level of self-centredness that hinder their capacity to carry out intimate relationships in more expressive, reflexive, and reciprocal forms. When George asks Mae to confront their relationship on an emotional level – what it means, whether it's meaningful – Mae tells her that when they lie together, they feel 'quiet, deep inside'. It is a romantic scene, complete with fairy lights and a kiss reminiscent of an American high school drama. Except as the audience we know that Mae is increasingly unable to relax in George's company, and in a later comedy routine self-loathingly confesses to being 'exhausted . . . from like trying – like I'm basically trying to be what I imagine her dream version of her high school boyfriend is', before humiliating George by questioning her bisexuality for laughs as part of a 'tell-all' comedy routine.

Similarly, in *Work in Progress*, after a weekend during which Chris has taken care of her every emotional need, Abby inexplicably betrays him by going through his possessions to discover his deadname from his medicine bottles. When Chris expresses a sense of betrayal, Abby is unable to accept responsibility despite her guilt. She shows up at his work uninvited, implies that whether she goes ahead with her planned suicide or not depends on him agreeing to speak to her, and when Chris clearly but compassionately asserts that the relationship is over, Abby screams his deadname in the street as a final act of cruelty. Interestingly, and perhaps somewhat differently from *Feel Good*'s representational dynamics, the show hides Chris' deadname from us, the viewers, suggesting that we are meant to align affectively with Chris' disapproval and hurt, rather than become accomplices in Abby's cruelty. This is further emphasized by Abby's attempt to secure support from her ex-partner (a lesbian woman of colour), who refuses Abby's self-centredness: 'still, after all of these years, you've managed to make it all about you.'

In the penultimate episode of season 1 of *Feel Good*, George straightforwardly asks if she makes Mae happy, to which Mae replies 'like, not really'. The first season of *Work in Progress* similarly ends with Chris promising Abby: 'No one will ever feel as broken as you do.' Thus, Abby's statement in an earlier episode proves to be prophetic: 'I've had sex – but not everything about me has changed.' Despite the euphoric scenes of queer sex, pleasure, love, humour, and friendship, neither Mae's explorative sex life with George nor Abby's middle-aged sexual awakening lead to substantial changes in their happiness over the series – good sex doesn't seem to make things better. Moreover, just as both characters continue to engage in discussions about their broader misery with others, they increasingly refuse their new partners' support, as well as ignoring their boundaries or needs. Good sex is thus also the beginning of imbalance and non-reciprocity in these relationships that eventually turn pretty bad for everyone, and both shows seem to toy with the *im*possibility of emotionally fulfilling queer relationships in the context of broader suffering. In *Feel Good*, Mae likens their relationship with George to 'pushing on a bruise', figuring both the pain and pleasure of their time together by comparing it to an injury without emotional or physical permanence (a summary that contrasts strikingly with their recurring flashbacks of teenage sexual abuse). Equally, in season 2 of *Work in Progress*, Abby summarizes her relationship with Chris in flattened terms: 'we're two people who could only go that far – I have my limits and you have yours', undoing the titular possibility of progression initially promised in the series.

Ward argues that although queer people also 'act out and hurt each other in numerous ways, including violence, addiction, lying, and so forth . . . the key difference between straight culture and queer culture in this regard is that the latter does not attribute these destructive behaviors to a romantic story about a natural and inescapable gender binary' (2020: 25–6). Indeed, both *Work in Progress* and *Feel Good* deviate from the *hetero*pessimism we analysed in Chapter 1, in that Abby and Mae at least get to have meaningful, pleasurable and mutually respectful sex with their partners and the inevitability of an imbalanced relationship is not foregrounded. At the same time though, the transformative, if not utopian, escape and promise of queer romance and sex is concluded in both series as not really all that long-lasting. For Abby and Mae, queer sex might not be disappointing, but at the same time it doesn't necessarily offer any meaningful escape from the broader experience of an isolated, unhappy life. Both shows, perhaps, share the same affective structure as *Fleabag* with its heteropessimist dynamics, imbuing the private, domesticated, and sexual realm with the promise of holding the pain of the broader world at bay. As for straight cis women, such a promise is doomed to fail, yet it continues to be the primary form of attachment in a world where (queer) social and communal spaces and ways of relating are often unavailable. Sex and romance, then, appear not only not enough to overcome or significantly improve Abby's, Mae's and Fleabag's relationships to both themselves and others, but they also fail to eventually live up to their early promise as an escape from the confines of structural and emotional precarity.

In the previous chapter, we described Fleabag's continued attachment to heteronormativity as *cruel* hetero-*optimism* – to borrow from Lauren Berlant's (2011) 'cruel optimism', which describes the condition of maintaining an optimistic attachment to objects that are actually obstacles to one's flourishing. Mae's and Abby's optimism is not necessarily attached to some promise of future romantic love, like we argued Fleabag's eventually is, but instead they imbue sex with a similar emotional weight: for these characters, sex needs to continuously remain pleasurable, as well as exciting and daring, to keep them emotionally afloat. Yet, as Lorde (1984) reminds us, the erotic cannot be the end point, the only salvation from our personal and social suffering. If a queer escape via the erotic seems ultimately untenable, or indeed just as disappointing as the escape to heterosexual romance *Fleabag* seems to end with, what route then remains for the characters to get and feel better?

Impossible escapes

Before trying to find their salvation in sex and relationships, Abby and Mae have both invested heavily in the neoliberal self-improvement logics of mental fitness, recovery, and betterment. Abby has spent her life in talk therapy that has not helped her address her compulsions and has participated in Weight Watchers classes that make her feel like a failure. Mae has been working hard at their recovery, yet perversely enjoys professional success the more their mental health derails and the more they come to embody a self-destructive 'addict', 'trans', 'lonely millennial' – which their booking agent identifies as 'very now'. Both of them seem to fail at the neoliberal impetus to 'get better'. In discussing the queer pedagogy and utopia in *Sex Education* (2019–23), a series we explore in our final chapter, Tanya Horeck borrows from Jack Halberstam to argue that 'failure' – sexual, social, heteronormative –

in the series radically 'resists the facile mantra of individual "positive thinking"', and instead asks us to consider how 'failure can be productive in terms of generating new forms of knowledge' (2021). For Horeck, the sexual imperfection in *Sex Education*, combined with its frank and non-judgemental discussions of sex/sexuality, offers new queer possibilities for thinking about queer sex and life beyond the neoliberal promise of better futures. Similarly, it could be argued that Abby and Mae's failings to 'get better' in straightforward ways resist the facile neoliberal demands of wellness, as well as the underlying ableist, classed, and gendered logics of productivity and self-improvement – particularly as they have been imparted onto 'good' queer subjects.

Abby and Mae have both tried to get 'better' through the resources they have been promised will deliver it: self-reflection (or self-absorption), homonormative monogamy, weight loss, therapy, and hard work (Barker et al. 2018). Yet it is precisely the attachment to such practices that often makes them poor partners and friends: George and Mae's, and Abby and Chris' romances both rest on imbalanced, privatized, and gendered practices of care, perhaps partially because neither Abby nor Mae finds comfort in the more formal healthcare structures they have engaged with so far. It is notable that they both seek support from institutions that fail to accommodate and/or relate to their queer desires and experiences, offering empty (or no) platitudes in the face of their significant struggles and pain. Mae is enabled by ill-equipped peers in Narcotics Anonymous and leaves their cosy rehabilitation clinic within days of arriving. Abby's unhelpful therapist dies in the middle of her session (it comically takes Abby some time to notice), and she is alienated by the feminized, heteronormative positive thinking logics of her local Weight Watchers chapter. In the absence of more meaningful (queer) support, both characters struggle to feel better with the self-destructive means at their disposal (drugs, compulsions), before resting their hopes for well-being on their new, privatized romantic relationships – with queer partners who ultimately fail to be secure enough themselves to meet such hopes.

One way of reading the main characters' refusals to get better (despite the great sex they are having) is through Sara Ahmed's (2010) discussion of the figure of the 'unhappy queer'. For Ahmed, 'the freedom to be unhappy would be the freedom to live a life that deviates from the paths of happiness, wherever that deviation takes us' (2010: 195). In this reading, Mae and Abby's unhappiness is not simply a problem, but a queer possibility that derives from a social system set up around the promise of happiness which excludes queer, non-binary and trans people. Indeed, they both seem to refuse or ignore at least some aspects of both heteronormative and homonormative narratives of maturity and respectability, 'measured by what one has given up in order to keep the family system going' (Ward 2020: 129). Abby's story in particular is marked by an implicit, generational refusal of the normative, US-focused 'It Gets Better' discourse of the early 2000s – for Abby, it certainly didn't. As the kinds of subjects who should/could/would live better lives in the supposedly more queer and trans-inclusive present, Abby's and Mae's continued refusals to let go of the pain and patterns of their pasts arguably reveal the facile apolitical logics of twenty-first-century LGBT politics, where 'the illusion that same sex object choices have become accepted and acceptable (for example that civil partnerships would mean queer civility) both conceals the ongoing realities of discrimination, non-recognition and violence, and requires that we approximate the straight signs of civility' (Ahmed 2010: 106).

In this way, the shows challenge straightforward attachments to a post-queer sensibility, which in Kate McNicholas Smith's words emerges 'through homonormativity and postfeminism' and 'functions to situate the struggles of queer and feminist politics as redundant as it mobilizes its progress narrative of gay rights' (2020: 7). While neither Abby nor Mae's struggles are straightforwardly the result of homo/transphobias (and indeed, although both of their friends and families are frequently coded as *potentially* homo/transphobic, they are ultimately mostly welcoming and supportive), at the same time neither is doing *well* in the sense figured in the supposedly prevalent post-queer, homonormative sensibilities of the present. In this vein, both shows also reject stereotypically positive or progressive narrative endings, whether in regards to individual wellness or romance, in favour of more ambivalent and mundane culminations: Abby informs us that it was really just the daily onslaught of random 'shit' that kept her from taking her own life in the context of a flailing and unequal US healthcare system, while Mae compassionately confronts their abuser as a first step in overcoming their PTSD, vomits on the road, and then goes for a nice drive with George.

However, perhaps contrary to Ahmed's (2010) reflections on the possibilities of queer unhappiness – that is, unhappiness as a freeing emotion that offers space to deviate from the empty paths of normativity and to develop queer ones instead – in other ways, Abby and Mae continue to largely attach to the 'post-queer' premise that queer and trans subjects can be accommodated within normative frames of domesticated happiness (McNicholas Smith 2020). The shows' endings on ambivalent but compassionate notes of recovery and resilience can be contrasted with their overwhelmingly privatized and domesticated depictions of care and pleasure. In other words, while the shows' warm portrayals of Abby and Mae's surviving resist simplistic narratives of better mental health for normative white, middle-class queers, at the same time they both demonstrate considerable ambivalence towards and disinterest in the possibilities of more radical, vulnerable or politically generative queer socialities.

For instance, both Mae and Abby show little interest in their partners' emotional needs beyond the context of sex, and both go on to ultimately cross their partners' boundaries by exploiting vulnerable aspects of their gender or sexuality (Abby's taunting of Chris with his deadname; Mae's tell-all comedy routine in which they get laughs from calling George 'culturally straight'). Similarly, in season 1 of *Work in Progress*, after Abby grows the confidence to finally confront a cis woman in a bathroom for what she understands is an attempt to refuse her entry on the basis of her butch presentation, she then performs a complete 'self own' in her 'unyielding insistence on painting herself as the scene's consummate victim' (Kessler 2021: 46), by competing with a presumed trans woman and a disabled teenager for who struggles the most in using public bathrooms, screaming 'my life is worse than everybody else's!' In *Feel Good*, Mae often manipulatively uses guilt and a one-dimensional understanding of 'love' to take advantage of the less-experienced George and their family, and steals from, ignores or uses supportive (and similarly precarious) friends and colleagues. This is not to say that Mae and Abby are 'bad queers' who do not deserve our empathy, understanding or sense of humour. Rather, we discuss these limits to the promise that queerness can produce happiness, for the characters themselves or for the people around them, when it is disconnected from wider infrastructures and communities of care.

In a review for the *Wall Street Journal*, John Anderson argues that 'one of the more thoughtful and engaging aspects of "Work in Progress" is its insistence that the things that really matter in relationships aren't always about sexual orientation, sexual fluidity or awkward sex' (2019). But if one of the 'more thoughtful' things about such shows is not sex or sexuality, and neither character attaches to queer sociality or community more broadly, then what are we to make of the promise of happy queer sex lives? Yes, the sex on screen is queer, and most of all fun (as well as often funny). Yes, it is joyous and pleasurable, and a key source of the characters' happiness for a time. But the majority of

Abby and Mae's interactions with others are interlaced with loneliness, shame, and significantly uneven practices of care, suggesting that their queer lives are quite disconnected from broader queer relationalities, reciprocity and social or political change. The privatized realm of queer and lesbian care and hot sex not only proves to be no escape from the ravages of homo, bi, and transphobia but also becomes increasingly unable to remedy Abby and Mae's unhappiness more generally – further challenged by the cringeworthy ignorance that they both display towards the experiences of others, and particularly their poor treatment of the other queer people who care for them.

This is all the more pertinent for the ways in which queerness itself is arguably depoliticized and individualized by the two main characters in the series. While both Abby and Mae understand themselves through the language of gender diversity and queerness, they both struggle to connect to wider queer sociality, community, and politics. Identifying as a 'queer dyke', Abby professes pains about her experiences of gender-based bathroom phobia, usually to her dismissive straight cis sister. But her social life is limited to a small circle of mostly white, middle-class lesbian friends, and she appears isolated enough from broader queer culture and politics that she is frequently unacquainted with terms and ideas that circulate amongst Chris' young, racially diverse, genderqueer political scene. It is telling, for example, that Abby's rage over the homophobic character on *Saturday Night Live* is wholly individualized – it put *her* (not queer people generally) at risk.[2] In *Feel Good*, Mae similarly does not seem to have (m)any queer friends, spending most of their work and social time with straight cis men. And while Mae is cynically identified by others in the comedy scene as a political act to promote in the era of visible queer cultures and post-MeToo politics, they themselves feel largely (often understandably) disconnected from or ambivalent about such politics. These individualized and privatized dynamics temper the character's ability to fully tackle and escape the wider neoliberal logics of individualized progress and well-being they find themselves in.

In some ways, then, *Feel Good* and *Work in Progress* confront us with an individualized and domesticated version of the promise of queer escape that is closer to a heteropessimist framework than it might at first appear. While refusing simple post-queer progress narratives of 'It Gets Better', Abby and Mae's desires struggle to fully break out of wider normative, privatized, neoliberal frames. These representations are in many ways what Kessler calls 'butch middle-brow', which is considered 'a contemporary aesthetic and affective sensibility distinguished by the cozy reception it enjoys among the straight, white, liberal viewers and critics to whom Showtime presumably pitches its product' (2021: 47). The hope remains that all other (material, racial, and monogamous) things being equal, good sex, and the romance and coupledom that follow from it, will be a point of salvation in an otherwise precarious and overwhelming world, along with a general 'apathy about social justice projects' that Ward (2020: 126) associates with straight culture. Ward goes on to argue that this apathy makes 'heterosexuals the worst people to get stuck next to at a dinner party', because of their 'wilful focus on keeping things light and comfortable' (2020: 126–7), and we wonder here whether Mae and Abby's retreat to the sexual and private spheres precisely in moments when they might benefit from engaging with broader queer socialities and politics could be read similarly.

Queer arrivals?

While we began this chapter by suggesting that both *Work in Progress* and *Feel Good* place queerness in the affective frame of queer/lesbian escape (perhaps citing earlier notions of separatism), what appears to be missing from Abby and Mae's lives is the political, collective, or even radical and transgressive connections that imaginaries of lesbian and queer escape promise. Theorists like Rich (1980) posit non-heterosexual desire as an escape from the confines of heteropatriarchy, framing lesbian and queer existence as a response to heteronormative domestic and sexual cultures in ways that privilege lesbianism in particular as a *political* category, perhaps even more so than an intimate one. Conversely for others such as Lorde (1984), lesbianism and queerness might be imagined as entangled social, political, intimate projects that would allow their subjects to live outside of heteropatriarchy's sexual and gendered confines and to find happiness in a communal sociality that rejects restrictive, individualized terms of partnership, labour, and domesticity. While some theories of lesbian separatism have come to rest on contradictory attachments to an essentialized experience of womanhood, the affective promise of lesbian and queer socialities, particularly for subjects who have experienced the (sexual, gendered, regulatory) violences of heterosexism, remains potent – the 'queer power, freedom, abundance or relief in the face of heterosexual misery and myopia' that Ward (2020: 114) also discusses. In their depictions of abundant queer sexual pleasure and joy, both *Work in Progress* and

Feel Good thus provide an important, affectively charged challenge to the miseries of straight culture, the 'emotional flatness [and] antiflamboyance' (2020: 116) that Ward argues typifies straightness, exemplified for instance by Fleabag.

Moreover, while the characters in the shows struggle to fully escape the privatized and individualized forms of care and desire dominant in heteronormative neoliberalism, both series also present more enduring sites of care, collectivity and politics *outside* of sexual and romantic relationships. In *Work in Progress*, Chris already exists in an affirming queer community – one in which his friends are careful and caring about his emotional needs. Abby appears to envy this world, where flashback scenes to her more limited lesbian life in the 1990s seem to ask: Would Abby have been a happy(/ier) queer if she had grown up in an era of more collective queer experience exemplified by Chris' life? In *Feel Good*, it is George who comes to discover community in her painfully earnest and somewhat cringeworthy, but ultimately well-meaning, teachers' social justice group, where she discovers her interest in activism and builds her self-esteem and sense of purpose outside of her isolated relationship with Mae (or the self-serving, detached irony of her wealthy, straight friends and family). Through this, George comes to reframe the unequal and unhappy terms of heteronormativity that her friends and family ascribe to as not all that different from her isolated, dishonest, and imbalanced entanglement with Mae, eventually rejecting Mae's misguided proposal of marriage: 'there has to be room for stuff I like.' At the end of *Work in Progress*, Chris similarly articulates the impossibility, loneliness, and misery of carrying the responsibility for Abby's wellness without his community for support. While sad for Mae and Abby, in many ways these scenes pose an important challenge to ideals of domestic and privatized care and romance, acting as catalysts for Mae and Abby to find other forms of companionship and support, too.

In this 'against the grain' reading (Gibbs and Lehtonen 2019; Wearing 2013), we suggest that it is the arrival or existence of the more minor characters of Chris and George in forms of queer political community that seems to hint at more radical social and political possibilities of escape – if only Abby and Mae would join them. In our desire for Abby and Mae to join a more collective journey of queer escape, we learn that while queer trauma, sexual shame, fear, and mental health issues can be explored in sexual intimate relationships, they cannot be resolved through them alone. As Eva Illouz (2012) argues, in neoliberal capitalism love – and we would add sex – hurts as it is imbued with the promise to solve the weight and contradictions of the neoliberal world we live in. In other words, sex (as good as it might be) cannot alone solve problems and pains that are ultimately social and political in nature. In a world where (queer) social and communal spaces are far and few in between, it is romance and sex that continues to be the primary form of attachment, the only thing that promises fulfilment and happiness outside of normative, neoliberal demands – as well as, cruelly, the thing that fails to deliver on such promises. What Mae and Abby experience, then, is a lesbian and queer escape emptied of some of its collective and political dimensions, a queerness unable to fulfil their and our utopian longings, what José Esteban Muńoz' calls the 'insistence on potentiality or concrete possibility for a future' (2019: 1).

Our argument here is not that we should reject the attachment to or desire for good sex; good sex, and relationships that centralize good sex, might be a very good thing indeed. But at the same time, if 'the impetus for many of queer culture's best insights is the desire not to reproduce the failed practices of straight culture' (Ward 2020: 141), we wonder what possibilities remain to imagine and build more social and communal forms of queer sociality and connection – including through, but not limited to, sex? In the next chapter, we continue exploring this question from the perspective of cis gay men, as we investigate how the protagonists of *Please Like Me* (2013–16) and *Special* (2019, 2021) find, not good or even better, but at least *good enough* sex amongst the ableist pressures of hetero- and homonormativity.

Chapter 3

GAY MALE SHAME AND GOOD ENOUGH SEX IN *PLEASE LIKE ME* AND *SPECIAL*

Introduction

If straight women like Fleabag are stuck in heteropessimist imaginaries of bad sex, and lesbians and non-binary queers like Mae and Abby wrestle with only partially fulfilling fantasies of queer escape, how do cis gay men navigate the expectations of sex today? Long associated with sex in secret, with disease and contagion, in recent years the image of the gay man who confidently owns his sexuality has become an emblem of good sex in TV, as well as in public cultures more generally. While Stanford Blatch in *Sex and the City* (1998–2004) and Will Truman in *Will and Grace* (1998–2006) were still mostly comical, desexualized characters, from *Queer as Folk* (1999–2000; 2000–5) to *Looking* (2014–16), we got many representations of hot gay men confidently celebrating their bodies and exploring the many pleasures that contemporary (mostly white and middle-class) gay culture has to offer. Such representations of gay sex push against heteronormative expectations of sex, not through heteropessimist commentary or fantasies of queer escape, but by outdoing them. While shows like *Queer as Folk* and *Looking* do explore the anxiety and shame that young gay men navigate in homophobic society, for the most part they emphasize the pleasures of sex as a route to self-discovery – where being 'out' provides a more fulfilling sexual future. If straight society wants to keep us and our sex stigmatized and hidden, these gay characters seem to signal, we should simply live bigger, more fabulous, and most of all *sexier* lives. Bad sex, in other words, is for straight people.

This push for good and even better – fabulous, adventurous and exciting – sex goes hand in hand with gay pride, the rise of the pink economy, and the achievement of LGBT rights such as same-sex marriage in the wake of the AIDS crisis in the United States and across Europe. In queer scholarship, these developments are often discussed as the co-optation of a more radical gender and sexual gay liberation politics within the rise of homonormative (Duggan 2004), homonationalist

(Puar 2007), and homocapitalist (Rao 2015) politics of the 1990s and 2000s. According to these authors, gay, mostly white and middle-class, cis male subjects located in the Global North are granted partial acceptance in society through their inclusion in capitalist consumerism and the nation-state. The drive to 'better sex', however, is not simply a move towards inclusion into heteronormativity, but the outperforming of heteronormative standards where gay men are expected to not just have the *same* but even *better* sexual lives than straight people. The promise here is that the shame and pain produced by living in a heteronormative homophobic society can be overcome, or at least ameliorated, through good and even better sex.[1] This promise – further exemplified by the complex cultural anxieties about, and fascination with, the pressures of the perfect gym body, Grindr orgies or chemsex parties – becomes particularly pronounced in an increasingly neoliberal and precarious present where other forms of queer collectivity and relationality are becoming less and less available (Hakim 2019b; Upton 2023).

But do gay men really do it better? The TV shows *Please Like Me* (2013–16) and *Special* (2019, 2021) offer some pertinent reflections on the imperative of good and better sex, and the disavowal of sexual shame and insecurity in gay male culture that goes along with it. Positioned at the crossroads of, unreachable dominant heterosexual norms and the cultural imperatives of gay pride and sexual promiscuity, Josh (*Please Like Me*) and Ryan (*Special*) trouble common representations of gay men as both sexually confident and successful. These shows centre on, and are written by, neurodivergent and disabled white gay cis men who struggle to live up to the ideal of the sexually confident gay man. Josh in *Please Like Me* (written and created by Josh Thomas, who has since talked about his ADHD and autism) finds sex and intimacy awkward and confusing and, instead of living it up on Grindr, must take care of his suicidal mother in the suburbs of Melbourne. Ryan in *Special* (written and created by Ryan O'Connell), works to hide his cerebral palsy, is out as gay but has never had sex, and struggles with his desire to create an independent, let alone fulfilling, sex life while living with his mother on the outskirts of LA. Rather than meeting the gay ideal of 'better' sex, both characters are in complex relationships with their mothers, mull over their 'imperfect' bodies, and linger in sexual shame, cringe, and self-deprecating humour.

Our reading of these shows extends long-standing debates in queer studies on the threat and value of gay shame (Halperin and Traub 2009; Love 2009; Ngai 2004; Sedgwick and Frank 1995) through an explicit focus on sex. We show how an embracing of shame can bring about new forms of sexual pleasure, not through the often-unattainable ideal of good and better sex but through forms of *good enough* sex – sex that, playing on Donald Winnicott (2016), is, all things considered, sufficient and pleasurable, rather than perfect or fabulous. In *cripping* (Kafer 2013; McRuer 2010) the expectations of good sex, we show how for the disabled and neurodivergent characters of these shows shame cannot be pushed aside but needs to be embraced for different forms of sexual connection and relationality to be possible.[2] Yet, we also reflect on the limits and contradictions of this emotional and sexual unmasking by highlighting the deeply ingrained layers of whiteness and capitalist productivity that constrain the scene of emotional and sexual liberation in both shows. Can 'good enough' sex actually fend off the threat of shame and carry the psychic and affective weight it is invested with?

Gay shame and even better sex

Both *Please Like Me* and *Special* centre around their protagonists' quest for good sex. In the first episode of *Please Like Me*, we meet Josh being broken up with by his girlfriend, Claire, who proclaims: 'I kinda think we have drifted . . . and also you are gay.' Once forced out of the closet, nobody seems much bothered or surprised about Josh's gayness, and so his anxiety comes to revolve more around fulfilling what it means to be gay rather than being gay in itself. In other words, instead of worrying about the stigma and social sanctions that being gay in a heteronormative society carries with it, Josh seems most anxious about having to live up to the expectations of being a successful gay subject, let alone a successful *sexual* gay subject. This anxiety is mainly expressed in insecurities about his body and sexual abilities. He worries about 'looking like a fifty-year-old toddler' and is afraid of putting things up his butt. Rather than reassuring him, his family and friends tend to reaffirm his insecurities. His mother wonders in front of him about whether he is bad in bed, and his ex-girlfriend jokes about how the first time they had sex, they weren't actually having sex but that Josh 'was just rubbing between me and the sheets.'

In a particularly telling scene, his cranky aunt Peg speculates on the size of his testicles, wondering whether Josh might have Klinefelter syndrome, a genetic variety in which children are born with XXY chromosomes. This scene highlights the entangled anxieties about sexuality, gender, and embodiment that mark Josh's life. While the show never directly names his neurodivergence, the show has been popular with a neuroqueer fanbase that has claimed Josh as one of their own on Reddit and other fan forums (Jones 2022).[3] After all, it is Josh being at odds not just with heteronormative but also with neurotypical society that makes the character so appealing and his quest for sex so relatable. He is socially awkward and compulsively blurts out comments in conflict with neurotypical expectations. He worries about having the wrong social and emotional responses, struggles with textures, bodily and sensory issues, and is generally depicted as feeling out of place in sex, as well as in broader life.

Neurodivergence, mental health, and disability also feature prominently in the show more generally. Josh's coming out is overshadowed by his mother's attempted suicide. Her well-being fluctuates across the series, as his sexual self-discovery consistently gets interrupted by visiting his mum at home or at a mental health clinic. Despite his concerns about his mother's health, Josh also makes friends amongst his mother's new peers. It is here he befriends Hannah, a depressed lesbian played by Hannah Gadsby (who themselves has also come to identify as autistic and has created a show about the experience). Hannah, like Josh, struggles with heteronormative, ableist and neurotypical norms – often in ways that allow the key characters to have meaningful conversations that social convention would ask them to avoid. Like Hannah and his mother, Josh is often more at home in the world of structured day visits and frank discussions about mental health than he is when faced with the optimistic sexual demands of being a twenty-something gay man.

The first season of the show revolves around Josh meeting the toned, white and normatively handsome Geoffrey, who shares an office with Josh's best friend and housemate Tom. When Geoffrey comes over for dinner, Josh ends up in bed with him. Josh is awkward about Geoffrey's unexpected advances, keeps finding reasons to avoid having sex with him and is partly embarrassed and partly relieved when he gets a lip bleed as Geoffrey tries to kiss him, spoiling their first sexual encounter. Yet, despite their failed attempt at sex, Geoffrey stays adamant about his desire for Josh. They continue to meet and try to have sex – to loud opera music and dimmed lights to keep Josh's anxiety about intimacy and anal sex at bay – but keep on getting interrupted and struggle to connect. Despite Geoffrey telling Josh that he loves him, Josh is hesitant about their relationship and frequently embarrassed by Geoffrey, telling his best friend Tom: 'I don't think I really like him . . . I think I am just grateful that he has so many muscles and that he is willing to kiss me.' Josh, in other words, does not actually desire Geoffrey but simply desires being desired by him (reflective of Fleabag's similar claim we discussed in Chapter 1).

In *Unmasking Autism*, Devon Price (2022) describes how struggling to know one's own desire is not just a crucial condition of a closeted queer but also that of a masked neurodivergent experience where one's wants and desires are suppressed to avoid being shamed in heteronormative and neurotypical society. This hesitance and uncertainty of naming one's desires is also crucial to Katherine Angel's (2021a) critique of 'enthusiastic consent' which we discuss in the introduction and in Chapter 6, in relation to women. Josh, too, is caught in such confusion. As suggested by the title of the show, his desire is without a clear object or direction and is instead structured around the plea to 'please like me', ideally by someone who ranks high in the sexual desirability scale of gay culture. However, once this wish is met and someone does desire him, Josh does not know what to do. In other words, despite his desire to be desired, he does not know how to *be* once he is desired. As a result, he ends up toying with Geoffrey whom he calls after being rejected by another man at a gay bar, just to break up with him shortly after as 'he is just always so there'. Sex and intimacy for Josh, then, seem not just hard to attain, but, like for many gay men, less about actual desire and more about a sense of self value that shields against feelings of unworthiness and shame (Odets 2019).

Ryan in *Special* is stuck in a similar predicament. In the first episode, we meet him lamenting to his physiotherapist that 'I am not able-bodied enough to be hanging in the mainstream world, but I am not disabled enough to be hanging out with the cool PT [physical therapy] crowd'. His self-deprecating irony stems from his struggle to live a life not defined by society's and his own perceptions of his disability, let alone a fulfilling sex life. Still living with his mum, he is about to move out to start an unpaid internship at the website *Eggwoke*, focused on publishing confessional stories. Ryan struggles with the demands of the new job and avoids disclosing that he has cerebral palsy. After he gets publicly shamed for being unable to carry out some physical tasks and is confronted by his boss, Ryan reveals he got hit by a car (which he did, but which is not the reason he has difficulties opening envelopes neatly). His boss is delighted about this mistaken confession: 'everybody come hug Ryan. He was hit by a car, and now he has a weird, sad limp forever.' The lie of the car accident allows him to claim that he was not disabled once, presumably making his disability a tragic incident rather than a core part of who he is.

It also makes for a good story. As Alison Kafer argues, the stories we tell of disability are important, because 'how one understands disability in the present determines how one imagines disability in the future; one's assumptions about the experience of disability create one's conception of a better future' (2013: 2). The story of his accident sustains the broader 'curative' imagination in which 'the very *absence* of disability signals a better future' and 'the *presence* of disability . . . bares too many traces of the ills of the present to be desirable' (2013: 2, emphasis original). Cheered on by his boss, Ryan writes his first article: 'Getting Hit by a Car was Fucking Awesome!' The story goes viral and secures him praise, and Ryan seems more secure in the knowledge that his disability has afforded him something he perceives as valuable. His overall story becomes one of survival and overcoming this tragic event. Difficult questions of structural injustice in his new workplace are sidestepped, and Ryan is, at least initially, happy to have his story be one of 'compassion and charitable feelings' (Schweik 2009, cited in Kafer 2013: 10). While Ryan is now exploited as an object of 'inspiration' (Young 2014), it moves him closer to what he perceives as a 'good' future.

Hidden and exploited in his professional life, Ryan's disability troubles him even more in his search for sex and intimacy. When his physiotherapist suggests that he try Grindr, he laughs: 'I love that you think I have enough self-esteem to be on Grindr', and continues: 'What would my profile even say? I am gay *and* disabled, but I promise not to drool on you until the third date?' Ryan's biting irony communicates his frustration of being a virgin in his early thirties, a shame for any self-respecting millennial, let alone a gay millennial. But it also reveals the shame he feels about his disability – his perception of the way his body fails to act in line with an idealized, ableist gay norm. At work, Ryan befriends Kim, a self-declared 'voluptuous brown girl' who has made a writing career out of body positivity and tries to help him in his quest for sex. When Kim notices how uncomfortable Ryan is at their boss's pool party, surrounded by meticulously trained pool bodies glistening in the sun, she takes him to the side for some coaching in body positivity. When she tells him: 'take off all your clothes and tell me everything you love about your body', Ryan struggles to list more than his nipples, and replies with a flat-out 'no' when she asks him if he feels better. Kim's self-love mantra falls silent when it comes to Ryan's experiences of disability – asking him to reframe the things he hates about his body, to overcome the 'tragedy' that has befallen him. In doing so, Kim ignores the lived experience of impairment that shapes Ryan's experience of his body and surroundings (particularly in the context of the gay male desirability he is confronted with at the party).

As Kafer (2013) argues, while attention must be given to the structural and relational impacts of disability, if we fail to acknowledge the pain, fatigue and experience of the body, we leave much of disabled people's experience unexamined. Perhaps if Kim made 'room for people to acknowledge – even mourn – a change in form or function' while also acknowledging 'that such changes cannot be understood apart from the context in which they occur' (2013: 6), Ryan's shame could be felt and placed in a social context revealing of its origins. But in asking Ryan to simply push away his feelings of shame, the focus on positive feelings adds to that shame: Ryan now feels bad not only about his body but also about feeling bad. Incidentally, Kim later learns the racialized limits of her mantra, when some thin, white girls tell her how *inspiring* they find her – if someone like *Kim* can feel good, well then, *they* certainly should. In this biting commentary on the positive psychology model underlying body positivity as it is translated through bodily, racialized, and ableist frames, the show demonstrates how negative experiences of social shame cannot just be turned into positive feelings of pride or happiness.

The narrative arc of Ryan's quest for sex culminates when he bumps into a man he has texted on Grindr at the pool party. When his Grindr acquaintance takes him into a bedroom, Ryan awkwardly undresses as his hook-up comments on his 'cool scar', and they start kissing. Yet, the hook-up ends abruptly when the other guy ends the sex he initiated, with Ryan left asking, 'was it that bad?' The interaction is not desired, and sex (here at least) for Ryan has no future. At first encouraged by Kim to change his attitude, only to be shamed and dismissed, Ryan is then deemed not good enough *at* and therefore not good enough *for* sex, ostracized from the sexual spectacle unfolding at the pool party around him. As McRuer (2010) argues, shame for queer disabled people is produced not just by heteronormativity but also by norms of 'compulsory able-bodiedness' that infuse gay communities where disabled queer life is relegated to the shifting dynamics of fetishization and erasure. Ryan's disability is interesting as a 'scar' but not when it informs his lack of experience in interacting during sex.[4]

Both Josh and Ryan, then, are represented as failing as the ideal gay sexual subjects of good and even better sex. They are not the attractive, sexy, confident men associated with contemporary gay male culture, nor are they driven, glamorous, or even camp enough to make up for this lack. Instead, they are anxious about their bodies and associate sex with shame and insecurity rather than pleasure and prowess. Both Josh and Ryan constitute the vexed figure of what Sara Ahmed (2004) calls the 'unhappy queer', produced as counterfoil for the construction of happy heterosexuality. Yet, rather than simply juxtaposed to the supposedly happy heterosexual, Ryan and Josh are primarily framed as negative counterparts to the sexually liberated gay subject of good and even better sex. As such, they are produced precisely through a combination of shame and sexlessness that no self-respecting gay person is meant to want.

The figure of the unhappy queer highlights that Josh and Ryan cannot be the subjects of good gay sex exactly because they enact the wrong affective register to accrue value in the economy of gay male sexual desire. In other words, they are not just not normatively 'attractive' enough, but also too sad, too awkward, and too self-hating to have good sex, imagined through the imperative of pride, confidence and self-love. As Ru Paul declares to a global audience of gay men at the end of every episode of *Ru Paul's Drag Race*: 'If you cannot love yourself, how in the hell are you gonna love somebody else?' What is meant as a mantra for overcoming the shame that heteronormative society imposes on queer existence can also work as an imperative and yardstick that queer men have to live up to, to be seen as lovable in the first place.[5] Josh and Ryan are stuck in this double-bind: Without a way to love themselves, how are they are gonna love somebody else, or find somebody else who loves them?

Finding good enough sex

Unable to access the promise of good sex through proud and happy gay male subjectivity, both Josh and Ryan find other ways to create sexual and intimate connection. In season 2 of *Please Like Me,* Josh continues to struggle with his sexual desire. He now has a crush on his housemate Patrick, who in his straight-acting manner and masculine physique easily picks up hot guys in gay bars and on Grindr, having good and even great sex in the flat. In a telling juxtaposition, we see Tom having sex with his girlfriend and Patrick fucking a hot man he picked up at the bar, while Josh is failing at changing his baby stepsister's diaper. While heterosexuals have good and gays even better sex, Josh has poo on his fingers. Yet this situation is about to change when Patrick momentarily falls for Josh's charm. Patrick is disarmed by Josh, letting him into his vulnerability by showing him how he failed at his high school gymnastics routine. They get drunk and make out. When Josh tries to make out again the next morning, Patrick tells him that his breath smells and that he does not want to have sex with him: 'I really like you, I like spending time with you, I like hugging you, I like kissing you, I just don't want to have sex with you.' Like Ryan in *Special*, Josh is rejected as not good enough for sex. He is clearly hurt, rants about how 'sexually repulsive' he must be and how he is going to go extinct like pandas as they 'refuse to have sex with each other', and ultimately stops talking to Patrick.

Josh's behaviour towards Patrick is represented as clearly childish and emotionally immature. His behaviour is out of line with the cultural codex of casual sex in gay male circles, where sex as well as the rejection of sexual advances should be easily shrugged off and not taken too seriously (Delany 1999). It is also out of line with the feminist codex that nobody has the 'right to sex', which Amia Srinivasan discusses as the notion that 'no one is obliged to desire anyone else, that no one has a right to be desired' (2022: 90). Yet while Srinivasan argues that nobody has the right to sex or to be desired, she also insists that the question of 'who is desired and who isn't is a political question, a question usually answered by more general patterns of domination and exclusion' (2022: 90). In stopping to speak to Patrick, Josh struggles to fully accept that he has no right to have sex with Patrick, yet he also finds a way to refuse the hierarchy of desirability that structures contemporary gay male sexual cultures. Deemed unworthy of good sex, he refuses not just Patrick but also the chase for good and even better sex altogether.

Instead, Josh develops other forms of intimate and sexual connection. Srinivasan suggests that if sexual desire is also a political question infused by patterns of power and hierarchy, 'the fact is that our sexual preferences can and do alter, sometimes under the operation of our own wills – not automatically, but not impossibly either' (2022: 91). And, whether fully consciously or not, over the course of the seasons, Josh's desire does alter. Instead of wasting his energy on Patrick, Josh strikes up an intimate relationship with the equally awkward Arnold, who stays at the 'mental home' where Josh's mum now lives. Arnold struggles with an anxiety disorder and, from time to time, voluntarily comes to live in the ward. The two become friends, bonding over being bullied as kids, as well as being generally at odds with the world around them. They go on dates and have their first kiss at the zoo. Letting the other into their own vulnerability, they connect. When Patrick tries to make up with Josh at a later point, Josh decides against him and desires Arnold instead.

Michael Warner suggests that shame can create a 'special kind of sociability' that 'begins in an acknowledgement of all that is most abject and reputable in oneself' (2000: 35). He argues that in the ideal scenario, queer shame can work to bring 'into great intimacy by their common experience of being despised and rejected in a world of norms that they now recognize as false morality' (2000: 35). Josh and Arnold weave such bonds of intimacy out of their shame, fear, and insecurities. Josh is there when Arnold has panic attacks and accompanies him on his journey of coming out to his adoptive parents. In a key scene, Josh convinces his own dad, Alan, to play Arnold's father in a practice run for Arnold coming out. Josh directs his father as if in a play, to be dismissive of Arnold and his voice gradually softening: 'as the song changes, gradually change your mind.' What starts as a planned act becomes reality when his dad is actually moved by Arnold's performance, who himself eases into singing Sia's 'Chandelier', revealing his own emotional turmoil. Teary-eyed, Josh's dad hugs Arnold, telling him he is proud of him for being a good person – unclear whether he is now playacting for Arnold or talking to his own son, Josh. As Emily Nussbaum points out in *The New Yorker*, in this scene we are 'witnessing the miracle: the performance of family love becoming real, behind the mask of another man, as Alan makes the leap from "accepting" his gay child to adoring him, seeing him fully' (2018). For a moment, the deadpan and awkward irony of the show breaks and relational bonds are being formed (between Alan and Arnold) and healed (between Alan and Josh himself).

Josh's relationship with Arnold in some ways mirrors his relationship with his mother who he also takes care of, with Josh's friends joking that he has a 'rescue complex'. Yet, as we can see in the singing scene just described, Arnold also rescues Josh, and perhaps Josh is able to shift the dynamics of caring/cared for with his mother through being cared for by someone else, too. With Arnold, Josh can be weird, he can go on rants, let his external monologues flow – and he *can have sex*. After a couple of dates, Arnold organizes a romantic date in an abandoned warehouse. Josh is overwhelmed by the situation, asking out loud if this is where 'we are gonna have sex . . . for the first time' before bursting out into the 1990s hit 'Kiss me' by Sixpence None the Richer. Arnold laughs about, and with, Josh's unmasked excitement. We see them kissing, undressing and getting lost in random comments, before carefully having anal sex. Negotiating pleasure and shame, Josh asks, 'It's ok?' to which Arnold replies, 'Yeah, it truly is, just never ask me if I am okay during sex again'. Sex here is neither glorious and sleek, nor perfectly intentional. Instead, it is full of shame but also of pleasure, reciprocity, and connection.

In this representation, we get a sense of what, drawing on Winnicott (2016), we call 'good enough sex'. Winnicott uses the concept of the 'good enough parent' to describe forms of parenting that produce a nurturing environment for child development while counteracting the pressures and dangers of idealized forms of parenting and motherhood. The concept of 'good enough sex' similarly describes a form of sex that is nurturing, consensual, and pleasurable, while fending off the pressures of good and better sex, where sex is imbued with impossible standards and expectations. This concept is of particular relevance to gay male sexual communities which Walt

Odets (2019) describes as infused with the notion of sport, where sex is understood and practised as a competitive and purely physical performance. Yet, it is also key to thinking about the imperative of good sex in contemporary society more generally, where, as Meg-John Barker, Rosalind Gill, and Laura Harvey (2018) show, sex and sex advice are often structured around neoliberal notions of performance, success, and pleasure maximization.

We get a similar representation of 'good enough' sex in *Special.* After his fruitless attempt at finding sex on Grindr and at the pool party, Kim suggests that Ryan sees a sex worker. On the day, he is visibly anxious, dressed in a suit that seems to articulate the anxiety of a job interview rather than preparedness for hot sex. Yet, once Ryan actually meets Shay, who is caring and relaxed (even when Ryan accidentally kicks him in the face trying to undress), Ryan eases into the situation (Figure 3.1). We see them having anal sex, negotiated explicitly *with* the physical requirements of Ryan's body. Sex here is not a performance, nor the result of a perfect romance, but a careful negotiation of desires, needs and pleasures. Shay later tells him that he has other clients with CP, and, importantly, agrees with Ryan when he says he will have other (not solicited) sex in the future. In this scene, we get one of the rare representations of generative sex with sex workers that is key to the sexual cultures of disabled people

Figure 3.1 In *Special*, Shay, a sex worker Ryan has hired for his first sexual experience, is gentle, understanding and playful, even when Ryan accidentally kicks him in the face. *Special* © Warner Bros. Television /Netflix 2019–21.

for whom sex work can be a safer space for exploration and intimacy (see e.g. Garofalo Geymonat 2019). With Shay, there is no performance pressure, but care and desire are present instead (see also Davies 2021). Ryan learns a new way of being with a person who is a professional at not just good and better but, most importantly, *good enough* sex – sex that gives Ryan a sense of security from which he can develop a new relationship with himself, his body, and others.

Relieved by his experience, Ryan later meets the dancer Tanner at a straight bar. They end up in bed together, and what starts as a one-night stand develops into a complex relationship. Tanner figures that their night together was Ryan's first time going home with a guy at a bar, but rather than being freaked out by it, they spend the day bonding over coming-out stories and gay divas. And while Ryan never fully unmasks in front of Tanner, who is in an open marriage with another man, they strike a loving relationship sharing vulnerabilities, exploring each other and having good enough sex. For both Ryan and Josh, then, sex and intimacy are possible after all – not through the overcoming of shame and vulnerability but by sharing in it. Between the imperfect nature of their desires and the imperfect ways in which they are desired is exactly where their sexual confidence is developed. If you can't be loved by someone else, how the hell are you gonna love yourself?

The limits of gay shame

While both Josh and Ryan find ways to work through their shame, their vulnerability and shame also have restorative limits as they are rooted within the wider social context of whiteness and neoliberal productivity. Josh is not just freaked out by sexuality but awkward about nearly everything in his life – specifically about his position in the white settler colonial society of Australia, where what Aileen Moreton-Robinson discusses as the 'perpetual Indigenous dispossession' (2015: xi) haunts the national, non-Indigenous imaginary of belonging. *Please Like Me* is littered with racial and racist references that spurt out of Josh and other white characters on the show like from a repressed unconscious. His mother and aunt make racist jokes about his dad's Thai wife, Mae, Arnold randomly talks about feeling bad for people in Africa, and Josh awkwardly discusses how he 'thought that Gondwanaland is what Aboriginal people call Australia'. This awkward and often-offensive discussion of race and racism is not confined to the show itself, but also featured in the media discussion around it.

For example, during a panel for a BingeFest event at the Sydney Opera House in 2016, Josh Thomas stated that the reason there were so few people of colour in the show was that 'finding an experienced actor that's not white is really hard', amongst other comments about casting and racial stereotypes. His statement led to public pushback in and outside of Australia, and he later apologized for being 'dumb, illogical' and 'insensitive' (Eyewitness News 2020).

Dumb, illogical, and insensitive also describes how Josh behaves towards characters of colour in the show itself. While his gay shame is disarming and even productive of new forms of relating, his white shame and anxiety are not just painful to watch but also destructive of social and intimate relationships. This becomes most clear in his direct contact with the few characters of colour in the show. Taking care of his Thai-Australian half-sister, he wonders: 'she does not look like my sister.' And when Josh goes on a date with a Wurundjeri man, Ricky, he begins the date with a monologue about how 'anxious' he feels about the history of colonialism, questions Ricky intensely on whether he can hail a taxi (seemingly regurgitating headlines from a 2016 controversy in Melbourne (Wahlquist 2016)) and rants how 'everyone is still so racist, not me, obviously cause I am here on a date with you'. His date, unsurprised but uncomfortable with the rapid derailment of the conversation, attempts to highlight the offensiveness of Josh's comments – 'is [this] a date? Or the world's worst application for Young Australian of the Year?' – and finally interjects with: 'if you keep going on about this, I am not going to have sex with you.' They have sex anyway, but when an unreflective Josh tells his friends he got in contact with Ricky again ('Remember that boy who is Aboriginal – which doesn't define him I just need a very quick way of letting you know which boy I'm talking about'), Ricky declines to see him.

Jack Halberstam (2005) describes gay shame as a specifically white male formation. Halberstam argues that queer discussions of gay male shame often get stuck in white male anxieties, while sidelining the feminist and queer of colour critiques that have articulated ways to work against the social forces that produce shame, rather than getting stuck in a shame/pride binary. Halberstam's provocation aimed at moving beyond shame is at risk of prematurely leaving behind the complex, sticky and ambivalent power shame has over many queer people, including lesbians and queer people of colour (Love 2009; Probyn 2005; Stockton 2006). Yet, it offers a way to understand some of the potentially destructive ways in which white gay male shame, particularly in the context of coloniality, can also operate through the projection of shame through racialization. Halberstam discusses how white gay artists like Andy Warhol come to 'project shame, castration, and vulnerability onto the feminized and racialized body' (2005: 229). The same can be said about Josh who often makes his own shame the problem of racialized others.

As such, *Please Like Me* offers a pertinent cultural object through which to unpack how gay shame can intertwine with colonial shame and guilt in Australia, where white queer belonging often obscures how whiteness imbues experiences of inclusion or exclusion, despite its depiction as 'predicated on an anxious form of embodied belonging that only exists in particular "settled locations"' (Riggs 2006: 52).[6] As Sara Ahmed (2004) argues in the context of colonial memory and shame in Australia, the expression of shame has acted as a performative *inexpressive,* aimed at restoring the national image (of the apologizer) rather than reconciling the wrongs committed in the ongoing project of settler colonialism (see also Probyn 2005). In this, the show has notable parallels with another popular Australian queer export, *The Adventures of Priscilla, Queen of the Desert* (1994), in which the subversive celebration of (white) queer and gay identities in Australia works in relation and through, we would argue, violently sexist depictions of an Asian woman character and an 'unsettled' engagement with Aboriginal communities and land (see e.g. Moreton-Robinson 2015; Riggs 2006). In both of these popular depictions of white queer Australian life, racial anxieties leak into the narrative through stories involving racial difference and dispossession that cannot be properly named. In the case of *Please Like Me*, these racial anxieties similarly haunt Josh's interactions without in any way changing his behaviour or attitudes, or becoming a lens through which his shame or struggles can be understood (Kohnen 2022). Josh says he *feels* bad but doesn't seem to (want to) change. Ricky's ultimate rejection of Josh is presented as a seeming reminder of Josh's sexual and romantic failings, while his behaviour *towards* Ricky haunts the rejection by never being revisited in the show. As Ahmed argues, 'what is shameful is passed over through the enactment of shame . . . allowing the endless deferral of responsibility for injustice in the present' (2004: 120).[7]

Ryan's engagement with shame in *Special* is different if not necessarily less troublesome. His whiteness is not a key source of his shame, and he connects with Kim who shares her own struggles of being a larger woman of colour in the LA media industry. She confesses that, despite her talk of body positivity, she feels the pressure to present herself impeccably and has a shopping addiction, resulting in several tens of thousands of dollars of debt. While there is a gendered and racialized dynamic in how Kim often comes to assure Ryan (in ways we extend in the more in-depth discussion of a similar dynamic in *It's a Sin* (2021) in Chapter 4), he also comes to assist her, and they bond together in their differently located, yet also shared, senses of vulnerability and shame (Maple 2019). Significantly, both are struggling with how the glitzy LA media world forces them to market their experiences of racism, homophobia, sexism, and ableism as 'trauma porn' for clickbaiting online journalism.

As Francesca Sobande (2019b) has shown, contemporary media culture works through the 'woke-washing' of public communications in which it is the personal and collective social justice struggles of marginalized groups that accrue increasing market value. *Special* critiques the turning into commodities of stories of struggle and shame, while never being able to fully shake off this dynamic. Both Kim and Ryan, after all, are only able to open up and unmask their shame and vulnerability as part of their income generation and market appeal, where the more successful they become in their lives and respective careers, the more they do so. For both Kim and Ryan, an investment in this vulnerable writing quickly becomes a literal 'tick box' exercise (Ahmed 2012) for their employers: Kim is explicitly told she is the 'girl . . . woman stuff' writer at her laughably white and masculine new job at *Listicle*, while Ryan's boss urges him to reduce his writing on disability at *Eggwoke* to 'top ten times I fell down'. Eventually, neither Ryan nor Kim finds a sense of empowerment through the version of vulnerability politics they are asked to perform: it boxes them in and elides the increasingly precarious realities from which the embracing of such vulnerability is performed.

Moreover, while Ryan comes to unmask more of himself, he remains haunted by the shame that his disability carries. When his boss sets him up on a date with her deaf cousin, Ryan is outraged, struggling to even look at him across the table and speaking only to his interpreter. He later confronts his boss about her insensitive attempt at matchmaking, telling her that 'I can still do better than a deaf guy'. The scene is jarring. Ryan's otherwise deplorable boss directs him to the online discourse *about* disability that he thought he was (dishonestly) directing, encouraging him to 'Twitter' his 'internalised ableism'. In this scene, we can see that Ryan's desire to frame his disability as an abjected bodily 'thing' is in conflict with the views of others who understand him as disabled. Ryan's desperation to identify his disability as a purely medical bodily impairment that can be overcome (or at least monetized) is reiterated across the series – whether through his story of the car accident, his refusals to identify as disabled or accept reasonable adjustments at work, or his distancing envy of the 'cool PT crowd'.[8]

Our argument here is not to further shame Ryan for his struggles to make sense of himself. Rather, it is to demonstrate the limits of Ryan's desire to strictly medicalize (and distance) his experience of disability from his sexuality because of shame. Because when his hierarchical view of disability and sex is applied to his deaf date, that shame hurts others too. Indeed, in contrast to his date's willingness to navigate a world of diverse embodiment (the ASL interpreter is working to make *Ryan's* experience of the date smoother, given that Ryan is not part of the Deaf community), Ryan is only able to see his date as having a deficit on a hierarchical list of impairments – one that is *worse* than his own. Differently to desiring a sexual future that may be less *disabling* for everyone (as in, where fewer stigmas and barriers exist that prevent him and others from participating in sex), Ryan invests in the 'curative imaginary' (Kafer 2013) expressed in the desire for a sexual future for himself where he is distanced from the shame of impairment (his own or others'). His deplorable boss, then, is probably right. Ryan's 'ideal' man and world remains one that is avoidant, or better yet untouched by, the disability 'thing', as he calls it. But how are you gonna love yourself if you can't love anyone who is like you?

The threat of bad sex

Yet, when Ryan goes on a date with a perfect kind of (non-disabled) guy, who claims to love Ryan's writing and initially seems great, the guy suddenly starts fetishizing Ryan's wearing of leg braces, listing off Ryan's physical impairments while inside him and saying how he 'knows it's weird' to be into disabled guys. Ryan continues to have sex with him, but lying in the bath later on, repulsed by the encounter, he tries desperately to scrub the memory of the man's kisses on his scars away. Here, someone did treat his disability as a fetishized 'thing', and it wasn't good sex at all. After these experiences, Ryan eventually confronts his own ableism and joins a group formed around experiences of disability, *The Crips*, which celebrates their cripness and pushes back against non-disabled society. He tells them about the date, and the sharing of fetishization is a comfort – that sex *was* bad, but not *because* Ryan is disabled. Ryan goes back to Tanner, who at least has more compassionate ways of engaging in good enough sex with him, acknowledging some vulnerability.

And yet once Ryan finds the conceptual language to make sense of his disability, he finds it hard to continue his relationship with Tanner, who is largely uninterested in educating himself on issues of disability. Tanner prefers to see Ryan as 'normal', and shows off his fluid dance moves at a prom organized by *The Crips* in a misguided effort to include himself – not recognizing why this might offend. The incompatibilities between Tanner's (and originally Ryan's) desire to not make disability a thing within their relationship, and Ryan's growing recognition that it might be a big thing for him, come to a head when they go on a trip to the countryside. The atmosphere is tense, particularly when Tanner continues to elide Ryan's experiences of embodiment, to avoid that which he perceives will shame Ryan, insisting that he is the clumsier of the two. Ryan is increasingly frustrated by Tanner's desire not to see his experiences of disability for what they are. Yet, he shuts Tanner out of this frustration, contrasting with the mutual vulnerability that typified their earlier encounters. When they try to have make-up sex, Tanner suggests that Ryan tries topping him. Ryan is ecstatic when Tanner tells him: 'that's my boy . . . I think you have a future in topping.' In season 1, this is exactly the kind of future Ryan would have wanted: where his body is just like anyone else's; a future where disability isn't a 'thing'. Both seem to enjoy themselves, and maybe there is a future in sex, maybe better sex can save their relationship.

Yet, once they are done and Ryan pulls out, there is shit on his penis. Ryan, immediately repulsed by the situation and haunted by the spectre of bad sex, is overcome with shame and anger and blames Tanner for the mishap – implying he was unprepared for sex. Tanner is hurt and reminds Ryan that he did not make him feel bad or ashamed when he struggled with sex earlier in the relationship. The acknowledgement of shame is too much for Ryan to discuss and shortly after he breaks up with Tanner. Tanner's complicated treatment of Ryan's body becomes concentrated on this moment of bodily abjection. The body (his own and others') continues to mess up Ryan's imagination of perfect sex – the gross, the bodily, the frustratingly present, the clumsy remain things that Ryan can't quite name but that also can't be hidden when it comes to sex. Tanner accuses Ryan of refusing to talk about his disability meaningfully, keeping Tanner in a place where he will only ever get it wrong. While in many ways he might be right, just as in many ways Ryan *should* break up with Tanner, it is bad sex that makes it possible for him to do so. Because the shame of bad sex is too unbearable to hold, it is an acceptable reason to dump your hot boyfriend, while his ableism and poor treatment of Ryan up until and after that bad sex is not.

Haunted by the unrelenting shame of bad sex, Josh and Arnold's relationship in *Please Like Me* ends in a similar way. At the end of the third season, they are also on holiday in the countryside, camping with their friends. Josh is emotionally distant and increasingly embarrassed by Arnold for reasons that remain unclear to both Josh and the viewer. When they try to have sex, we see them awkwardly doing so outdoors, bent over a tree branch, looking towards a grey and windy beach. Arnold cums, but when he tries to return the favour, Josh is not into it, tensely trying to jerk himself off for a bit, he chuckles and pulls up his pants. Here, sex is no longer good enough, but *bad*: full of shame and tension, void of pleasure and connection. And like in *Special,* it is bad sex that comes to mark the end of the relationship. When Josh is crying in the tent the night after, Arnold asks him, 'what is wrong', to which Josh replies that he thinks they need to break up. Arnold tells Josh off for his cruelty and has an angry panic attack: 'you are always worrying about your fucking forehead, it's not even your worst feature', and 'anytime everyone is happy and calm you say something mean', ending with the warning that in his 'pathological quest for stimulus . . . you are never going to be happy Josh!' – before breaking down in tears and apologizing.

By the end of both series then, these characters have found ways to work through and with their shame, yet remain haunted by the scene of bad sex and still also get occasionally caught up in its potentially destructive force. Both Josh and Ryan are gay male antiheroes who don't travel far from the situation they started with, though possibly with a bit more love (for themselves and others), and a few new pathways to finding it. While recovering from the key narrative turn of the series – his mother's death – Josh finishes some grief counselling sessions, moves back in with his best friend Tom, and continues his quest for good and better sex on Grindr and in the gay bars of Melbourne. Ryan, on the other hand, stands up for himself and quits his job, recuperates his relationship with his mother, and chooses friendship (for now) with the cute, clued-up Henry from *The Crips* meetings, less afraid of negotiating the future of sex. Walking home, Ryan manages to dodge a car this time, but it is ultimately unclear what his next 'story' will be. Perhaps Ryan will find out what a crip queer future might look like for him, and Josh will sustain a small community that will get him through the days of grief ahead of him – not yet the ideal gay subject of better sex, but also not the sexless and isolated panda he is afraid of becoming. Both remain conflicted while continuing to cause hurt to others, yet both have also found ways to unmask, engage their shame, and find, if not glorious, then at least *good enough* sex and intimate connection.

What our analysis highlights, is that like other emotions, shame is enmeshed within the wider power constellations it emerges out of. It can help us open up and relate to others, be the source of connection and shared vulnerability – rather than something that will either prohibit or promise the (sexual) future one seeks. As such, we should be careful with its erasure in an aim for gay pride and even better sex, while also being cautious about simple celebrations of shame as the radical counter to the potentially oppressive politics of pride. As Heather Love reminds us, 'if shame will bring us together, it is also the case that it can, will, and does tear us apart' (2007: 14). Rather than simply embracing shame, we need to stay with its ambivalent force and, like Josh and Ryan, aim to learn how to navigate the complex ways in which it infuses the scenes of sex and relationality. One way of doing so is through the creation of forms of good enough sex from which different forms of relationality, connection, and subjectivity can emerge – sex that circumvents the performance pressures of good and better sex imperatives and that can hold on to the messiness, tension, disappointment, and potential for hurt and hurting others inherent in intimate relationality. From the position of 'good enough' sex, a future of loving *yourself* and *someone else* may be possible – after all, if you can't fuck it up, how the hell are you gonna learn to love in the first place?

Chapter 4

WHEN SEX WAS STILL GOOD IN *IT'S A SIN* AND *POSE*

Introduction

In previous chapters, we have reflected on the sex of the present as awkward, difficult, or unfulfilling – a site of pleasure and intimacy but often also cruel disappointment. In contrast, in *Pose* (2018–21) and *It's a Sin* (2021), two shows that chronicle everyday friendships and queer communities in, respectively, 1980s New York and London, the sex and intimacy of the past is positioned as the space of pleasure and hopefulness. This hopefulness is present despite (or rather in relation to, as we explore below) the 'bad' sexual politics of the era, with its wilful disregard and hostility for minoritized sexual and gendered subjects. In this way, *It's a Sin* and *Pose* explore a decade which is easily remembered as a time of only loss and suffering for trans, queer, and gay people in the context of the AIDS crisis, as also being one of reciprocity, resilience and, yes, good sex.[1] In *Pose*, 1980s cinematic and sitcom conventions present the found family of the Ballroom scene as a place of magical, transformative, multidimensional intimacy – one that buffers against the violence, racism, and poverty faced by its predominantly Black and Latinx queer and trans community. *It's a Sin* draws more recognizably on the legacy of HIV/AIDS-themed melodrama to tell a story of sexual discovery and friendship amongst a group of friends living in London during Thatcher's reign. As the years pass from the late 1980s towards the 1990s, both series use nostalgic cinematic and televisual cues to depict queer characters who confront the communal and personal tragedy of the epidemic in different ways.

In this chapter, we investigate how both series mobilize nostalgia for this past through affective narratives of *progress* and *loss* to tell stories of queer (communal if not individual) survival. For audiences situated in the 2020s, we suggest that the key emotional pull of this narrative is the depiction of a time when sex was still *good* – a force of transgression, community, and political liberation, despite, or even because of, the lethal danger it carried. While others seek to explicitly examine the representations of HIV/AIDS in these series (see e.g.

Bollas 2022; Duckels 2022; Pearl 2023), we are more interested in the sexual and representational politics of these historical pieces as they appear in the 2020s (see also Harrison 2023; Pensis 2019; Stamm 2020), particularly for how they contrast with the representation of bad sex in the contemporary moment we have discussed in previous chapters. Cognizant of José Esteban Muñoz's reminder that a queer utopian potential is often 'distilled from the past and used to imagine a future' (2019: 1), both *Pose* and *It's a Sin* reframe narratives of sexual regret and individualized blame common to mainstream Anglo-American representations of HIV/AIDS from the 1980s, emphasizing good sex and sexuality instead. That is, by demonstrating the possibilities of transgressive sex in terrible times, the series provides a paradoxical push away from and pull towards this tragic era, offering important and unique imaginations of the possibilities of sex today.

In viewing these shows as a nostalgic re-remembering of a time when queer life and existence was hard and fragile, but queer sex was still good – transformative, radical, and potentially liberatory – they relate differently to our focus on bad sex. On the one hand, these shows seek to correct or repair historic representations of queer sex and intimacies of the 1980s as only tainted by loss and illness. On the other, by extending the site of intimacy to queer care, as it is contrasted with the failings of normative intimacies and state-provided healthcare, they present a *bad* sexual political context we are allowed to feel we have *progressed from*, while simultaneously presenting a sense of *loss* for a simpler time of queer community. In doing so, both series produce a complex affective pull for audiences of the 2020s. In this chapter, we ask if *It's a Sin* and *Pose* bring to light *good* sexual, political, and affective experiences within bad political times because weary audiences who lived through the era deserve it? Or, do they provide an anachronistic story of this past for a new generation who may unexpectedly long for its return? Here, we argue that these shows offer both – revealing a complex affective longing for a presumably lost sexual time and politics. The AIDS crisis of the 1980s emerges here as an impossible object of attachment, as feared as it is desired, which might tell us more about current frustrations with bad sex than about the actual sex of the time.

Good sex in lethal times

It's a Sin opens with eighteen-year-old Ritchie on a ferry from the Isle of Wight. His father hands him a packet of condoms in acknowledgement that 'it [sex?] is different on the mainland', though

Ritchie is not particularly worried about the unwanted pregnancy his father's warning assumes. With high expectations for himself amongst the entrepreneurial drive of Thatcher's Britain, to a presumedly head-shaking audience, Ritchie throws the condoms into the sea. While his first attempt at anal sex with a man (his later lover Ash) ends in embarrassment, Ritchie is soon making the most of London's burgeoning gay scene – dancing his way through the early 1980s and having lots and lots of sex. Ritchie's friends are similarly having fun. Roscoe, a queer, British Nigerian man runs away from his restrictive parents to hook up with (and gleefully screw over) a closeted Conservative minister, alongside 'having' a series of other closeted, privileged men, including his landlord, while Colin, a gentle Welsh tailor on Savile Row, discovers the possibility of a domesticated gay future by befriending an older couple who live semi-openly in their South London neighbourhood. Sex and sexuality in the early episodes is playful and speedy, presenting sex as a site of exploration, transgression, and pleasure. Particularly for Ritchie in episode 1, a rolling montage depicts drink sharing, kissing, dancing, and threesomes. Under an operatic 1980s disco remix, shifting between the glowing lights of the disco and the drab, sweaty walls of his undergraduate dorm room, the early years of Ritchie's growing sexual fulfilment are marked by his increasingly expressive outfits and never-ending hook-ups.

Yet, these representations take place against the backdrop of the emerging horrors of the AIDS crisis, though Ritchie is seemingly unbothered by the whispers that something is afoot in America. The messy house parties, fun hook-ups, and shitty jobs that Ritchie and his friends experience foreshadow the shattering portrayals to come of Ritchie and Colin's illnesses in later episodes. Gabriel Duckels argues that *It's a Sin* represents early sex scenes 'as an excess', thus contrasting these earlier fluid and plentiful sexual representations with a scene a few episodes later where Ritchie 'lies in hospital, wondering aloud "how many boys [he] killed"' (2022: 124). Like Duckels, we agree that the brevity of the series, combined with its presumed *knowing* audience, could lead to a representation of sex as a site of regretful danger – arriving as the result of apolitical 'luck', as Monica Pearl (2022) argues. Yet, while initially Ritchie begins to avoid people he perceives as ill and brutally rejects his own boyfriend on these grounds, his friends (such as Roscoe) continue in their exploration of an unashamed sexual life at the same time as organizing fundraisers and protesting at funerals. Ritchie's conservatism is also increasingly shamed by the more politically defiant queers who surround him, and the final scenes of the series present transgressive forms of sexual and political interpretation even for Ritchie, whose shame we witness unravelling as the show progresses.

Most importantly, when Ritchie is dying in his mother's home, he uses his final words to tell her just how good all that sex was and just how much fun he had having it. While Ritchie's mother attempts to care for him in secret, retaining the nostalgic objects from his childhood, and refusing to acknowledge he is ill, Ritchie continues to demand the presence of his queerness in their home (Figure 4.1). Eventually asking

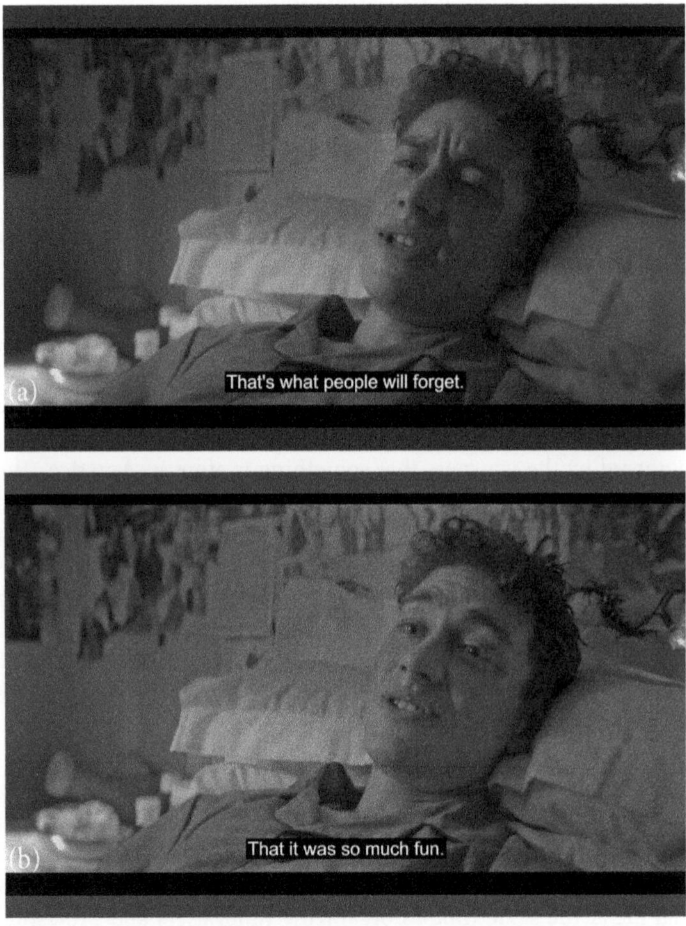

Figure 4.1 (a, b) In the final moments before his death, Ritchie, lying in his childhood bed, speaks to the joys of his queer sex life. *It's a Sin* © Red Production Company/Channel 4 2021.

his mother if the neighbours 'know what's wrong with me?', Ritchie resists becoming 'a secret':

> I had so much fun. I had all those boys. I had hundreds of them. And do you know what, I can remember every single one of them. Some boy's hair, or his lips. The way he laughed at a joke . . . His face as he cums. Seeing him across a club six years later and thinking . . . 'oh, that's him'. And he's with someone. And he looks happy. And I think, 'ah that's nice'. Cos they were great. Some of them were bastards. But they were all great. That's what people will forget. That it was so much fun.

While Duckels discusses this scene in terms of Ritchie 'declaring that he regrets nothing while acting as though he regrets everything' (2022: 125), we would differently argue that the 'overall ambivalence' of his ending remains significant. Particularly for queer viewers, who *already know* such scenes are meant to end with a learning about personal regret and safer sex, there is much pleasure in watching Ritchie's homophobic mother shudder at his explicit discussion of the pleasures of gay sex – apparently, the last conversation she will have with her son. Mirroring the meme-worthy first episode where Roscoe runs away from home in a skirt after telling his homophobic parents to 'fuck off', here we might feel pride as the young man who once cleared his bedroom of 'filthy' gay magazines uses his final words, in that same room, to speak only of the joys and pleasures his queer sex life gave him, and of just how much sex he had. In these moments, the show offers queer audiences both unexpected and ambivalent attachments. We *presumed* Ritchie would die with shame and thus feel a sense of joy when he refuses to do so, signalling the shifting representational possibilities of gay shame we discussed in Chapter 3. In this, we feel an overwhelming sense of progress – that this is Ritchie's ending, when written today. But if Ritchie's defiance stems from reclaiming the joys of a time that is over (and one we 'will forget'), is there also a sense of loss that we might have missed it?

Pose begins a little later in the 1980s and so the characters are already aware of, and living through, the loss and grief of the epidemic. This choice is significant in the series and for the characters, in that the crisis is neither presented as a loss of innocence or an isolated danger – particularly for racially minoritized trans and queer subjects navigating homelessness, violence, and bigotry (Bailey 2013). In episode 1, Blanca, an underrated junior member of a successful 'House' in New York City's Black and Latinx Ballroom scene, discovers she is HIV positive in a typically cold scene of clinical diagnosis. Resisting the expectation to disappear in shame, Blanca takes the initiative to begin her own legacy as Ballroom Mother – securing a humble apartment and adopting her own house of 'children'. Her daily life across the series revolves around securing the House's success in Ballroom competitions and supporting her children in their diverse ambitions. Perhaps the most important element of the framing of sex in *Pose* is the way in which the *continued* search for good sex (and lives) over the years is emphasized without explicit concern for the 'bad' or lethal sex of the era. Indeed, Blanca discusses the importance of safer sex with Damon, but is more worried about his failure to take his prestigious studies seriously once he has a boyfriend. She encourages and worries about Angel as she navigates the interpersonal dangers of dating cis men in the context of transphobia, recognizing this as a greater risk to her well-being than her sporadic engagements with sex work. For the characters of *Pose*, sex and the 'risks' of sex are lived alongside the search for intimacy and material comfort in the context of the diverse inequalities of the time. Blanca continues to long for a partner, while her close friend Pray Tell loses his to AIDS. Blanca fears for her children, but for complex reasons. In *Pose*, the 1980s remain a lethal era, but the threat of bad sex is just one of its causes.

But, most importantly, and just like in *It's a Sin*, sex is often just good. For example, when Ricky discovers he is HIV positive and Pray Tell struggles to overcome his anger at his own deteriorating health, it is sex – in this case intergenerational sex between two Black men living with HIV – that restores them. Afterwards, the camera tenderly lingers on their bodies, and both go on to thrive (seemingly for some years) with the support that sex and intimacy provide them. While the relationship is complicated by Pray Tell's status as an elder within the community and Ricky's social role as Blanca's child, the shaming they experience from their community is counteracted by tender scenes between them: Ricky cooks for Pray Tell the next morning; Pray Tell secretly gives his hard fought-for cocktail of medication to Ricky; Ricky eventually discovers and holds Pray Tell's body in a way that mirrors their first sexual encounter – a visual recognition of their continuing bond. We would argue that good sex (and the good *of* sex) is important here as a representation of survival, pleasure, and holding, particularly within the limited representational field for marginalized queer and trans of colour characters of the 1980s. As Jennifer DeClue argues, where the 'tacit pressure' of respectability still haunts a need to 'exclude or mute or justify images and narratives of black queer and trans life, desire, and sexuality' (2020: 46), the complex sex scenes between Ricky and Pray Tell might reflect 'a queer lifeworld in which the transformative potential of queer sex and public manifestations of such sexuality were both a respite from the abjection of homosexuality and a reformatting of that very abjection' (Muñoz 2009: 34).

While suffering appears early and consistently in *Pose*, sex is not emphasized only as a site of risk but also as one of connection, pleasure, and care, illustrating how the presumed grief for lost futures implied by HIV/AIDS melodramas has historically lacked such intersectional interpretation (see e.g. Bailey 2013; Muñoz 2019). For Black and Latinx trans and queer characters such as Pray Tell, Angel, Papi, Ricky and Damon, sex is also how they form connections in times of broader social crisis or discover different parts of their gendered and sexual selves. For example, House mother Elektra makes a substantial living (and finds great personal satisfaction) as a dominatrix hired by wealthy, white men when her fetishizing long-term partner leaves her. Angel and Papi navigate a supportive normative relationship, which remains complicated given Angel's imagination she was not entitled to experience one. One key funeral scene of the series takes place in the context of a likely transphobic hate crime during sex work, not an AIDS-related death, thus exploring the many forms of structural and social violence queer and trans people of colour are exposed to.

In what frequently crosses into the genre of magical realism, muted scenes of funerals and hospital visitations appear alongside the rolling flirtation, sex, glitter, and extravagance of the ballroom, with the ghosts of lost friends and lovers occasionally returning to enjoy it.[2] Eva Pensis is more critical of the 'aspirational' 'anachronisms' of the series, seemingly required for such a representation of good sex to be possible, arguing that the show swaps 'survival codes developed by street queens for the conventional scripts' (2019: 23) of love and transnormative desire. Angelos Bollas argues differently that such anachronisms allow *Pose* to provide 'a more humane and whole depiction' (2022: 115) of characters living amongst the intersecting sexual, political, and social violences, and joys of the era. Indeed, in the interplay between joy, mundanity, violence and extravagance, as well as 'moments to just be; moments of pleasure, rumination, and boredom' (Gonsalez 2020), we agree that more often *Pose* provides audiences with a transgressive and healing representation of 1980s' sex and its many pleasures.

Intimacy and the question of care

Both series also explore care and intimacies outside of romantic and sexual relationships, with most of the characters living in supportive and chosen communities. In these ways, the shows often seem to act as a historical corrective to narratives of suffering and isolation so common to stories of queer life during the AIDS epidemic. In *Pose*, Blanca (despite having little material wealth or security of her own) opens her home to a cast of young queer adults who are variously navigating homelessness, sex work, and addiction when she meets them. In this, she displays a seeming endless wealth of generosity and understanding of her children's means of survival – destigmatizing strategies of theft or sex work that bring material and personal comfort to their home. Such a corrective narrative is exemplified by the show's repetition of sitcom-like scenes of idealized domesticity: warmly lit conclusions to episodes feature the characters meeting around the dinner table in Blanca's home or in a local Chinese restaurant, fading out to conversation and laughter (Figure 4.2). Reminiscent as these are of domesticated scenes of cis/straight families in 1980s and 1990s television (e.g. *Fresh Prince of Bel-Air*; *Full House*; *Roseanne*), 'through *Pose's* sitcom-like rhythm across three seasons, the (implicitly cis,

Figure 4.2 In *Pose*, the dinner table in Blanca's flat serves as a space of community, where warming scenes of familial comfort frequently fade out to laughter. *Pose* © Color Force/FX 2018–21.

white, seronegative) viewer can forget the serostatus of healthy HIV+ characters rather than anticipating the spectacle of their immediate death' (Duckels 2022: 125).

In *It's a Sin,* we get similar representations of queer friendship and intimacy. Here, it is Jill, the female best friend of the otherwise mostly gay male characters, who carries the extended frame of intimate care. Ritchie meets Jill when they are both studying drama at university, and they move into the Pink Palace (a messy Victorian flat which Roscoe has proudly secured through a sexual encounter with the landlord) with their friends Ash, Colin, and Roscoe. Here, the dinner table similarly serves as a space of debate, laughter, education, and later grieving. Like Blanca, Jill takes on the disproportionate responsibility for this familial centring. She is shown informing herself and the group about the 'new' illness, cooking, and cleaning for friend Gloria when he becomes ill. Jill is both 'the receiver of trauma and the broadcaster of bad news' (Harrison 2022: 88), showing a sense of humour towards the chaos the house embroils her in – but notably never having any chaotic experiences or attachments of her own. Yet, differently to *Pose*, such domestic scenes often sustain an affect of foreboding common to melodramas: Ritchie announces a new acting role he will be too ill to take; Ash declares book censoring arriving at his secondary school with the introduction of Section 28 in the UK prohibiting discussion of gay sexuality in schools; the group gathers cash for a trip to see Ritchie that they will never complete. Reading *It's a Sin* alongside *Pose,* we can see how such scenes operate as similarly deliberate political and cultural correctives or remembrances of intimate queer life. Reminiscent as they are of familial American and British soap opera conventions, such scenes similarly seem to say: '*look, we did all this too. It wasn't all just bad sex and death.*'

Of course, through a feminist lens, it is possible to critique both *Pose* and *It's a Sin* for almost exclusively relying on gendered and racialized intimacies and a sentimental frame of care as a response to the characters' material and physical suffering – even as they play with idealized domestic conventions. In many ways, Blanca's children thrive exclusively because of her interventions, and there is an unquestionable romanticization of maternal care as a feminine impulse in both series, alongside a romanticization of the structural poverty that underlies it (Pensis 2019). In *It's a Sin*, Jill's role as carer is largely unquestioned (by her or others) and even occasionally mocked by the recipients. In the context of *Pose*, it is important to consider the ways in which both the series' and the broader Ballroom scene's recuperation of gendered and sexualized terms, including the practice of Mothering, has always acted as an implicit critique of the 'realness' of idealized, racialized, familial, and gendered domestic cultures, as well as an acknowledgement of 'the actual labor in which its members are constantly engaged to create an alternative existence for themselves within their marginality' (Bailey 2011: 384).

These gendered, racialized, and sexual connotations were famously debated by bell hooks (2009) and Judith Butler (1999) in response to some of the documentary source material for *Pose*, *Paris Is Burning* (1990). Here, motherhood is claimed by a woman whose claim to femininity or family is frequently denied, and the (actually adult) 'children's' embrace of Blanca's role takes place in the context of rejection from their biological families and broader racist and transphobic society. In these ways, Blanca's performance of motherhood both idealizes and rejects forms of racialized, classed, and gendered respectability: while Blanca is certain that she will put food on the table (often humorously badly), she also at times embraces stigmatized forms of survival (sex work, theft) as ways to achieve this. Her performance of motherhood also sits within a discursive and representational field of Black and Latinx parenting in relation to the US welfare state of the 1980s, similarly repairing racist representations of 'failing' minoritized families and queer isolation through its insistence on nurturing and self-reliance (see also Bailey 2013; Cohen 1997; DeClue 2020; Lane 2019). In this way, *Pose* could be argued to present a version of idealized domesticity through a frame of queer kinship, as a 'repetition of hegemonic power which fail[s] to repeat loyally and, in that failure, open[s] up possibilities for resignifying the terms of violation against their violating aims' (Butler 1999: 337). As such, intimacy and care in the series straddle a difficult recuperation of normative genre conventions that have otherwise been denied for its characters, challenging some of their implicit exclusions, and 'assuming greater agency in the dialectic between subjectification and identification' (Bailey 2011: 384; see also Lane 2019).

Nonetheless, nostalgia for such care and its labour remains consistently, and romantically, gendered in both *Pose* and *It's a Sin*, where the representation of Jill's care has been similarly critiqued by others (see e.g. Harrison 2023). While Jill's care undoubtedly brings a corrective in representing the previously untold practices of queer care that writers such as Ann Cvetkovich (2003) and Marlon Bailey (2013) highlight, the series seems to rarely question its gendered and racialized unevenness – especially because Jill's sexual, gendered, and racial location as a Black woman is uncommented on (rather than, how Blanca's is explored precisely in relation to these structural expectations in *Pose*). So, while in some ways offering a corrective to the invisibilization of (mostly queer) women as key political and caring agents within the epidemic, the series' failure to give Jill a life outside of such care places some limits on this recuperation – especially because her care is presented as so passionate, limitless, and enduring. In the penultimate scene of the series, Jill expresses her frustration at filling in a gap left by a careless society: 'the wards are full of men, who think they deserve it.' Yet she, like Blanca, ultimately appears resigned to this role, when at the end of the series she offers her hand to an unknown man on the hospital ward, just as Blanca ultimately trains to become a nurse. In this way, and similarly to many other shows we discuss across the book, intimacy in *It's a Sin* and *Pose* both recuperates and makes visible forms of gendered and racialized care and intimacy in the absence of broader structural support – while remaining politically ambivalent about them.

Narratives of loss and return

While the question of gendered and racialized forms of care and labour is key to these nostalgic narratives, our interest in these shows is not about whether they are politically sound, historically accurate, or morally pure. Rather, we are interested in what these representations tell us about the affective politics of sex and sexuality today. These shows are of course anachronistic and unable to do full justice to the complex social and political landscapes of the time. Pensis, for instance, argues that at points *Pose* 'opts for a narrative perspective that elides the ways that antiblackness, transphobia, and misogyny interact and punctuate everyday life for its central characters' (2019: 21). They point out that, 'family-friendly trans narratives, we are told, even family-friendly sex work narratives (is there such a thing?), must downplay the ordinary violence and structural inequity (e.g. lack of health insurance or credit) that drives the show's gender non-conforming people of color into sex work to begin with' (2019: 21). Similarly in *It's a Sin*, we get representations of distinctly 'easy' engagements with the limitations and violences of Thatcher's Britain, such that nostalgia for it can be secured. Roscoe, Colin, Ash, Ritchie, and Jill are consistently working and laughing through the social violences of the era. For example, when Colin becomes ill from AIDS-related seizures and is essentially arrested in a hospital in Wales, Jill secures a legal team to rescue him – and the Welsh police and hospital are dumbfounded and reluctantly respectful of the lawyers' claim to Colin's human rights, quickly letting him return home. Money to visit Ritchie in the final episode similarly comes easily, when Ritchie's agent benevolently hands them several hundred pounds just in time. And while Roscoe suffers from explicit racism in his encounters with a Conservative politician, he resolves this by literally peeing in Margaret Thatcher's tea. In these instances, the deprivation and misery of Thatcher's Britain appears somewhat remediable – allowing for an acknowledgement but ultimately also a potential watering down of the structural contexts these characters navigate.

Instead of asking about the accuracy or truthfulness of these representations, then, we are more interested in the question of what kinds of structures of feelings they make tangible in relation to the sexual politics of the past. In both *It's a Sin* and *Pose*, we are presented with a complex narrative structure that features the past as both a threat that we have overcome and a radical time that we have lost. In her work on narratives of gender and sexuality, Clare Hemmings (2011) describes such narrative structures of *progress* and *loss*. On the surface, both *Pose* and *It's a Sin* operate as progress narratives of a time that we have presumably left behind, a time in which queer life and sex were lethal, hard, and brutal – yet likewise, they present this as a time of community, transgression and care that seems to be lost in the present. In her reading of the film *Pride* (2014), Aura Lehtonen (2023) finds a similar structure of affective longing for a political past, and argues that the film's nostalgia for an easily built political solidarity between gay city folk and Welsh miners in the 1980s maintains elements of the story as a longing for lost solidarities and potential of the past, while at the same time allowing us to experience a sense of progress vis-à-vis the achievement of LGBT rights. The narratives of *Pose* and *It's a Sin* similarly present us with 'nostalgic attachments' which 'tell us as much (or more) about the political desires of' the present – in our case, the 2020s – 'as they do about the 1980s' (Lehtonen 2023: 115).

Certainly, in providing an image of a time when sex was lethal, yet still *good*, transgressive, joyful, and full of political potential and connection, these shows divert from classical representations of this time. *Pose* and *It's a Sin* stand out for their willingness to return to the politics of sex in the 1980s for queer people – and in *Pose's* case for Black and queer people of colour. Both series have been lauded for complicating straightforward narratives of the decline and personal isolation of the era through their emphasis on queer collectivity, care, and erotics, reflecting academic literature which seeks to similarly recuperate the era along these lines (Bailey 2013; Cvetkovich 2003; Gould 2009; Muñoz 2009; Schulman 2021). However, much of the nostalgic pull of *Pose* and *It's a*

Sin is secured through a *knowing* reference to this legacy for audiences aware of common representations of the AIDS epidemic. In this, *Pose* and *It's a Sin* operate through what Hemmings refers to in her reading of feminist political narratives as 'technologies of the presumed' (2011: 16). For Hemmings, practices of (in our case, cinematic and televisual) citation both build on and contribute to collective narratives of progress that we *should* all agree on.

For instance, when Blanca learns she is HIV positive in the first episode, she responds with a wilful desire for her community, not tears of fear or shame. The scene is noticeable precisely for countering common cinematic scenes of cold, clinical HIV diagnosis and expressions of sexual regret and despair. But Blanca's diagnosis goes largely unmentioned for much of the first season as she develops her successful Ballroom House and home. While characters' illnesses do progress across the years – in this, the series often demonstrates temporal realism (Bollas 2022) – Blanca and her children mostly navigate success, failure and heartbreak, continuing to dream of social mobility while refusing to accept personal or communal decline, in striking contrast to cinematic portrayals of HIV/AIDS viewers may be more familiar with. In these ways, the series reflects Kara Keeling's analysis of the representational importance of queer Black futures in the context of social marginalization, where 'those for whom the future remains to be won in each moment . . . will continue to dream "freedom dreams" of a better day ahead' (2019: 89–90). Indeed, *Pose*'s final episodes display miraculous material comfort and romantic and professional success for the characters, which we would argue are deliberately citational of 1980s/1990s 'yuppie' themed cinema, where straight, white subjects exuded success through adherence to Reaganite excess, materialism and individualism (e.g. *Pretty Woman*; *Wall Street; Working Girl*). In its fantastical, citational, future-looking temporalities, *Pose* presents us with important utopian narratives that evoke not just fear and the spectacle of death, but also a longing for these times.

Such citations also reverberate through the story of Ritchie and his housemates in *It's a Sin* – named after the iconic 1980s Pet Shop Boys song which alludes to gay shame. Certainly, Ritchie's story of white, urban gay discovery resembles classic melodramatic portrayals of the lost privileges of 1980s queerness, just as the overall narrative of the series adheres fairly strictly to the genre with its familial loss, sexual deception and AIDS-related decline (Pearl 2023). While early on the series is more playful with this (e.g. when Ritchie's Thatcher-voting parents suffer comically as he 'comes out' to them as an actor in their tidy living room),

Ritchie's personal story is overall sustained as one of *retreat* from sexual liberation, as the AIDS crisis comes to his door. At first callously cynical and later emotionally unable to process the death of his housemate Colin, unlike Blanca in *Pose*, Ritchie remains wedded to an apolitical, individualized frame (and life) across the series, promising he is 'going to live!' while audiences already know that, within the genre conventions of 1980s AIDS melodrama, he will die.

For these reasons, Duckels (2022) and Pearl (2023) both critique *It's a Sin* for replaying these melodramatic legacies, providing a 'reactionary rather than interrogative position [on] the history that it constructs' (Duckels 2022: 124). Forced back to his mother's home as his illness progresses, Ritchie is isolated from his community and sexuality, as his mother hides him from the neighbours. In these and other ways (isolated hospital wards, lesions, and bodily fluids), the series does linger on bodily abjection, shame, familial deception, and sex as a site of 'bad' and danger, reflecting earlier melodramatic portrayals. However, as we have argued earlier, the show reaches a conclusion in its final episodes that to some extent challenges this frame. It is Ritchie's best friend Jill's story that concludes the series, with the ongoing gendered care of a queer community surviving the disaster, and Ritchie ultimately singing the pleasures of the sexual life his queerness afforded him, subverting the otherwise melodramatic ending. In these ways, *It's a Sin* similarly uses cinematic citation to narrate a story of sexual dissidence and communal strength. Here, too, the sexual politics of the past are not featured as simply an outdated era we have progressed from, but also as something we can long for in the present. In Hemmings' (2011) terms, then, in these contemporary responses to the genre of the AIDS melodrama, we not only get a sense of progress and loss, but also potentially even a longing for *return*.

Who is re-remembering otherwise?

This of course raises the question of *for whom* these shows evoke the feelings of loss and return: What political work do these representations do as they appear in the present? Indeed, just as Rahul Rao (drawing on Anjali Arondekar) has been 'critical of the manner in which the archive has become freighted with hope, as if it contained the secret whose revelation might effect transformation' (2020: 20), in the context of sexual colonial archives, the correctives and good sex narratives of *It's a Sin* and *Pose* rely on a citational practice and history that we, as an audience, *feel* we were previously missing. The transformative potential of *Pose* and *It's a Sin* seems reliant on our recognition of them not as an uncovering of a historical truth but rather as, as Keeling suggests, 'a creative seeking that generates the past one seeks' (2019: 94). In the final sections of this chapter, we thus ask what work these creative correctives perform for differently situated audiences. Indeed, so far we have considered the series as revealing not just of feelings of fear and comfort for having overcome this time but also of affects of loss and longing, as the shows present 'new' ways of looking at what *we all already knew* about the bad sex and politics of the era.

In a late scene in *It's a Sin*, Ritchie's parents discover that he is ill. Ritchie's mother, Valerie, oscillates between promises of unconditionality towards Ritchie ('you are not infectious to me') and rage, as she stalks the hospital ward, looking for someone to blame. The latter scene is made more powerful by Valerie's desperate attachment to the racialized, gendered, and classed respectability that Ritchie's queerness compromises. The typically undemonstrative Valerie appears belligerent as her husband sobs in the waiting room, and demands to see a doctor to a bemused nurse. Talking to Jill, Valerie attempts to rationalize Ritchie's queerness – 'boys are terrible . . . and then [they] grow up' – revealing her simultaneous disdain for, and cruel attachment to, heterosexuality, discussed in Chapters 1 and 2. But when Valerie insists she *didn't know* Ritchie was gay (or ill), a working-class mother who has been listening interrupts and demands that Valerie answer: 'If you didn't know he was gay . . . what were you lookin' at?'

The woman's demand, another corrective, anticipates an audience that does not align with it but one that aligns with Ritchie and his friends. Similarly to Ritchie's death bed confession, here we feel a sense of progress, since we now know that during the Thatcher era upwardly mobile Britons were wilfully choosing not to look at the ravages of the epidemic, as it did not impact them. Indeed, in an earlier scene, the iconic 'Don't Die of Ignorance' commercial first airs, and Ritchie exclaims: 'My Mother's watching this!' We switch to Valerie and Michael, eating dessert and reaching for the TV guide – they are not looking at all. Thus, unlike in earlier melodramatic representations (e.g. *Angel's in America*; *Philadelphia*) that on some level empathize with cis/straight society's desire to *not see*, Valerie is asked to answer for such wilful ignorance. This move is made even more forceful in the end of the series, when Jill, heartbroken about Valerie's refusal to let her visit Ritchie, in return refuses Valerie any sympathy, promising her: 'all of this . . . is your fault.'

For Rebecca Harrison, Ritchie's 'abject' mother reflects the series' misogynistic investment that 'rather than interrogate how the crisis was caused by white supremacist and patriarchal capitalism that all of the characters in the show . . . perpetuate . . ., blames bad mothers who refuse to do their duty to young men' (2023: 91) – perhaps in an echo of its centring of gendered care practices we discussed earlier. However, if we see Valerie (as Harrison does) as a proxy for the neoliberal individualism the era represented, Jill's obvious overstatement – 'they *all* die because of you' – could be read as a more nuanced recognition of the structural ignorance of the time, and of the understanding frame afforded to the violences of that society in earlier cinematic and televisual representations. Jill's refusal to allow Valerie the right to mourn, coupled with Ritchie's defiant claim to the *good* of all that sex, allows for more complicated affective engagements for audiences. As we argued earlier, such a corrective allows queer audiences not only to sob for Ritchie's loss but also to feel an outlet for our anger and a sense of progress. For straight/cis audiences, these moments act as a demand: to answer for what they, at the time, chose not to see. And yet, the corrective only works because we have been asked to feel, or have been allowed to feel, otherwise in the past. We can now, finally, uncover, understand, and hope, as Rao (2020) suggests in the context of archival searching related to sexuality and coloniality, that transformation will emerge from these realizations.

The final episodes of *Pose* also play with genre expectations and memory, but in notably different ways to *It's a Sin*. By the final season, two of Blanca's children have moved into a large, bright penthouse apartment filled with 1980s paraphernalia and are raising a child, and another has been on tour in Paris, as the group celebrate a wedding in an iconic New York Hotel and become mentors to younger queers. Blanca completes her nursing studies and joins her friends for a *Sex and the City* style brunch (Figure 4.3). The ending of the series – mostly fantastic, joyous, and expensive – provides viewers with a vision of success for the characters, who do not just survive, but are also supported, loved, and much wealthier as the hospital wards fall quieter by the late 1990s. Like in earlier domestic scenes, here, *Pose* is arguably performing narrative 'realness', reflecting on the marginalized forms of community that buffered against the ravages of the crisis, while highlighting their typical exclusion from cis, straight, and white stories of 1980s and 1990s success.[3] The locations of these scenes (a yacht club, elite New York Hotel, Hamptons beach house) were normalized in 1980s and 1990s

Figure 4.3 The joyous, aspirational settings of *Pose* feel deliberately citational of earlier cinema and television. Here, the characters discuss the '*Sex and The City effect*' while out at an expensive Carrie Bradshaw-style brunch. *Pose* © Color Force/FX 2018–21.

television and cinema, yet appear somewhat anachronistic within the genre of queer television and certainly in contrast to the downtown locations of a Times Square peep show and LGBT community centre which began the series.

In this, Blanca and her community come to be one of few successful depictions of the Black and Latinx trans community most impacted by the crisis, given the chance to live out their cinematic fantasies despite societal (and audience) expectations that they could not. In prioritizing survival and joy, unlike *It's a Sin*'s defiant end, *Pose* is deliberate in these anachronistic choices – such as when the characters (mis-)reference *Sex and the City* when they go on their celebratory brunch. Following Muñoz's reminder that queerness is 'not simply a being but a doing towards the future' (2019: 1), these 'figments of imagination, of someone's desires for us to exist' (Hong 2015, cited in Keeling 2019: 94) potentially allow particularly trans and queer of colour audiences not only to remember but perhaps also to feel the pleasures of an otherwise that should have been possible – 'an insistence on potentiality or concrete possibility for another world' (Muñoz 2019: 1). Or, as Jafari Allen argues of Janet Mock's 'careful' 'editorial hand' in the series:

> the most important and impactful aspect of [*Pose*'s] wide viewership is the careful and apparently necessary ethical pedagogical work it does: the *Pose* camera seemed to teach millions of viewers *here's how to care, here are the questions to ask and how to ask, here's where to look at us. Here is where you must look within.* (2022: 210, emphasis original)

Yet, if both series perform a pedagogical re-remembering of the era's violences, responsibilities and joys, are its assumed affective impacts reliant on an audience familiar with its cinematic legacy and silences? Indeed, with the distance of four decades, both *It's a Sin* and *Pose* also offer stories about queer history, as well as potential new attachments to it. While we have emphasized the nostalgic genre cues and citational practices of the series, which allow for narratives of progress and correction, is it possible that as Pearl movingly argues, 'for some of us, the AIDS crisis is a memory soaked in blood; for others, it is history they have not had to learn' (2023: 111). We have argued that for queer, especially queer of colour, audiences who lived through the 1980s and 1990s, both series might provide a range of affective correctives. In subverting familiar scenes of diagnosis, coming out, and shame, the shows offer a fantastical 'otherwise' that seems to say, '*this is how it should have been for you*'. Queer viewers can rejoice when Blanca and her friends get their happy endings, or when Jill and Ritchie say what should have been said, precisely because history tells us that this wasn't always the case. For a queer generation that lived through, but was not acknowledged for, the intersecting traumas of the era, such viewing likely culminates in a sense that maybe things did get a bit better, after all.

Yet, in the context of the broader scene of bad sex we have developed across this book, such reparations are less straightforward. The fantastical 'otherwise' through which the politics and sexual politics of the era are depicted in the shows risks being taken more straightforwardly as a representation of something that simply *was*, especially since life in both *Pose* and *It's a Sin* somehow looks like, in spite of everything, *so much fun*. Where these genre subversions are taken at face value (a meme-worthy, defiant 'coming out'; a queer family conversing and laughing around a dinner table; or the upending of a racist interaction at a yacht club), they risk looking *better* than the disappointing sexual political scene of the present. Indeed, it is precisely because much of the sexual and gendered shaming, racism, and poverty of 1980s London is missing or benevolent in *It's a Sin* that the Pink Palace can appear as an effortless, inclusive, intergenerational party made all the better for the lack of smartphones and more affordable mortgages.

Following Lehtonen (2023) in her analysis of nostalgia in the film *Pride* (2014), and Pearl (2023) in their analysis of transnormativity in *Pose*, the series also seem to mobilize a nostalgia for a 'simpler' time of queer sexual politics precisely by neglecting the bad sex and politics of the 1980s. Similarly of *Pose*, Laura Stamm questions the work of fantasy in the series because it might 'evoke a sense of longing' for 'a moment when the queer community was politically energized' (2020: 617) in ways that suggest this time is both better and over today. But, when 'trans women, and trans women of color specifically, are continually left out of contemporary conversations about HIV/AIDS', then 'representing their stories as past serves to further erase their need for treatment and activism in the present' (Stamm 2020: 616). In the context of the retrenched homophobias and transphobias that queers navigate today, and the inequalities that continue to structure contemporary experiences of HIV/AIDS, audiences may find themselves feeling a sense of loss in the face of these fun and joyful representations of queer communality, good sex and success – a lingering, albeit guilty feeling of '*maybe it used to be more fun*'.

In this, we agree with Duckels that both series are embedded in a 'politics of memory': 'if melodrama is associated with nostalgia for a time "before" – a fantasy of a home always already lost – then the pre-antiretroviral, pre-PrEP, pre-gentrification, and pre-Internet settings of *It's a Sin* and *Pose* function as romantic spaces of innocence and embodiment' (2022: 123). Thus, both shows present us not just with an important corrective: an enjoyable reparation of earlier representations for weary audiences, or transformative visions of a future not yet reached. But, in other ways, they also perform an affective pull *towards* the violences of the era, even when they are honestly and dramatically shown. Depending on what attachments audiences have to the racial, gendered, and sexual politics depicted, or to the bad sex and disappointments of today, we may find ourselves longing for the good sex, community and politics we could have or should have had – nonetheless grateful that we don't have to return. And so, despite their refusal to individualize blame or straightforwardly attribute suffering to (therefore bad) sex, at the same time these shows are less about what really was and more about what we want to have been.

Pose and *It's a Sin* are abundant in their attachments to what has been notably missing from the contemporary representations explored in previous chapters: community, sex as a transgressive force, queer and trans joy as a form of resistance, forms of solidarity forged outside of normative frames. As such, they give us space to imagine a politics where sex is still *good* and transgressive, as well as leaving us with a lingering, paradoxical feeling of nostalgic identification and loss, in the context of bad sex today. As such, they might distract from but also provide inspiration for how sex could be made better in the present. In the next chapter, we continue exploring such themes of sex and nostalgia through engaging with the return of our 'bad' (but much missed) TV exes in *Queer as Folk* (2022), *The L Word: Generation Q* (2019–23) and *And Just Like That . . .* (2021–).

Chapter 5

SEX WITH YOUR EX IN *AND JUST LIKE THAT . . .*, *THE L WORD: GENERATION Q*, AND *QUEER AS FOLK*

Introduction

In the final episode of the 2022 remake of *Queer as Folk*, Brodie – the show's hot and cocky but complex protagonist – spontaneously decides to move to the UK to escape the chaos that his life in his native New Orleans has caused. He explains to his friend and business partner Bussey that he is going to Manchester because he thinks he 'should be with all the broody Morrissey gays' and only speaks 'English and Gay'. Brodie then pulls out his phone to show Bussey a Grindr profile of Nathan, thirty-nine, located in Manchester, 'muscular, dom, hunk'. The picture is a real-life, present-day image of Charlie Hunnam, the actor who played fifteen-year-old Nathan Maloney in the original UK version of *Queer as Folk* that ran from 1999-2000. 'I mean, come on', says Brodie, to which Bussey quips: 'He a'ight for a white boy.' Brodie's plan to move to Manchester, the birthplace of *Queer as Folk*, can be read as a comforting, nostalgic closing of the loop between the three versions of the show for the viewer. Brodie's desire for the adult Nathan mirrors not just Stuart's desire for the teenage Nathan over twenty years ago, but perhaps also all of our desire to not quite yet let go of the – complex and troubled – original.

This 'Easter egg' scene (Achouche 2017) articulates a web of attachments between the remake and the UK and US originals, highlighting the sexual – as well as racial, transnational, and generational – politics of the recent flurry of reboots and sequel shows, which this chapter investigates. In the previous chapter, we explored portrayals of queer sex in *It's a Sin* (2021) and *Pose* (2018–21) that look back to the 1980s and 1990s as a time when sex was a site of transformative intimacy, survival, and community. This chapter continues exploring themes of nostalgia and recuperation: the three shows we investigate here are remakes of the (in)famous 1990s and 2000s postfeminist and post-queer liberatory shows, in which sex tended to be represented as overwhelmingly *good*, as well as overwhelmingly white, middle-class and gender normative. *And Just Like That . . .* (2021–) picks up seventeen years after the original series of *Sex and the City* (1998–2004), positioning its political ambiguity as generational through its struggling central characters – once modern and trendy, now old and out of touch. *The L Word: Generation Q* (2019–22) initially refuses to dwell on the troubled past of its predecessor *The L Word* (2004–9), but eventually tries to heal some of the old wounds more explicitly – as well as quite literally returning many of its original characters to their exes. Finally, the production of the 2022 *Queer as Folk* as a *remake* of, rather than a sequel to, the original British (1999–2000) and American (2000–5) versions of the show allows it to engage with the ghosts that haunted the originals differently: with a new more diverse cast, new location, and few explicit connections to the original (apart from, perhaps, the above scene).[1]

While many would hesitate to return to characters and contexts marred by often implicit, sometimes explicit transphobia, racism, classism, and homophobia, here we wonder what is behind the impulse to return to representations that reflected limited, often exclusionary queer and sexual politics, in the context of today's diversified representational demands. Why go back to an ex we now know wasn't that great for us? This chapter explores the complex affective dynamics of these remakes and sequels and asks whether the desire to return indicates an attachment to the more straightforward and homogenous sexual, class, gendered, and racial politics of the past – at the same time as such politics are marked as outdated and old-fashioned in these reimaginings (Loock 2018). On the one hand, the recent remakes and sequels are positioned as a chance to redeem oneself, to represent better, to do better politics – and indeed in many ways they are better: more politically aware, more intersectional, more trans-inclusive and so on. On the other hand, they cultivate a web of nostalgic attachments to their often-problematic originals, perhaps even a yearning for their simpler representational demands and better, more liberatory sex. Here we discuss the forgettings, learnings, and recuperations that the reboots stage in relation to their originals, asking what is gained and lost, politically and affectively, in these attempts to return to, recuperate, and have sex with a bad ex.

Outdated or forgotten

In the first episode of the *Sex and the City* sequel, *And Just Like That . . .*, references to the three main characters, Carrie, Charlotte, and Miranda, being old and outdated proliferate. Charlotte suggests Miranda should dye her grey hair before she starts her master's in human rights. Miranda resists Charlotte's urging, but fumbles through her first class at Columbia as if a caricature of an offensive and politically out-of-touch boomer. She first misgenders a fellow student – 'Someone's quick with the pronouns!' – and then mistakes the Black professor for a student because of her braids. Later on, Miranda reflects on the experience: 'I think I was just so worried about saying the wrong thing in this climate that I said all the wrong things.' Miranda's uncertainty seems to represent the character's *generational* unease with the supposedly 'woke' 2020s, as if speaking to a fellow fifty-something audience who were also having more fun *before*.[2]

Doing better with the demands of the era, Carrie is now using Instagram and is on a podcast titled 'X, Y, and Me'. The podcast involves Carrie ('representing the cis women'), her fellow guest Jackie Nee ('representing the cis het men'), and the host Che Diaz ('queer, non-binary Mexican Irish diva, representing everyone else outside these two boring genders') talking about gender and sexual roles. Every once in a while, the discussion is punctuated by a sound effect naming a 'woke moment!', where Che explains the more complex political dynamics behind a simplistic shorthand used in the discussion: 'And yes, I know that no one person can represent all the genders and sexual orientations or an entire race, and . . . I fully acknowledge that we are complicated diverse beings here on this wondrous planet, all just striving to be our very best self. Many of us just trying to get laid.' Carrie appears uncomfortable and hesitant to go into any kind of detail about her sex life – a far cry from the supposedly candid coverage of sex and relationships in her column in *The New York Observer* in the original *Sex and the City*. Not only is *Carrie's* discomfort with *sex* unexpected, her articles never had to work this hard to make us laugh, generating nostalgia for a simpler time when discussions of sex were seemingly only ever light-hearted and funny.

These early interactions of the main protagonists of *And Just Like That . . .* set the scene for much of the first season, where they continue to struggle to keep up with the demands of today's supposedly more nuanced and complex politics of difference and diversity. Interestingly, while the original *Sex and the City* was mostly devoid of the kind of explicit reference to gender, sexual, and racial politics that abound in the sequel, the characters regularly had a lot of sex – most of it good – whereas in the sequel they appear outdated, but sex is largely absent from the early episodes. It is, in fact, Miranda's now teenage son

Brady who gets the show's first sex scene in episode 2, which Miranda points out to Steve: 'Jesus! Can you hear that?' to sounds of Brady's bed banging against their shared wall. The lack of much explicit sexual representation early on in the reboot is certainly a departure from the original, known for its frank discussions and episodic portrayals of multiple characters' sex lives (Alexander 2021; Waters 2021) – perhaps also reflected in the show's removing any reference to sex from its name. This shift is further amplified by Samantha's departure from the series, the most sexually open and explicit character in the original, and perhaps the only one to cultivate a desire akin to Jane Ward's (2020) 'deep heterosexuality', involving an explicit, comprehensive appreciation and lust for men's bodies. In contrast to being at the forefront of the 'new' sexual politics of the 1990s, the liberated women of *Sex and the City* are (at least initially) out of touch and out of sex in the 2020s.

In contrast to *And Just Like That . . .*, the other two shows examined in this chapter approach the relationship between the old and the new through forms of amnesia and deliberate forgetting. The 2022 version of *Queer as Folk* is a remake, not a sequel, and its setting in present-day New Orleans (in contrast to the late 1990s Manchester and early 2000s Pittsburgh of the original UK and US versions) facilitates a different kind of racial politics, in particular. In an early sex scene, protagonist Brodie is hooking up with a white man donning a Black Lives Matter tattoo. In the middle of the act, he asks Brodie to 'punish my white ass. Mm, my ass takes up so much fucking space. It's so fucking privileged. Let me pay reparations with my tight hole'. Brodie rolls his eyes, ends the encounter and asks the guy for hotel money. He refuses, to which Brodie quips: 'I thought you were an ally.' This almost ironic representation of the changed and charged racial politics of the present positions the viewer as a knowing conspirator in Brodie's 'eye-roll' (Ahmed 2014).

Not dissimilarly, *The L Word: Generation Q* initially mostly ignores the troubled past of *The L Word*, only making comedic reference to plot lines in the original – such as Alice already having had 'vaginal rejuvenation in '04, have vaginas changed since then?' in response to being asked by a producer to interview a vaginal rejuvenation expert on her talk show. Thus, although all three shows are self-conscious of the changed landscape of representational politics they are operating in, they frame their characters' relationship to it differently. While the characters of *And Just Like That . . .* struggle to adjust, the new characters of *Queer as Folk* are embedded within the sexual politics of the 2020s, and the women of *Generation Q* are disavowing their problematic pasts, having already 'been there' in the 2000s – further indicated by their easy friendships with a generation of younger queer women.

In contrast to *And Just Like That . . .*, the characters in both *Queer as Folk* and *Generation Q* also have plenty of sex, much of it seemingly pleasurable. This echoes the original series, which were both lauded and criticized for their frank depictions of queer sex (Bahr 2019; D 2022; Glock 2005; Jones 2019; Montgomery 2019; Nicholson 2019b; Pattillo 2022) – with the new versions adding diversity to their sexual representations. *Generation Q* opens with a period sex scene between Dani and Sophie (Figure 5.1); *Queer as Folk* features a central sexual and romantic relationship between Ruthie, a white trans woman, and Shar, a Black butch non-binary character whose parental term is Zaddy; and both shows involve sex between disabled people.[3] At least initially then, while sex remains in a mostly uncomplicated manner *good*, both shows make only cursory reference to their troubled pasts. These early storylines are perhaps at least somewhat reminiscent of the kind of diversity politics that Sara Ahmed describes as 'a politics of feeling good, which allows people to relax and feel less threatened, as if we have

Figure 5.1 The reboot series of *Generation Q* opens with Dani and Sophie having great sex while Sophie is on her period. *The L Word: Generation Q* © LMR Original/ Showtime 2019–23.

already "solved it" and there is nothing else to do' (2006: 121). Rather than explicitly addressing the criticisms the originals faced for their lack of racial, gender, and class diversity, the new shows sprinkle in enough diversity in the form of new characters to indicate a *visually* changed landscape, if nothing else.

Repair and recuperation

Despite the early indications that none of the reboots are too keen to deliberately delve into the past, the desire to go back to the ex eventually drives all three of them. *Queer as Folk* makes this desire explicit in the final episode, when Brodie plans his move to Manchester, and his sexual desire for the now-adult Nathan brings the show full circle with the original. Nathan first appeared in the original show as the fifteen-year-old target of twenty-nine-year-old Stuart's sexual desire, to much controversy, with the first episode of the show airing on the same day that the House of Lords debated the *Sexual Offences Bill 1999* to equalize the age of consent for homosexual sex to sixteen in the UK. The adult Nathan appearing on Grindr as an out-and-proud 'hunk' is suggestive of a desire to repair the remake's (as well as our) relationship to the original *Queer as Folk*. Here, the show seems to suggest that like Brodie, we too can continue to attach to the original representation, despite its highly controversial depiction of an adult man's desire for a teenage boy (Montgomery 2019; Pattillo 2022; Staples 2019b). In the context of MeToo and the renewed negotiations of contemporary and historical norms and practices of consent, we learn that Nathan is doing 'ok'. If we weren't quite ready yet to let go of the original, affectively, if not politically, then here our worries about this depiction are presented as unfounded.

Similar, and arguably more clear-cut, returns appear in the other two shows, with the most obvious one in *And Just Like That*... taking the form of the relationship between Samantha and the rest of the main protagonists being repaired. The first episode of the show mentions Samantha's move to London, 'for work', but many viewers would have been aware of rumours that circulated about a feud between the actor who played Samantha, Kim Cattrall, and the rest of the cast (see e.g. Chung 2023). The show mentions Samantha, and her (newly) complicated relationship with Carrie, intermittently, but eventually brings her back in the season 2 finale. She appears in a car in London, having been unable to get on a plane to attend Carrie's big goodbye dinner. 'Ta and cheerio, and have a great night', Samantha says to Carrie over the phone, in a scene that Guardian columnist Rebecca Nicholson calls 'minimal effort for maximum impact' (2023). There is no shock or surprise in the interaction for either Carrie or Samantha, as if they have been conversing, off screen, for ages. The repairing of their relationship would have certainly been a surprise for many viewers of the show, where Samantha's sexual transgressiveness had been so conspicuous in its absence, and where the feud between the cast had clouded attachments to the original series.

Max's return to *Generation Q* in a season 3 episode carries a similar positive and warm-hearted affect to those engendered by the returns of Nathan and Samantha. The original show's depiction of Max's transition attracted criticism from many, drawing as it did on stereotypical narratives of testosterone use, gender-based betrayal, and reactionary comparisons to 'trans-racialism', particularly in the context of Max being one of very few openly trans characters on screen at the time (Bernard 2009; Dry 2022; López 2022). As if to add insult to injury, Max's final storyline in *The L Word* involved him getting pregnant by a cis gay man and facing a barrage of gender dysphoria but also abhorrent, often transphobic, treatment by many of the show's other characters. In *Generation Q*, Max now has four children and seems happy and together. He acts as a mentor figure to Micah, who is in the process of trying to have children. As the two discuss the complexities of trans parenthood, Max talks about how special their interaction is to him: 'I'm the one who gets to tell you how great it's gonna be. Your whole life. You get to reinvent everything for yourself and be your own kind of . . . your own kind of parent and your own kind of man.' Whereas Max in the original felt like he was written as a warning to viewers about the apparent social isolation of transition, he now gets to tell (us) how 'great it's gonna be'. Later when he bumps into Shane, he states: 'I feel like I've lived a thousand lives since I've seen you last.' Shane goes on to deliver an apology on behalf of the show's core group of protagonists – as well as perhaps on behalf of the show itself: 'So for what it's worth . . . I just want to apologise. For how we were back then.'

These small moments of recuperation are reminiscent of Eve Kosofsky Sedgwick's (2003) notion of reparative reading, in Rita Felski's words, 'a stance that looks to a work of art for solace and replenishment' (2015: 151). Rather than straightforwardly tearing apart and critiquing the problematic representations in the original show, in these instances the reboots try to recuperate aspects of them, offering viewers small moments of repair and reassurance – most of which require a knowing viewer to read the subtext of the scenes. The aim of these recuperations is to make the viewer feel good – and in the case of Nathan, Samantha, and Max, this seems to have been mostly successful. Indeed, Daniel Sea, the actor playing Max, themselves describes the character's return as 'reparative' (Dry 2022). Without such moments of recuperation, engendering a kind of collective sigh of relief, we might remain uneasy about our attachments to the original shows, with their frequent myopias about racism, sexuality, transphobia, and classism. '*Don't worry*', these moments seem to say, '*we can all move on*'.

We might view Charlotte and Anthony's (Charlotte's wedding planner and friend from the original) storylines in *And Just Like That . . .* as similar moments of repair. In the sequel, the originally sexually and romantically conservative Charlotte appears much more open, confident and relaxed about sex, buying condoms for her teenage daughter and openly chatting about giving her husband Harry a blowjob in the bathroom. The latter shocks her previously more open and liberated friends, perhaps suggesting that Samantha's departure (and the sexual progressiveness she represented) hasn't left such a big hole after all. Anthony, originally a brash, critical, and judgemental gay man employed as a stylist for wealthy women, begins a relationship with younger man Giuseppi, but initially refuses to play the role of a 'bottom' when they have sex: 'Jesus Christ, because I'm not the woman okay?' Eventually, Anthony learns to let down his walls and try new kinds of sex with Giuseppi. Here, two of the more conservative characters from the original show demonstrate to viewers that the show has left behind some of its outdated views, for instance about homosexuality (see e.g. Alexander 2021), just like Charlotte and Anthony have left behind their prudishness and attachment to fixed sexual roles, respectively.

This sense of a harmonious closed circle between the original shows and their remakes or sequels is further reinforced by the crossovers between the three different shows. Several actors appear in more than one: Kim Cattrall not just briefly reprises her role as Samantha in *And Just Like That . . .* but also plays Brodie's unaware upper-class mother in *Queer as Folk*. Chris Renfro appears both as Brodie's good friend Daddius, who dies in a nightclub shooting in *Queer as Folk*, and as Alice's brief younger situationship in *Generation Q*. And Armand Fields plays Max's partner Reese in *Generation Q*, as well as Brodie's business partner Bussey in *Queer as Folk*. As viewers returning to the worlds of all three shows simultaneously, we can almost imagine the shows as taking place in the same universe, all together inviting us to retain our nostalgic attachments to the late 1990s and early 2000s representative landscape, where sex was good, politics was distant, and everyone was having fun. Zoe Williams writes similarly about the continued popularity of *Friends*: 'It's hard not to mourn . . . the spirit of the 90s, with its relentless optimism and comically low stakes. It felt like a time when nothing could go wrong, and anything that did would be worth it for the anecdote' (2023). Likewise in these three shows, through their recuperative narratives and introduction of more explicit 'diversity', the remakes present us with a way to hold onto this spirit (or the *imagination* of the 1990s/2000s), cultivating a kind of yearning for a time of apparently more straightforward politics and simpler representational demands.

Learning to do (it) better

But this desire to go back and repair our relationships with the troubled originals sits uneasily with the awareness that perhaps not everything can – or should be made good. *And Just Like That . . .* begins with depictions of marital bliss between Carrie and Mr Big, her obsessive on-again, off-again love interest throughout *Sex and the City*, whom she eventually married in the first *Sex and the City* film (2008). Mr Big dies of a heart attack while on an exercise bike in the first episode of the reboot, and much of the season focuses on Carrie's journey through grief. Arguably Mr Big's departure was narratively necessary, as Olivia Petter argues in the *Independent*: 'for the reboot to be more than just an exercise in nostalgia, heaving with self-congratulatory in-jokes and open-goal observations about these (now) middle-aged women trying to remain tapped into the zeitgeist, the writers needed to do something drastic. Something Big' (2021). Big's death allows the show to explore new themes of loss and ageing – but it also does away with the relational dynamic between Big and Carrie, which may not have fared so well in the 2020s. The obsessive attachment to a white, rich, and emotionally unavailable Mr Big as the ultimate goal of female desire does not fit into the no-longer *post*feminist present. Mr Big is positioned here as the ex that no one wanted to go back to – or in Clare Hemmings' language, not a 'good object worthy of being recovered' (2011: 73). For the show to make sense today, Mr Big had to die.

The explicit references to a changed political landscape in all three shows function narratively in a similar way, as self-referential nods to aspects of the original shows not worthy of recuperation. This indicates to audiences how much learning has happened between the originals and the new versions. *Generation Q*'s third season provides probably the most unambiguous example of such learning. Sophie and Dani are discussing the film *The Wedding Planner*, which they both 'fucking love!', when Sophie interjects, 'Wait, but also problematic culturally . . .', to which Dani responds: 'Oh, yeah, but everything in the 2000s kind of was.' The pair go on to discuss the casting of Puerto Rican Jennifer Lopez as Italian in the film. This exchange could be read as the show remarking on its own problematic past, where it faced criticism for casting actors Sarah Shahi and Janina Gavankar, of Persian Spanish and Dutch Indian origin, respectively, in the Latinx roles of Carmen and Papi – as well as for the stereotypical characterizations themselves (Marquez 2014; Ortega 2008). Here the affective tone of the show moves from a reparative one more towards its counterpart – that of paranoid reading where, in Sedgwick's words, 'critique itself becomes a canopy, a dwelling, a resting place, a home' (2003: 50). Here the reboots come to view the originals through a lens of suspicion and critique.

Such moments are indicative of wider progress narratives in the shows, intended to reassure viewers that things have changed for the better. While progress narratives tend to present a linear view of historical or political change, and are 'told with excitement and even relish' (Hemmings 2011: 35; see also Lehtonen 2023), the tone and affect in these shows are often ironic, almost cynical. In *Queer as Folk*, Mingus – Brodie's younger love interest – tells his mother that he passed a test without having to 'pull the queer card again', to which his mother replies: 'Wow, a D+ you earned all on your own without weaponising your marginalisation. It's like we're back in the 90s.' These lines are delivered with a metaphorical wink at the audience, as if to suggest that we should all know that some contemporary political demands have gone too far. Like Carrie's discomfort with the cringeworthy 'woke moments' in the *X,Y, and Me* podcast, these scenes are suggestive of a cynical, almost post-political frame, whereby attempts at radical political and social change are dismissed as impossible or embarrassing, and the status quo preserved via passivity (see e.g. Felski 2015). When considered together with the self-referential moments where the shows explicitly point towards the problematic racial politics of their originals, such cynicism starts to resemble Ahmed's discussion of institutional admissions of racism – where 'saying "we are racist" becomes a claim to have overcome the conditions (unseen racism) that require the speech act in the first place' (2006: 107).

Rather than radical social or political change, in the reboots it is often the private, domesticated, and sexual realm that holds the struggles of the wider world at bay – not dissimilarly to *Fleabag* (2016, 2019), or Abby and Mae of *Work in Progress* (2019, 2021) and *Feel Good* (2020–21), discussed in Chapters 1 and 2. In the first episode of *Generation Q*, Dani proposes to Sophie, but the ring doesn't fit. Sophie tries to reassure

Dani by saying, 'rings are just a symbol of the patriarchy'. Dani counters with, 'yeah but I still want you to have one', to which Sophie responds, 'yeah I'll still take it'. Here Sophie and Dani are aware of the patriarchal connotations of engagement rings, but both confirm their desire to take part in the ritual anyway. Again, it is good sex and its companions romance and long-term partnership which are imbued with the hope of (knowing) salvation – while at least some of the political and social changes that have taken place in between the originals and the reboots are brushed over or ridiculed.

The affective dynamics of these representations, then, are evocative of paranoid or suspicious reading, such that they tend to proceed along 'prescriptive as well as excruciatingly predictable' pathways, 'closing our minds to the play of detail, nuance, quirkiness, contradiction, happenstance' (Felski 2015: 141). There is nothing surprising about the learnings that the reboots present to us, and instead they tend to be delivered with a certain weariness – just like Sophie's formulaic acknowledgement of the patriarchal meaning of engagement rings. They are also echoed in *Generation Q*'s increasing return to a narrative focus on its original cast members (rather than the new characters) over the three seasons, and in the easy 'lessons' Charlotte offers about pronouns in *And Just Like That . . .*, as if sharing gossip to friends. Diversity has been visibly demonstrated (ticked off), and marked as a pit stop on the road to return to more familiar, comfortable dwellings – romance, marriage, and relationships with our bad but now recuperated exes.

Bad attachments

So far we have proposed that the reboot shows all attempt in some ways to both recuperate their originals and demonstrate to their audiences that learning has occurred in the intervening years – although, as we suggested above, sometimes the latter does not come across as entirely sincere. These representational and affective dynamics carry the underlying assumption of a certain end point, as if there is no possibility of further problematic representation in the new shows. Earlier we mentioned the significantly changed dynamics of racial representation in all three shows – for instance, in *And Just Like That . . .* all of the core characters' significant new friends are people of colour: Carrie's realtor and friend Seema, Charlotte's mom friend Lisa, Miranda's professor-turned-friend Nya, and Carrie's coworker and Miranda's love interest Che. The setting of the new *Queer as Folk* in New Orleans results in a much higher level of racial and ethnic diversity in the cast, and as already discussed, many of the new characters in *Generation Q* are also people of colour – as well as frequently played by actors of a similar ethnic background. However, these markers of representational progress sit uncomfortably alongside some (continued and new) exclusions and myopias.

In a third season episode of *Generation Q*, an old incident from the original series comes up, when Alice ends up in the middle of a social media storm using the hashtag #AliceSoEntitled. In season 5 of *The L Word*, she attends a secretive gay Hollywood party, where a famous Black basketball player, Darryl Brewer, is also in attendance. Alice later sees Brewer making homophobic remarks on TV, and decides to publicly 'out' him. The video she posts goes viral and results in Alice getting a guest spot on a talk show – a key development in her career, and presumably also in her eventually having her own talk show in *Generation Q*. In the present, Alice is unwavering in her opinion that she did nothing wrong and should not apologize. Although Sophie does in the end convince her to apologize publicly for the violence of a public outing, the *racial* features of the incident go entirely unremarked. That the racial dynamics of a white talk show host flippantly outing a Black sports star are not explicitly discussed in the story's rehashing might raise eyebrows for knowing viewers, especially since they *were* implicitly remarked upon in the original – whereas newer viewers might miss them altogether.

Likewise, *Generation Q* does not fare as well with its main trans character Micah as it does with the reparative storyline of Max, discussed above. Most of Micah's storylines circle around transness itself, including his struggles with his mother misgendering him and being pigeonholed as a trans therapist at work – otherwise he remains mostly a background figure to his housemates, Dani, Sophie, and Finley, with a narrative arc that occurs independently of the main friendship group. Interestingly, the other major trans actors on *Generation Q* play cis characters (Jamie Clayton as Tess, Sophie Giannamore as Jordi) – a move that was confirmed as deliberate by show creator Marja-Lewis Ryan, and subsequently questioned, for instance, by Drew Burnett Gregory: 'but is the desire actually to be cast as cis? Or is the desire to be cast as a character granted humanity beyond their transness?' (2020a), suggesting that when characters are only positioned as explicitly trans when their storylines are about transness, other aspects of their personhood are ignored.[4]

Relatedly, class remains a major blind spot in both *And Just Like That . . .* and *Generation Q*, with most characters being comfortably upper middle class and unaffected by the demands of the increasingly unequal, neoliberal world they inhabit. Season 2 of *Generation Q* introduces a new character, Tina's partner Carrie, played by Rosie O'Donnell. Carrie is a butch lesbian somewhat reminiscent of *Work in Progress*' Abby – she is a public defender, an alcoholic, and on antidepressants. She is generally lovely and kind, but struggles with the high-flying world that Tina's friends effortlessly move in, fumbling her way through social encounters by talking and drinking too much. Although it is clear that Bette's dislike of Carrie originates in her still being in love with Tina, there is a perhaps unwarranted level of condescension in all the major characters' dealings with Carrie – focused on her perceived brashness, basic tastes in food and physical characteristics. Although later the show goes on to at least try to repair its relationship to Max, the way that Carrie is treated carries a rather similar affective tone to how Max was treated in the original – as a butch, differently classed and gendered outsider, who simply does not belong. This signals a certain continuity between the reboot and the original, where 'the show's explicit transphobia was then closely aligned with its inability to tolerate butchness' (Bradbury-Rance 2024: 41).

Class remains otherwise uncommented on in the shows, except when Che struggles to pay for their apartment and returns to administrative work to make ends meet, or when Miranda (unrealistically for a character of her social and professional positioning) struggles to 'begin again' by moving into her friend's apartment and taking on an unpaid internship alongside her twenty-something classmates. Instead, financial uncertainty is presented as 'over' for the original characters, arguably in an attempt to humanize their distinctly upper-middle-class experiences. Scenes where the once 'financially messy' Carrie can now make a $100,000 donation to a charity on a whim; where Shane arrives in LA via private jet; or where Samantha can fly from London for the weekend to see her friends, are presented as largely unremarkable. The original socio-economic aspirationalism of these characters has now, naturally and obviously, transformed into extreme financial security, simply ignoring the turbulent economic realities that have taken place in between the reboots and the originals and which feature as central elements of many of the other shows we discuss in this book.

Perhaps somewhat ironically, the shows also features blind spots in relation to queerness and sexuality themselves. The major representational shift in *And Just Like That . . .* is Miranda's coming out and subsequent positioning as explicitly queer – in contrast to the original *Sex and the City*, where she was understood as 'queer coded' by many (see e.g. Aurthur

Figure 5.2 In the original *Sex and the City*, the lesbian-'coded' Miranda dons a short haircut, tie and pantsuit as she confirms she is 'definitely straight'. *Sex and the City* © Darren Star Productions and HBO Entertainment 1998–2004.

2022; Divalentino 2022; Gerhard 2005; Giampaolo 2023; Hirschman 2022). Queer coding adds enough characteristics, behaviours, and external features for a character to appear as queer to audiences who clock the references – in Miranda's case, pantsuits, a high-flying career, a no-nonsense attitude, and overwhelming social scepticism towards cis men – but without explicitly making the character queer (in fact, in season 1 of the original, it was confirmed that she was 'definitely straight' (Figure 5.2)). In the reboot, Miranda is in an unhappy relationship with Steve when she first meets Carrie's non-binary coworker Che. The pair end up hooking up in Carrie's kitchen, which Miranda describes as the most 'transcendent' sex of her life (Figure 5.3). After first pursuing an affair with Che, Miranda eventually breaks up with Steve, and goes on to become obsessed with Che in a way that is reminiscent of stereotypical romantic comedies (or even, the original Carrie). She leaves her family and friends behind to follow Che to Los Angeles, turns up at Che's flat unannounced, and generally spends her time ruminating on her self-worth and relationship, much to the frustration of everyone.

The desperate undertones of Miranda's first forays into queerness are certainly a departure for the character, with one critic describing the experience of observing Miranda's coming out as 'bittersweet' (Giorgis 2022). Similarly, Allegra Hirschman ponders, 'in a show

Figure 5.3 After having 'transcendent' sex with Che in Carrie's kitchen, Miranda becomes explicitly queer in the reboot. *And Just Like That . . .* © Michael Patrick King Productions/HBO Max 2023.

about female friendship they were always just talking about men, an issue Miranda often bemoaned. And now, just like that, we are meant to believe she was also a delusional romantic who just hadn't found her Mr. (or Mx) Big yet?' (2022). Thus, in making Miranda's queerness explicit, and by presenting it through rather typical coming-out and romance narratives, *And Just Like That* . . . manages to lose some of the character's original queerness – perhaps akin to the loss Gregory (2020) describes in relation to the one she experiences when realizing Tess and Jordi are meant to be cis in *Generation Q*. Further, Miranda's 'new' queerness finds its place in the sexual and domestic when she moves in with Che, where her original queer coding was emphasized by her independent, liberal feminist desire to gain a home, a social life, and a career, just for herself. After sex, the old Miranda would have checked her watch and got on with her busy day, channelling the lesbian affect we always already knew her for, whereas the naming of her queerness makes us miss her more (*and* the original show she came from).

In a similar vein, narratives about queer reproduction in *Generation Q* and non-binary characters in *And Just Like That . . .* seem to hint at, or gesture towards, more diverse and in-depth representations of queerness and gender diversity – but without quite hitting the mark in the end (see e.g. Bernard 2023; Factora 2021; Flint 2022). Relatedly, both shows seem haunted by the notion of non-monogamy, perhaps in a similar way to how *Fleabag* is haunted by lesbianism, as we argued in Chapter 1. It appears throughout *Generation Q*, in Alice's brief throuple with her partner Nat and Nat's ex-wife Gigi (following a steamy, alcohol-fuelled threesome in the back room of Shane's bar); and in cursory references scattered throughout Shane's storylines – with Tess finally asking her in the final season if she 'wants to do ENM [ethical non-monogamy]'. And in the second season of *And Just Like That . . .*, it is revealed that Che is still married to their husband Lyle, who states that the couple were 'poly pioneers'. In encountering these flirtations with different and complex queer representations in the reboots, the experience of many queer viewers (the authors included) has been one of frustration or disappointment – whereas in the originals such topics were often treated with an open disdain or even disgust that we could at least openly reject.

Going back to your ex

In the previous section, we engaged in some paranoid reading of our own, suggesting that in many ways the shows continue with problematic dynamics from the originals. So why return to such exes at all – a question that is made even more relevant by the shows' insistence on very literally returning many of their key characters to their exes. In *And Just Like That . . .*, Carrie ends up reconnecting with Aidan, her second main love interest from the original series, and the two pick up exactly where they left off – with Carrie eventually even wondering if she made a mistake by choosing Mr Big. In the third and final season of *Generation Q*, Bette and Tina reignite their on-and-off relationship from the original show, and Alice bumps into her ex, Tasha, from the original show at Bette and Tina's wedding, where the pair dance romantically suggesting a likely reconciliation. Throughout the final season, Shane also goes back to her old antics of sleeping around, and cheats on Tess. Combined with the increasing narrative focus the show gives to the original characters, and contrary to the narratives that demonstrate learning and a desire to do representation differently/better, here the implication seems to be that ultimately, we cannot help but return to an ex (and really, always wanted to) – even if they were not that good to us in the first place.

These moments of more straightforward return seem reminiscent of Hemmings' discussion of return narratives, which in her words 'affirm a common present by affirming a shared past' (2011: 98). For Hemmings, a return narrative 'resolves anxieties . . . by asking its subjects to "take stock" and focus on justice over infighting' (2011: 98). In a similar vein, these shows seem to want to reassure us about our continued attachments to the originals, but unlike in the earlier examples of recuperation and repair that demonstrate to viewers that (some) things are better now, here the message seems to be instead that some things are worth keeping exactly the same. In this reading, these exes (Aidan, Tina and Bette, Tasha, and perhaps even Shane's promiscuity) are 'good object[s] worthy of being recovered' (Hemmings 2011: 73), and we as viewers can remain nostalgic about them because we can all agree that nothing quite as good has been offered by anyone or anything new since. Indeed, Carrie's, Alice's, and Bette's dating lives in the reboots all seem to offer nothing but weary disappointment and comedic relief, and Shane appears to be just as repelled by her domestic life with Tess as she was by that with Carmen in the original. In these moments, the shows seem to *reward* this return to their loyal audiences. Having been willing to travel elsewhere and try new things for a couple of seasons, doesn't it feel just *right* to return back to your ex?

The key 'good object' that all three shows seem to want to return to is good sex. As highlighted above, the reboots tend to represent sex itself very similarly to the originals: as something that is mostly straightforwardly and unproblematically *good*. Bad sex appears neither in the context of the cringe or awkwardness explored in previous chapters nor in relation to power dynamics and contemporary conversations about the boundaries between sexual violence and bad sex, discussed in the next chapter. Sex in the reboots seems instead to play a role akin to the nostalgic representations in *Pose* (2018–21) and *It's a Sin* (2021) discussed in the previous chapter – but of course here without the context of the AIDS crisis, which we argued helps position good sex as an important representation of survival and pleasure in the face of an overwhelmingly negative representational landscape. Sex in the reboots remains as it always was: mostly good and somewhat sanitized (with the period sex scene between Dani and Sophie providing a notable exception) (Figure 5.1).

Despite the sexually pioneering status of the original shows, for the reboots sex is not something to recuperate or learn to do better – it's fine just as it was. As if to further underline this point, the very last sex scene in *Generation Q* features Shane hooking up with the wedding planner at Bette and Tina's wedding – closely mirroring her dalliances with several bridesmaids and eventually the bride at a wedding in season 5 of the

Figure 5.4 Shane in *The L Word* is thanked by a grateful bridesmaid after sex. *The L Word* © Coast Mountain Films/Showtime 2004–09.

original *L Word* (Figures 5.4 and 5.5). In choosing not to change much about their *sexual* representations, the reboots also remove themselves from the more nuanced and complex conversations about sex that many of the other shows we explore in this book are participating in. Sexual political change in the reboots remains wedded to visible gender and racial diversity of the people having it, or as 'woke moments' peppered through the discursive. It is as if, despite the transgressive visual presence of sex in the originals, on this there is nothing new to say.

So why would we, as viewers, want to return to these unchanged, often bad, exes – if there is nothing new to discover? In the rest of this chapter we want to pose this question more explicitly in relation to our own complex desires to go back to these shows as viewers. Here, it is pertinent to pause to highlight the different attachments we three authors had to the reboots. One of us feels that the reboots' self-congratulatory tone and focus on representational progress means that their emphasis on good sex appears particularly out of touch in the context of contemporary debates – for them, there is no point in returning, as the reboots can only ever highlight what these shows cannot contribute to the era of bad sex. Another one of us thinks that the problematic and harmful representations of the originals should not be ignored or forgotten, but instead made central in the new versions and the stories they try to tell. In this, they maintain something akin

Figure 5.5 Visually and narratively mirroring the original series, a grateful wedding planner thanks Shane after sex. *The L Word: Generation Q* © LMR Original/ Showtime 2019–23.

to a paranoid relationship to the new shows, as if the problematic originals can never be recuperated and enjoyed without an explicitly critical, even suspicious, lens. The third author found some comfort in recuperating and returning to a bad object, because this allows their affective attachments to the original shows to continue today, holding on to the possibility of a reparative reading in the present.

Our very different responses to the reboot shows reflect the different styles of reading we have engaged in throughout the chapter, moving between outright critical or suspicious reading, more generous reparative reading, and at times not wanting to engage in any kind of reading (or watching) at all. These modes of reading perhaps also align with Hemmings' characterization of progress, return, and loss narratives, respectively. Similarly to her analysis of feminist narratives, in this chapter we have tracked 'the commonalities of utterance, the remarkably similar affects produced' (2011: 22) across the three reboot shows. As Lehtonen (2023) argues, perhaps the complex attachments of loss, progress and return that the reboots cultivate in their viewers tell us much more about our desires in the present, than they do about whether the original shows are worthy of recuperation or returning to. As Elizabeth Nelson suggests in *The New York Times*, remake shows 'face a clear creative bind. The reboot that changes nothing will be uncanny and lifeless; the one that thinks itself more clever than its predecessor will turn out cynical and sour' (2023). It is thus our, the viewers', desire to return (or not return, or return with some conditions) that is highlighted and intensified by the reboots, rather than necessarily any intrinsic failure or success of the shows themselves. As Hemmings argues, 'there is no "outside" of these processes, no single (or even multiple) alternative story one could tell that would finally "get it right"' (2011: 22). Perhaps similarly here, there is simply no way of doing reboots that would finally 'get it right', and satisfy all of our complex, differing desires towards them.

So what are we to do with these complex, and at times contradictory, desires, to simultaneously leave behind, castigate, and recuperate sex with the ex? Could going back to an ex be done differently? Hemmings develops an approach that 'seeks to disrupt dominant narrative grammar and open up multiple re-readings of the present', asking 'what kinds of historical and political possibilities does such a move allow us to imagine or temporarily inhabit?' (2011: 23), while Felski enquires after reading practices that leave 'room for . . . the unexpected, the chancy and the contingent' (2015: 152). That is to say, we might likewise look for disruptions to the dominant affective and narrative grammar of the reboot shows in our own viewing and reading practices, rather than only in the shows themselves.

In her scathing analysis of Miranda's coming out narrative, Hirschman states that 'it's not the affair in and of itself. It's the overall tenor of this newly romantic, starry-eyed, and reckless Miranda that is undermining my own version of Miranda as already queer AND partnered with Steve' (2022). It is as if Hirschman simply refuses the reboot's version of Miranda, and (re)invents her own instead – a Miranda who has been comfortably queer for ages, while remaining married to Steve. Gregory (2020a) does something similar in imagining what it would have been like for Tess and Jordi to be written as trans characters, rather than as cis characters played by trans actors; and Autostraddle's Riese Bernard (2009; 2023) regularly reimagines disappointing storylines in her recaps, even penning a fictional letter from Max to *The L Word* creator Ilene Chaiken. Likewise, many viewers (the authors included) had already taken delight in imagining a deeply fulfilling, joyful life for Max, running parallel (or before we even got to) the developments on screen; or a near decade of explicit, communicative, ethical non-monogamy for Shane; and a close, intimate, long-term but long-distance friendship between Carrie and Samantha. And although *Queer as Folk* did not get a second season, we can certainly imagine the caring, cross-generational queer community built in the show continuing into the distant future – even in Brodie's, and our, absence.

These types of reimaginings perform similar functions to those brought about by fan fiction, or other active forms of media consumption highlighted in the introduction – such as the 'coviewing' practices explored by April Williams and Vanessa Gonlin (2017), whereby audiences engage in lively Twitter analysis and debate about Black womanhood at the same time as watching the newest episode of the popular TV show *How to Get Away with Murder*. Such practices of active viewership and reimagination are often understood to reflect limited representational paradigms, with fan practices filling the gaps to try and create something more inclusive and representative – such as with queer coded narratives and characters, who are frequently reimagined as explicitly, proudly, joyfully queer in fan-generated content (see e.g. Dhaenens et al. 2008; Floegel 2020).[5] While such practices certainly have a frustration to them, in that they often serve to highlight the shortcomings of what is on our screens, at the same time they can also help open doors to new pathways, invigorated imaginations and fuller, more nuanced representational landscapes. If we take the notion of reparative reading seriously, as a practice of consumption that 'looks to a work of art for solace and replenishment' (Felski 2015: 151), then is this not exactly what active viewership practices do? In this vein, perhaps the cancellation of two of the shows under analysis in this chapter (*Queer as Folk* after one, and *Generation Q* after three seasons) paradoxically leaves many of their storylines open for further audience reinterpretation, as well as of course for further adaptations in the era of the reboot, or as Zoe Williams describes it, 'the death of definitive TV endings' (2017).

Our discussion here thus also points at transformations in contemporary practices of media consumption, as discussed in the introduction, whereby audiences are less and less likely to simply accept the representations placed in front of them. As Natalia Samutina argues, 'contemporary communities of imagination not only receive and experience, but also actively transform and co-create imaginary worlds and live their lives in these worlds with great intensity, constantly expanding the spheres of their interests' (2016: 448). Arguably, such fan reimaginings are not that dissimilar to what reboot shows themselves do, in that both modes of televisual co-production 'destabilize the traditional understanding of a finite, quantifiable text' (Achouche 2017: 77). Indeed, it is these active transformations and co-creations that often result in the greatest pleasures in viewership – in being open to the unknown in the media representations we consume, we also open ourselves up to be transformed by the process of watching, rewatching, dissecting, refusing, and reimagining collectively. As Katherine Angel writes about the joy of sex, similarly the joy of engaging with meaningful, even if at times disappointing, media content 'might precisely be in discovering new, different ways to be touched: in being vulnerable to the unknown' (2021a: 114). In the next chapter, we explore representations of sexual violence in *I May Destroy You* (2020) and, returning to the notion of being vulnerable to the unknown and ambiguous, ask what implications and possibilities these representations might carry in the post-MeToo era.

Chapter 6

BEYOND THE BOUNDARIES OF BAD SEX IN *I MAY DESTROY YOU*

Introduction

If the last chapters have engaged with questions of good and bad sex, this chapter examines the boundaries of bad sex – in other words, when bad sex ceases to be sex at all. More recent shows have considered if and how the experience of gendered and sexual violence can be explored openly, honestly, and radically on TV (*Big Little Lies*; *Sharp Objects; Orange Is the New Black*). Amongst these, none stand out like *I May Destroy You* (2020), which follows Arabella and her best friends navigating the aftermath of sexual violence. Arabella, a young author who has garnered initial success with writing about her life as a precarious Black millennial in London, is spiked and raped in the toilet of a bar while on a night out with her friend Simon, avoiding a looming deadline. The next morning, she cannot remember what happened but has flashbacks that gradually reveal the violence that has been inflicted on her. In her journey through denial, anger, numbness, acceptance, and her quest for justice, she is accompanied by best friends Terry and Kwame. Both support her as best as they can, while also confronting their own experiences of consent violation. Written and directed by Michaela Coel, the show is based on Coel's own experience of sexual violence and follows the semi-autobiographical genre of shows like *Feel Good* (2020–21), *Fleabag* (2016, 2019) and *Please Like Me* (2013–16).

As Caetlin Benson-Allott (2020) highlights, *I May Destroy You* reinvents rape television by offering an intersectional, complex, and trauma-informed representation of violation. With its explicit focus on sexual violence, the show also significantly diverts from the bad sex shows that we have discussed in this book so far. While sexual violence is for the most part absent from most shows in this genre (*Please Like Me*; *Special*), it is brushed away or joked about in others (*Fleabag*). If it is featured, it often appears as a foundational yet unspecified trauma (*Feel Good*) or an ever-present threat (*Euphoria*; *Pose*). Indeed, the lack of direct and complex representations of sexual violence is not surprising, given the general lack of informed discussion of this topic in both television and film (Benson-Allott 2020), as well as the specific focus on bad sex that most of the shows discussed in this book have. The detached and often humorous depiction of sex as difficult, awkward and problem-ridden is threatened by any more serious consideration of when bad sex stops being bad sex, or rather sex at all, and turns into, or was always, rape and sexual violence. As discussed in the introduction of this book, from their inception shows like *Girls* (2012–17) struggled with delineating the division between *just* bad sex and sexual violence and abuse, dwelling on the blurring of boundaries instead of explicitly dealing with encounters that, both for those who experience them and for viewers, were not blurred.

I May Destroy You works against this trend by tackling the discussion and representation of sexual violence and its afterlife head-on. The show stands out by exploring experiences of sexual violence openly and radically, invoking contrast, humour, and narrative disjointedness to radically and delicately reframe common representations of sexual violence, challenging the essentialized victim/perpetrator binary through an intersectional exploration of sexual violence (and responses to it). In this chapter, we ask what implications and possibilities these new representations of sexual violence and trauma carry in the post-MeToo era. As such, this chapter emerges in dialogue with contemporary concerns about the (im)possibility of good sex in the wake of sexual violence (Angel 2021; Raghavan 2023; Srinivasan 2022). How can not just sex but also life be good again in the aftermath of sexual violence, and what forms of sexual politics are needed for this to take place? Here, we examine how simplistic frames of victimization, violence, and trauma can be challenged through more recent cultural forms that portray and enact a more intersectional politics against sexual violence. In doing so, the chapter reflects on justice and healing in the wake of sexual violence, pointing out the importance of friendship and infrastructures of care.

The boundaries of bad sex

Rather than simply shrugging or even laughing off bad sex gone beyond bad, like some of the other shows we have discussed earlier in this book, in the storylines of Arabella, Terry and Kwame, *I May Destroy You* directly asks and discusses serious questions about consent and the boundaries of bad sex. In the scenes after the night out, we witness Arabella being shaken up by flashbacks that carry her back to the scene of rape: through her eyes, we see a white man looking down on her and sweating, with the red walls of the toilet cubicle closing in on her. Her memory is hazy, and the night itself is depicted across three, incomplete timelines: Arabella laughing and dancing with friends, Arabella falling and stumbling, and Arabella writing in the office alone. Triggered by her inability to find her way home the next morning, or unable to explain a cut on her forehead, or a broken phone, Arabella tries to fight off and dismiss the flashbacks that begin to haunt her. When in a later episode she tries to distract herself by having sex with the pretentious author, Zain, who her agency has put her in touch with, he takes the condom off without telling her – committing stealthing, considered rape and a criminal violation of consent under UK law, as she later learns. Meanwhile, her best friend Terry, who first boasts about how free she felt when she had a threesome with two strangers in Italy, comes to the realization that said threesome might not have been as spontaneous as she thought but instead pre-planned by the two men who pretended not to know each other. Kwame, referred to as the 'king of Grindr' for his promiscuous, digitally driven, gay sex life, similarly struggles to make sense of a hook-up when his date won't let him leave the room, pins him down on the bed and humps him until he comes.

It is this aspect of the show that has garnered the most attention in public commentary. In *Slate*, Nonny Onyekweli discusses how '*I May Destroy You* Changed the Way My Friends and I Talk About Consent' (2020), recalling how the show made them reconsider situations they themselves have experienced.[1] This kind of learning is facilitated through the character's own difficult learning process. Arabella struggles to put into words what she has experienced, denying and playing down her memory loss in the following days. It is only when confronted with more and more evidence – like her smashed phone and ATM withdrawals on the other side of the city – that she comes to understand what happened to her. Similarly, Terry only slowly comes to the realization that her threesome might have been less consensual than she thought, confronting the difficult feelings that this realization brings when one of her dates affirms her experience. Kwame likewise struggles to make sense of how his once easy-going queer sex life has been shaken by the violation of consent during a Grindr hook-up. While he has a sense that what happened to him was sexual violence, particularly through his understanding of what happened to Arabella, we see him googling 'is non-consensual humping . . . rape' before eventually going to the police and confiding his experience to Terry and Arabella.

In these ways, the show also comes to trouble the idea of consent as the ultimate security against sexual violence and as the guarantee of good sex. As Katherine Angel (2021a) discusses, one of the problems with a singular focus on consent is that, while focused on stopping the violator of consent, it ultimately puts the responsibility squarely on the consenting person. In other words, ideas of consent place too much emphasis on women and other affected people to *know* what they want *and* to be able to enforce it – 'enthusiastic consent' (if performed) is the limited promise that sex might stay *good*. As Angel argues, this also means that if consent is violated, people experience not only the violation of their bodily autonomy but also remorse and shame for not having enforced their boundaries more clearly. Angel's argument points towards and critiques earlier, perhaps more simplistic, framings of sexual violence – framings that have also been critiqued, for instance, by Sharon Marcus (1992), Nicola Gavey (1999), and Priya Raghavan (2023). The imperative to consent, to know, and to act, can add shame for not having said 'no', not having been clear enough about what you desired, not possessing a body that acts as a straightforward conduit of your will in the moment, or not having known, yet, what that will was, or how you felt about it. Indeed, what if you cannot consent because you are drugged, if you do not know that the people you have consented to have made other arrangements beforehand, or if you have consented at first but then find it impossible to get out of the situation? Arabella, Terry, and Kwame's journeys through denial and shame cannot be separated, and they are at least partially infused with the reinforcing spirals of blame and self-blame that the discourse of not having protected one's consent can create.

What makes *I May Destroy You* so powerful is that it breaks such spirals by not shying away from venturing into difficult terrain. As Onyekweli notes, 'the show makes clear that consent procured under any kind of false pretences is stolen and is most likely a violation, while not labelling everyone who steals consent a monster' (2020). Exploring sexual violence through different and sometimes conflicting storylines that range from the clear-cut case of drug-induced rape to the more complex negotiation of consent, such as in the consensual yet non-consensual threesome that Terry finds herself in, the show encourages its audience to ask difficult questions. As Onyekweli recalls, it made her and her friends question the complexity of consent: 'What happens if a partner is dishonest about their relationship status? What happens if your partner is dishonest about their sexual history or a past partner? . . . What do you do if you realize, after the fact, that someone violated your consent?' (2020). In other words, when is sex no longer just bad sex but not sex at all? And not just how, but *when* will you know to call it such?[2]

In its complex representations of the different ways in which consent can be denied and taken away, the show goes against simplistic perspectives that would equalize all forms of sexual violence or portray (heterosexual) sex as a violence in itself – perspectives haunted by some forms of second-wave feminism (see e.g. Brownmiller 1975; Dworkin 1987; MacKinnon 1997). As Sharon Marcus points out, such frames tend to emphasize the 'essential' vulnerability of women by representing women as always 'already raped and rapable' (1992: 388), where to understand essential (feminine) vulnerability as the key element of violence 'is to make the identities of rapist and raped preexist the rape itself' (1992: 391). Quite the opposite, in *I May Destroy You*, we get one of the most evocative bad sex scenes in this genre, where sex is represented as an awkward, messy, and complicated, yet also enjoyable endeavour – namely when Arabella has sex with her Italian lover, Biagio, while on her period. After a drug-fuelled night, they are about to have sex when she tells him that she is on her period and that she 'is quite a heavy bleeder'. They try anyway, carefully with a condom, and rather than grossed out, he is intrigued by the blood clot that comes out of her after penetration. Together they investigate the blood clot, he touches it, wonders how soft it is and declares: 'oh I have never seen anything like that before.' Sex here is 'bad', but in a good way: messy, comical, difficult, but also consensual and intimate. Afterwards, she tells him, 'you have done really well today, don't hurt me' – foreshadowing that no guarantees exist that either he or other men she will encounter in the future will continue to be as respectful as he was in this moment.

The most intriguing aspect of the show, however, is not just that it invites us to look closer at the boundaries of consent, but how it engages with the question of how people live on after such a violation. After all, most of the show is focused not on the event of sexual violence but on what happens after – how people live in the wake of sexual violence and what this reveals about how not just sex, but life itself, might become *good* again. Here the show circumvents what Raghavan (2023) identifies as the key problem of most sexual violence discourse, feminist discourse included: the binary representation of victimhood and agency.[3] People who experience sexual violence tend to be represented either as the ultimate traumatized *victims* to be pitied and saved or as heroic *survivors* who fight against and ultimately overcome their traumatic experiences. What this overlooks is what Raghavan, drawing on Rajeswari Sunder Rajan, calls the 'radical subjectivity of pain', which often defies such clear victim/survivor binaries (Rajan 1993, cited in Raghavan 2023: 15). Instead, by understanding pain as socially and politically induced rather than ontologically given, this conceptualization highlights how people affected by sexual violence relate to the shared yet subjective condition of pain – which can shift, make worse, alter, and transform experiences of violence. *I May Destroy You* presents a complex portrayal of the radical subjectivity of pain and how people deal with it. Rather than simple solutions, it offers valuable reflections on what kind of justice and care are possible or needed in the aftermath of sexual violence.

The quest for justice

After the night of the rape, Arabella does not know what happened, let alone what she should do. After calling her friend Simon, who was with her that night, he reassures her that he brought her home. Yet, she realizes that his story does not match up with her flashbacks, nor with her credit card history. Once she understands that he has lied to her to cover up cheating on his wife and that she has indeed been left on her own, she calls her best friend Terry and goes with her and Kwame to the police. At first, Arabella's encounter with the criminal justice system is surprisingly positive. She is attended to by two calm policewomen, one of them Black and seemingly clued up on the complex trauma that sexual violence can induce. When she is first asked about 'the assault [she] recalls', Arabella responds, 'you are calling it something I never said', diverting that 'it's a very big thing to assume' and 'we should refrain from talking about things like that, we should be careful'. Yet, when asked more clearly about her flashbacks, Arabella realizes what she can no longer deny, hides in her sweater, and starts crying. Finding the language for what happened is not straightforward; it is marked as painful, yet also part of a process of working towards healing and justice.

Later on, Arabella gets a call that DNA has been found and the police have arrested a potential suspect on file for a similar crime. While at the police station, Arabella also gets confirmation that the stealthing she experienced is indeed a form of sexual violence and a crime under UK law. For a moment, it looks like the criminal justice system might deliver. Excited about the arrest and the affirmation she gets from the police officers, Arabella compliments them, asking, 'Who are you guys? Are you po-po or are you the rapebusters?' before bursting into a celebration and telling them how meaningful their advice has been, given that there are 'so many different types of sexual assault, you know'. The police officers respond: 'yeah the problem is when people don't know what is a crime, and what isn't a crime, they don't report it . . . and then people get away with it.' To make sure the perpetrator does not get away in this case, Arabella undergoes the difficult process of recounting the crime in detail, as well as physical exams – also requiring her lover, Biagio, to supply a DNA sample that can be tested against that of the potential perpetrator. The questions and exams are taxing, and Biagio will come to victim blame and shout at Arabella for not looking after herself and 'not watching' her drink. The story of victim blaming is a familiar one, but one initially countered by the assurances Arabella receives from the police and social media. Indeed, all of this must be worth it for achieving justice, for having her rapist punished and the perpetrator kept from violating other people.

Yet, Arabella's initial hope is cruelly thwarted when it turns out that the DNA the police have collected is not usable. The two policewomen read out the final report to Arabella and Terry, ending with no charges being made and the closing of the case – echoing wider UK statistics on sexual violence where between 1.3 and 8.2 per cent of reported cases lead to charges and only 1 per cent lead to a conviction (Hohl 2022). Arabella and Terry are distraught – shocked both by the suddenly stern and dismissive way in which they are treated by the police, as well as, perhaps, by how and why they came to invest hope in the police and the criminal justice system in the first place. As two young Black women in London, at several points in the show they are shown to be critical of the institutionalized whiteness around them, yet in the quest for justice they initially unquestioningly trust London's Metropolitan Police – found (in)famously to be 'institutionally racist' after the murder of Stephen Lawrence in the late 1990s (Macpherson 1999) as well as 'institutionally sexist and misogynistic' in the wake of the more recent murder of Sarah Everard (Casey 2023: 285). They are left with the conundrum that Angela Davis describes as the question of how 'a state that is thoroughly infused with racism, male dominance, class-bias and homophobia and that constructs itself in and through violence [can] act to minimize it in the lives of women?' (2000: 1). Arabella and Terry's suspicions, as well as perhaps those of viewers, have been reconfirmed, and while they do not know what they should do next, they do know that they need to leave the police station to 'an environment that sparks joy', as Terry says, turning their backs on the criminal justice system.

The inability of the criminal justice system to actually deliver justice becomes even clearer when Kwame turns to the police to report his experience of sexual violence. Sitting opposite a police officer who is clearly awkward and uncomfortable with taking on his case, Kwame is made to answer dismissive and intrusive questions, such as, 'this was about three weeks ago, yeah?'; 'when you went to his address you didn't say, "hello my name is"?'; 'did they penetrate you or . . . there's a big difference between sexual assault and rape' – the police officer emphasizing the difference with his hands. Kwame is ultimately told by the officer that a different person needs to deal with it: 'you know, there are other ways you could have reported this . . . We've got machines out there to make it easier for people to report these things without having to . . .' As a range of Black and abolitionist feminist scholars point out, the criminal justice system has been built for the protection of white upper- and middle-class women, often at the expense of racialized, particularly Black, men constructed as a threat to be contained (Crenshaw 1991; Davis 1983; Davis et al. 2022; Sexton 2017). The sexual assault of a queer Black man then confounds not just the police officer; it is also unintelligible to a criminal justice system operating on the construction of Black men as perpetrators, not as victims.

Further, the positioning of a queer Black man as a victim challenges common representations of queer, racialized promiscuity, as 'this group has not figured as frequently as white or heterosexual survivors into representations of sexual assault' (Meyer 2022: 4). This omission of queer people, especially queer men of colour, from depictions of sexual violence is one of the key issues within both feminist and non-feminist representations of sexual violence that *I May Destroy You* counters. Here, it becomes essential to recognize 'how systems of oppression such as heteronormativity and institutional racism play an equally important role as gender inequality' in constructions of violence, violation and power (Meyer 2022: 5). Kwame quickly realizes that he has made a mistake by coming to the police. Indeed, in contrast to Arabella's experiences with the police when reporting her rape, in Kwame's case the officer does not even bother to close the door of the interrogation room – despite a placard clearly stating that not doing so might put people 'in danger'. Not only will the police not help Kwame, they will likely do him further harm.

The politics of ambivalence

If the criminal justice system is not where Arabella and her friends will find resolution, then how might justice and healing be attained? Let down by the police, Arabella realizes that she might have to take the quest for justice into her own hands. After all, it was not just the police that taught her about sexual violence and helped her realize what happened to her but also feminist podcasts and online communities, where she learned about the different forms that rape can take and how other people affected by it have navigated their lives afterwards. After Zain takes the condom off during sex, for instance, Arabella initially learns about stealthing from a feminist podcast. Spurred on by another woman, who it is implied has had similar experiences with Zain, Arabella decides to no longer play along and to expose him. As Sara Ahmed (2021) suggests, when institutions are built on the normalization and silencing of sexual and gendered violence, complaints that can be heard beyond the closed doors of institutional structures often become necessary feminist action. At a reading organized by her publisher, Arabella has a vision of herself standing above herself, smiling in the toilet stall (Figure 6.1). Instead of from her novel, she reads out a

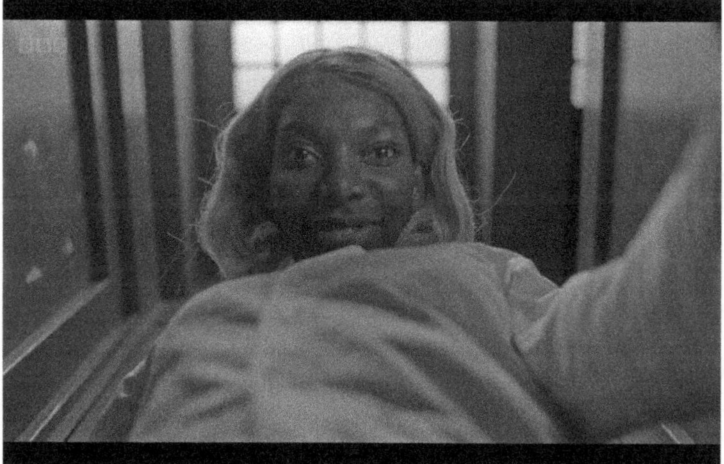

Figure 6.1 Before Arabella decides to name Zain as a 'predator' at her book reading, she imagines herself in the bathroom stall replacing the position of the rapist, looking down and smiling. *I May Destroy You* © Various Artists/BBC One 2020.

statement declaring: 'Zain Tareen is a rapist. He took a condom off in the middle of having sex with me. He placated my shock and gaslighted me, with such intention that I didn't have a second to understand the heinous crime that had occurred. I believe he is a predator.' Videos of her talk go viral online, and Arabella becomes an icon in the fight against sexual violence. For Arabella, in many ways, the public naming of Zain also comes to stand in for the other perpetrator she cannot yet name (and we later learn will never be named in such a way); indeed, it is a vision of the bathroom stall where she was raped that she imagines before naming Zain.

Yet, while her quest for public retribution is understandable, it is also clear that Arabella does not find complete restitution in this moment. Indeed, the redress and satisfaction that she derives from her social justice activism is both short-lived and laced with other more difficult feelings – all-consuming rage, self-aggrandizement, and social isolation. After she goes viral online, we see her become hooked on social media and spending more and more time posting about sexual violence and how to fight it. Arabella's engagements with social media are represented on a spectrum from helpful and informative early on, to increasingly self-destructive: as her energy is seemingly compelled from outside of her body, we see a disjointed series of flashing social media alerts reflecting her increasingly fast dialogue, rapid and surface-level engagements with others, and quick-fire, impulsive decision-making. It all escalates when dressed as the devil for Halloween, Arabella is consumed by her online social activism, losing track of herself, her thoughts, and her replies to fans (Figure 6.2). When a man in the bar compliments her for her costume, she replies: 'it's really amazing that you think your opinion should just be heard', then continues writing stream of consciousness posts about women's constant fear of sexual violence, male bias in tech design and calls for doxxing – the publishing of private information and addresses of potential perpetrators – via the hashtag #doxxthecocks.

In quick edits, we see Arabella slowly becoming the devil she is dressed as – powerful, fearsome, and vindictive – while her anonymous fanbase on social media cheers her on. It all comes to a head when her social media engagements start interfering with her friendships, and she pushes Kwame away for having slept with a woman without telling her that he is gay, equalizing his behaviour with rape. Here we witness the limits of feminist framings of sexual violence as purely *gendered*, which exclude the complex ways in which sexuality, race and power can infuse experiences of it (Meyer 2022). As a result, Arabella is unable to

Figure 6.2 Arabella is absorbed and overwhelmed as social media praise for her fight against sexual violence floods the screen. *I May Destroy You* © Various Artists/BBC One 2020.

consider how Kwame's date, Nilufer, admits to racially fetishizing him and makes homophobic comments after they sleep together. This no longer matters to Arabella, and neither does his remorse and admission that his actions were wrong. For Arabella, there is no complexity anymore, just good and bad, victims and perpetrators, angels and demons. As viewers we understand this resting place, but at the same time worry for Arabella (and Kwame) – it is clear that this simple division into good and bad might provide some temporary comfort, but ultimately it does not feel right.

Sarah Schulman (2016) discusses this form of black-and-white thinking in *Conflict is Not Abuse*. Starting from social justice epistemologies developed in the context of feminist activism and social work practice on sexual violence, she argues that a key insight derived from this work is that there is a distinction between abuse and conflict. While certain forms of sexual and gendered violence are clear cases of abuse and as such are rightly met with accusation and punishment, other forms of sometimes even violent tension are not abuse, but rather conflict – that can and should be better resolved through mediation and interaction. Given that it is not marked by an intractably unequal relation of power and oppression, the relationship between Kwame and Arabella, and perhaps also that between Kwame and the white woman he sleeps with, might be best understood not as abuse but as conflict according to Schulman's logic. This is something that Arabella also comes to realize: she is confronted with the overstatement of harm that underlies her accusation of abuse, when Terry (who sees through Arabella's coping mechanisms) reminds her of her own morally dubious behaviour at her birthday party. She locked Kwame in a room with another man who was flirting with him, knowing that Kwame was scared of sexual intimacy after his experience of sexual violence. Was Arabella here complicit with or even an agent of potential sexual abuse and harassment? If so, how could she then be the moral authority on the topic, a feminist icon fighting sexual violence that thousands of people look up to online?

What these scenes provide is a complex account of what happens when the binary legal categories of guilty/innocent enter social justice activism, and what social and personal effects this can have. While providing some form of justice and retribution, accusations of abuse are simply not enough to carry the wounds of violation or deal with the 'radical subjectivity of pain'. Arabella comes to realize the further pain her actions are causing both her and her closest friends, and turns to her therapist in an emergency meeting to talk about how she cannot be complicit with Kwame's behaviour as 'I don't keep that kind of shit around me'. Still dressed as the devil, she gets the advice to take a break from social media and look into what she does not want to know or acknowledge, the things she keeps under her bed, the 'dangerous things, dark things, anything that contradicts or threatens your perceived reality' and to cross the 'line [that] is drawn separating bad from good, friend from foe, men, women, black, white, them, us, criminal, victim, God, devil'. In psychoanalytic vocabulary, the therapist encourages her to leave behind what Melanie Klein (2002) describes as the schizoid-paranoid position where an object is either good or bad, but never both at the same time, so as 'to deflect, avoid feelings like guilt, uncertainty, self-blame', as the therapist puts it. Realizing that Kwame is both good and bad, friend and foe, allows Arabella to confront the ambivalence, conflictedness, and darkness that exists in herself and others that cannot be contained in a simple perpetrator–victim dichotomy.

Ambivalence is also central to Arabella's engagements with the rape support group she joins to talk through her experience with other affected women, led by her old schoolmate Theodora. Theodora is shown introducing the group as a 'safe abuse and oppression free space', talking about how rape and abuse are the 'most vile, abhorrent qualities of our species'. Yet, in flashbacks of her time in school, we learn about Theodora not just as a victim but also an agent of abuse. In these flashback scenes, we witness Theodora, who is white, frame a Black classmate for attacking her with a knife and raping her at school. When the boy is carried away to the school office to wait for the police, it is through the intervention of Arabella and Terry, who find video footage of what really happened, that he gets saved. They know that 'white girl tears' are what made him defenceless against Theodora's accusations – mirroring the long history of white women's claims of sexual violence being used to oppress and imprison Black men (Crenshaw 1991; Davis 1983; hooks 2000).

But, through her own experience of rape, Arabella comes to grapple with the more complex position of Theodora: while she clearly acted as an agent and perpetrator of violence and oppression within the structures of white supremacy, she was at the same time at least somewhat subjugated as a working-class girl, being paid to have sex, and have her photos taken by boys in her class – referred to as the 'poster girl for Childline' by Terry. Could Theodora be a victim and perpetrator at the same time? And if so, how to deal with her contradictory position in terms of class, gender, and race? In the end, it seems that Theodora's accusations towards the young Black man were made precisely because she knew that it was this story of sexual violence that would be believed, in the context of institutional racism and common narratives of predatory Black men. Her age, class, and social status as a sexually 'permissive' young woman meant that the truthful claims to harm she could make against other boys, perhaps would not.[4] This false accusation (followed by an unclear recanting of an earlier accusation against her own father) is, thus, a forceful reminder of precisely which gendered, racialized, and classed formations are necessary for accusations of sexual violence or harm to matter and be heard.

Arabella grapples with the complexity of these intersectional positions in a text she writes and reads to her literary agents. She discusses how, as a Black working-class woman, an identification with gender and sexuality has long felt like 'a betrayal to the council flat I was born' such that 'prior to being raped, I never took much notice of being a woman, I was busy being Black and poor'. Discussions of gender and sexuality, including that of rape and gendered violence, seemed like a luxury reserved for white women unencumbered by poverty, destitution and structural racism.[5] Struggling with the either-or framing of being a woman or being Black and working-class that she has grown up with, Arabella wonders whether 'it is time to serve a new tribe'. Lola Olufemi (2020) discusses the problems of single-issue politics that confront Black women like Arabella, with either-or framings appearing as a result of feminist movements that are often unquestionably white and middle-class, while Alison Phipps (2020) shows how particularly in activism around sexual violence, even in originally Black and intersectional movements like MeToo, it is often elite white women who come to dominate narratives and strategies. Dissatisfied with such binary frames of dominant social justice activism, Arabella comes to realize that what she needs is not a 'new tribe', but the community of Black friends and infrastructures of care that she has built in London, offering reflections on the often-overlooked importance of community and friendship in the context of sexual violence.

Friendship and care

Given that both the criminal justice system and the wider dynamics of feminist social activism can only ever partially fulfil Arabella's quest for justice and healing, she turns to self-care and therapy instead. In the first session with her therapist, she is anxious, not knowing what to do with the advice to take some time off from work (given that she needs money) or the suggestion to do more self-care activities like 'handicrafts' (which seems confusing and banal in the face of what has just happened to her). Nevertheless, Arabella takes on the suggestions and starts going to dance and sip-and-paint classes, and even picks up her childhood colouring-in pens from her mum's house. Audre Lorde famously declares that 'caring for myself is not self-indulgence, it is self-preservation and that is an act of political warfare' (1988: 130). Indeed, self-care gives Arabella a place of respite and distraction from the harrowing flashbacks, in the aftermath of her rape. Yet, as Rebekka Hammelsbeck (2016) points out, despite its origins in Black feminist organizing and theorizing, in a neoliberal world of individualizing achievement, success, and recovery, self-care has also become part of an individualized imperative to manage one's own well-being. Such individualizing narratives of self-care can add blame and pressure for not getting better – for not doing enough, for not caring for the self in the right ways, for not healing, as we also discussed in Chapters 2 and 3. The focus on well-being and positivity in much of self-care discourse can also work to brush aside the complex and difficult feelings brought on by the radical subjectivity of pain.

Arabella, after all, only starts to do 'better' once her therapist gives her the advice to no longer repress the negative aspects of her experience and to look into the darkness she has desperately tried to fend off. Rather than distracting herself and staying away from the site of injury, Arabella starts repeatedly and compulsively visiting the bar where she got spiked. What exactly draws her to this place remains as unclear to the viewer as it does to her – maybe she will find and be able to confront her rapist here, maybe coming here proves to herself that she *can* come back without breaking apart, or maybe she just comes back because not doing so is just as unbearable. It is also at this bar that she meets Zain again. He, it turns out, has published a book that Arabella admires, under the feminine pseudonym Della. Arabella is hesitant at first but then affirms to both Zain and herself that 'I'm not afraid of you' and that, having confronted the darkness, she is able to deal with him. She then asks him to come back home with her, where he gives her a plot diagram for creative non-fiction, and together they work on the multiple storylines of her unfinished manuscript. It is in this scene that we get a sense of the kind of transformative justice that scholars like Angela Davis et al. (2022) and Ruth Wilson Gilmore (2022) gesture at in their abolitionist perspectives on the criminal justice system. Arabella is not straightforwardly forgiving Zain, nor does she continue to frame and see him as a monster – instead, she finds a way to be with him, to work together and constructively on a different future.

Having rearranged the plot on Arabella's wall, Zain asks: 'I thought you were writing about consent?' 'So did I', Arabella replies. He confusedly utters: 'I don't understand it', to which she replies: 'I do, thank you', asking him to take the trash out as he leaves. Together with Arabella, we come to understand that maybe it was not (just) the question of consent that she was writing about, but also how people live on in the aftermath of sexual violence: healing, justice, and repair. From this perspective, *I May Destroy You* is not simply an investigation of the boundaries of bad sex, but most centrally a story about friendship and care. After all, it is only through the support, love, and company of her two best friends, Terry and Kwame, that Arabella is able to work through her experiences. Less close to her family, she does not discuss the rape with them; instead, she finds solace in the friendships and community she has built in Black London. It is here that the show differs from many shows in the bad sex genre, such as *Fleabag* and *Feel Good*, where the characters live largely isolated lives and have no one but their romantic partners to carry their need for intimacy and connection. It is such forms of privatized and domesticated intimacy in neoliberalized places like London, as we have argued across the book, that make sex *bad* in the first place, as they can never hold all the hopes and desires they are invested with. It is arguably also these privatizing dynamics that push sexuality and sexual exploration into an ever more precarious, competitive, and dangerous territory, open to exploitation and sexual violence. What saves Arabella in the end is that she and her friends, at least partially, defy this privatizing logic by having woven close ties and intimate friendships – despite the isolating pressures of neoliberal London.

While all three of them struggle to make ends meet, they meet up regularly, confiding in each other and forming what Premilla Nadasen calls forms of 'fictive kin' that 'step in to show support because of love, emotion, or obligation' (2017: 127). It is Terry, in particular, who takes Arabella to exercise classes, accompanies her to the police station, and comforts and confronts her when Arabella gets lost in the darkness. Throughout the show, we see the two growing together, reaffirming their interdependence through the mantra: 'my birth is your birth, my death is your death.' Yet, as viewers learn alongside Arabella, it was also Terry who betrayed her by telling their friend Simon that it is okay to leave Arabella alone on the night of her rape, echoing their night out in Italy which they frequently fight about – did Terry leave a drunken Arabella at the bar, or did Arabella get too drunk to follow Terry? But it is this lie about the night of Arabella's rape in London – hiding a moment of failed care – that hangs over their friendship and threatens the relationship dearest to both of them. In what is arguably the emotional climax of the show, we see Arabella and Terry meeting up at the bar: Arabella tells Terry that she met with Simon, 'what did he say?' Terry asks, knowing that Arabella now knows about her betrayal. Both start tearing up, before Arabella says: 'you are amazing, thank you for being a really great friend and looking after me this past year', adding, 'you birth is my birth, G', to which they reply in unison, 'your death is my death'. No longer afraid of the darkness, Arabella knows that their lives are too entangled, their friendship too important, to be ruptured, that it is their very interdependence that has and will get them through this time. While friendship can let you down and cannot alone protect you from sexual violence, it is also where a supportive ground for a different life can be built.

The importance of friendship and community is also reiterated in the ending of the show, which presents us with three different scenarios of how the crime of sexual violence could be resolved, or rather Arabella's fantasies thereof. All three scenarios start with Arabella recognizing her rapist at the bar where she got spiked. The first ending gives us a revenge fantasy where Arabella, Terry, and Theodora first drug the rapist, then drag him across the street where he collapses. They disrobe, kick, strangle, and ultimately kill him before Arabella carries his bloody body home and hides him under her bed. The second ending concludes with formal justice in an act of arrest by the police. Tricking him into trying to rape her again and then confronting him about his wrongdoings, Arabella gets him to confess and repent his crimes before he is carried out of her house by the police. In the third ending, we get a reconciliation story. The two meet at the bar, flirt, and go home together to have sex. He is gentle and soft, while Arabella penetrates him. The next morning she asks him to leave, and he does, followed by the dead body under her bed.

The multiple endings of the show point to the impossibility of final justice or healing after sexual violence. All three endings are satisfying and dissatisfying at the same time. While Arabella and us viewers enjoy the revenge, does this mean she will have to live forever with his dead body under her bed? While the arrest by the police feels right, the show has revealed the failings of the criminal justice system, and it ultimately feels inadequate in the face of his (im)possible remorse. And while the reconciliation story develops a scenario of healing where sexual agency is restored to Arabella, and where life and sex are finally *good* again, it is clear that this remains a fantasy, impossible in the face of the danger, hurt, and thirst for revenge that remain. Instead of giving a prescriptive answer to the question of what should be done in the face of sexual violence, the show keeps this question open and instead brings us to Arabella sitting on the patio of her home. She has decided to stay in and watch science documentaries with her friend and housemate, Ben – having completed this story, or several stories, or begun them – and this for one day is seemingly enough. Instead of a spectacular ending of revenge, justice, or reconciliation, what we get in the end is the mundane everydayness of living on in the face of violence. Christina Sharpe describes such a temporality in relation to Blackness and histories of transatlantic slavery as 'being in the wake' – a state of being in which 'the past that is not past reappears, always, to rupture the present' (2016: 33). Her insights into the ongoingness of the past in the wake of structural, racialized, and gendered violence are applicable to Arabella's experience in the aftermath of sexual violence. While we know that the pain is not and perhaps will never be over, we also know that Arabella will do the 'wake work' in which care is 'enacted laterally' (Sharpe 2016: 20), such that she has learned (or will continue to learn) to face the darkness, collectively: 'My life is your life, your death is my death.'

The question of how sex will be good again after sexual violence is, then, not just about better or more enthusiastic consent, about a 'better' criminal justice system or more social justice activism, but ultimately also about the infrastructures of care that can carry and hold both the pleasure and beauty, and the danger and violence that exist in sex and intimacy. It is these infrastructures of care and community that provide a way of living on in the face of horror and violence – even though we might never know when, or if, 'sex will be good again' (Angel 2021a), or if it might instead turn out to be bad or violating again in the future. For Arabella, facing the darkness, which includes the multiple and intersecting ways in which her actions following the assault impact both her and others, is one way of continuing through. In its recognition of the shifting temporalities, meanings, horrors, and interdependencies within the radical subjectivity of pain, *I May Destroy You* provides us with a radical depiction of intersubjectivity, care, and violence – and hope for the future. In the next chapter, we continue grappling with this question, and ask what better sex – in all its complexity – might look like for the sexual subjects of the future. Here we contrast the popular and glossy, yet also deeply painful and often violent, representation of teen sexuality in *Euphoria* (2019–) with the compassionate failures, humour and honesty of *Sex Education* (2019–23), and ask if these representations of teenage sexuality can teach us something about how to unlearn bad sex in the future.

Chapter 7

UNLEARNING BAD SEX IN *EUPHORIA* AND *SEX EDUCATION*

Introduction

Sex is everywhere in both *Sex Education* (2019–23) and *Euphoria* (2019–). Commentators discuss the shows' depictions of sex through the notion of a 'teen show sexual revolution' (Lewis 2023), with the two shows vying for the title of 'the absolute quintessential Generation Z show' (Qobrtay 2021). So is bad sex specifically. Neither show shies away from portraying less comfortable aspects of teenage sexuality – managing to avoid earlier tropes in its representation, which have tended to stick to euphemisms and suggestive comments in place of explicit sexual representation and discussion. *Sex Education* depicts teenage sexuality largely as anxious and uncertain, viewed through the lens of the show's main character Otis. In season 1, Otis starts running a sex education clinic for his fellow students, deploying the knowledge he has absorbed from his sex and relationship therapist mum – rather than from any sexual experiences of his own. In being both very knowledgeable about the subtleties of sex and sexuality and at the same time highly awkward in regards to his own sexuality, Otis is an unlikely hero of teenage sexual liberation – acknowledged by his friend Eric laughing gleefully about his 'super weird' difficulties with masturbation. In contrast, sex in *Euphoria* is often portrayed as detached, painful and even violent. The very first episode makes the normalization of sexual assault and harassment in the lives of teenagers explicit – main character Rue introduces her schoolmate Nate with the statement: 'I mean, I never liked him. And once during freshman formal he tried to finger me on the dance floor without my permission', while another peer mimics a blowjob during an active school shooter drill.

In earlier chapters, we have argued that representations of bad straight sex and unhappy queer characters continue to proliferate, despite and alongside the significantly diversified (sexually and otherwise) televisual landscape. In this chapter, we consider what has really changed in the representation of sex and sexuality through an examination of the representation of teenage sexuality in *Sex Education* and *Euphoria*. Adolescence is typically understood as a time of sexual confusion and awkwardness, and here we explore what we might learn from the portrayals of anxious and complex teenage sexuality in these two shows. *Sex Education* provides some of the more hopeful, even utopian, recent representations of sexual politics, with commentators celebrating 'its candid discussions about sexuality [and] the creation of queer spaces' (Johnson 2023; see also Horeck 2021), the show delivering 'the most realistic depictions of sex on screen in recent years' (Lewis 2023) and being 'ridiculously timely' (Qobrtay 2021). Conversely, *Euphoria* has been labelled 'Gen Z's most honest portrayal of teen life' (Young 2024) while simultaneously receiving criticism for its glossy, drug-fuelled, 'excessively sexualized' (Johnson 2023) portrayal. Here, we ask what these two contrasting representations might teach us. In this, we not only reflect on what better sex might look like for the sexual subjects of the future but also inquire into the ways in which we learn (about) sex. What sexual pedagogies can be identified in the awkward but sincere *Sex Education* vis-à-vis the shocking but glossy *Euphoria?*

We explore the sexual representations present in the two shows, focusing on the instances of teaching and learning about sex that *Sex Education* and *Euphoria* present to their viewers. Here, we argue that both shows might be understood as reimaginings or reinventions of youth for millennial and older viewers, offering opportunities for redemption – particularly for queer viewers frustrated with the limited representational landscapes of their own teenage years. *Sex Education* does this through cheery optimism, and the promise that through knowledge and critical reflection the future of sex can be improved. We counter this with an examination of the rejection of futurity in *Euphoria*, discussing the show's much more reckless and dark portrayal of sex, shrouded in flat and cynical weariness (not dissimilar to some of the other shows discussed earlier on in the book through the notion of heteropessimism). Contrasting *Euphoria*'s weary pessimism with *Sex Education*'s relentless optimism, we ask what space there is to learn about sex within these affective and pedagogical landscapes. What sexual pedagogies exist across these two affective modes of sexual politics, and how do we rethink the pedagogies of sex in a way that leaves space for hopefulness and reflexivity, as well as openness and vulnerability?

Generation bad sex

In the first episode of *Sex Education*, as they are arriving at school on the first day of the year, Eric declares to Otis: 'I keep telling you, man, everyone has had sex over the summer. Everyone except you.' Later he expresses worry for Otis while gesturing around the schoolyard, where multiple couples, dressed in bright clothing, are kissing and touching each other, or even having sex: 'Like, look around. Everybody's either thinking about shagging, about to shag, or actually shagging' (Figure 7.1). In the first few minutes of the episode, Otis has not only struggled to masturbate but also managed to send his mother Jean's younger hook-up Dan into a state by asking if his attraction to Jean is 'Oedipal', causing Dan to refer to Jean as 'mum' as he is saying his goodbyes. The interactions between Otis and Jean establish their relationship as involving frank and open discussion about sex, while at the same time Otis himself appears embarrassed about his own body and sexuality. Otis tries to counter Eric's questioning of his inability to masturbate by suggesting that Eric also lacks sexual experience, to which Eric responds: 'At least I can touch my own body.'

Figure 7.1 Eric and Otis arrive at bright Moordale High on the first day of term, optimistically discussing the sexual opportunities it provides. *Sex Education* © Eleven Film/Netflix 2019–23.

This contrast between Otis' wide knowledge about sexual practices and dynamics, on the one hand, and his own lack of sexual confidence and experience, on the other, is amplified later on in the first season when he begins to offer support and guidance to his peers struggling with a range of sexual problems, ranging from performance anxiety and peer pressure to vomiting during oral sex. In partnership with Maeve, he establishes a sex and relationship clinic in a disused school bathroom, charging fellow students money for sexual advice. Clearly, the young characters of *Sex Education* are not afraid to talk about sex, embracing this new opportunity for sexual counsel with enthusiasm – even if the actual practice of sex at times eludes them. The frankness with which the characters discuss sex in all its complexity is refreshing, and a clear contrast to many earlier televisual representations of sex, let alone teenage sex – with Otis in particular appearing kind and non-judgemental of the sexual exploits of his peers in his counselling sessions (see also Horeck 2021).

Not entirely dissimilarly, the characters of *Euphoria* also discuss sex, but often these interactions are much more wrought and challenging than the joyful and humorous atmosphere of *Sex Education*'s sex talk. Rue's love interest Jules quips to Kat, who is a virgin: 'Bitch this isn't the 80s. You need to catch a dick', mirroring the peer pressure Otis feels to gain sexual experience, although in an altogether darker, more judgemental tone. When Cassie and McKay are about to have sex for the first time, he asks her, 'Are you always this wet?' to which Cassie responds: 'Kinda. It's super embarrassing. Does it turn you off?' Although McKay initially replies: 'Not at all. It's cool', later on he seems embarrassed and frustrated by Cassie's openly expressed desire: 'Why you gotta make everything so sexual?' These scenes present a much more challenging sexual landscape than that of *Sex Education*, with the adolescent characters having to regularly confront simultaneous expectations of childlike purity and emerging adult desire; sexlessness and sexiness. The girls of *Euphoria* particularly appear to be caught in this double-bind, echoing Rosalind Gill's argument that 'sexual "empowerment" has itself become a normatively demanded feature of young women's sexual subjectivity, such that they are called on routinely to perform confident, knowing heterosexiness' (2012: 737).

Many of *Euphoria*'s characters also engage in somewhat reckless or even explicitly risky sexual behaviour. Jules, a new trans girl in town at the beginning of season 1, is shown to regularly meet and have sex with much older men from dating apps. At least one of these encounters ends with Jules in tears over the rough way in which she has been treated by the man – Cal, who we later find out is Nate's father and an important man in the local community. In a later episode, Rue asks Jules about these encounters: 'Is the sex, like, good?', to which Jules responds: 'I don't know. It's, like, it's not even the point, you know? It's more about, like, everything that leads up to it. That's the good part.' Jules' reflections evoke those made by Fleabag, discussed in Chapter 1, confessing that she is addicted to 'the performance of [sex]. The awkwardness of it. The drama of it. The moment you realise someone wants your body', and then adding, 'Not so much the feeling of it'. In *Euphoria*, we repeatedly witness the same emotional detachment with which Fleabag approaches her sexual encounters, but this time with teenage girls rather than an adult woman – perhaps in line with Jane Ward's argument that 'the affect of straight culture is marked . . . by a kind of emotional flatness, an antiflamboyance' (2020: 116). In another episode, Nate and Maddy are having sex: he presses her face down onto the bed, while Maddy's eyes glaze over, as if she is just *bearing* rather than enjoying the experience (Figure 7.2) – not dissimilarly to Fleabag's sexual encounter with the Bus Rodent over the counter of her café, except here without Fleabag's witty and self-referential commentary. Sex seems to be almost entirely transactional for Maddy: it is about power and what she gets in exchange for it rather than any possibility of pleasure during it.

Figure 7.2 Nate presses Maddy's head down onto the bed while they have sex, and her eyes glaze over. *Euphoria* © A24/HBO 2019– .

Moreover, neither show avoids depicting negative experiences associated with being a young queer or trans person, the difficulties of teen pregnancy or indeed experiences of sexual harassment and violence. *Euphoria*'s Jules faces both explicit transphobia and snarky comments related to her being trans, as does *Sex Education*'s Eric in relation to being gay. In a flashback montage on *Euphoria*, multiple older men are shown to sexually harass young Cassie, and Nate chokes Maddy at a carnival, while in *Sex Education* Aimee is sexually assaulted by a man with a 'nice face' on a bus. Both shows also include an abortion storyline, with Maeve on *Sex Education* and Cassie on *Euphoria* both attending an abortion clinic following accidental pregnancies. However, in line with the shows' overall differences in tone and aesthetic style, these experiences are presented and framed quite differently. *Euphoria*'s worldbuilding involves the positioning of such experiences as commonplace and unavoidable, with Rue's voice-over often remarking on them with weary resignation. In this vein, when Cassie is questioned about 'any history of depression' at the abortion clinic, she answers: 'I guess, the normal amount.'

In contrast, such storylines on *Sex Education* often appear as an arc of redemption, healing or personal growth. In relation to Maeve's abortion, regret is explored in a meaningful and complex way: she experiences grief, but it is not totalizing. Similarly, when Aimee is sexually assaulted, she first attempts to normalize the incident, joking about it frankly with Maeve, who quickly convinces her to go to the police. Amy then becomes increasingly distressed by the event, no longer enjoying sex and now uncomfortable travelling on the bus. Her 'healing journey' begins when she starts talking about the experience to her friends, with many of the girls at school sharing similar experiences of harassment and violence. This depiction normalizes such experiences – as does that on *Euphoria* – but in contrast to *Euphoria*'s affective tone of weariness, here the characters also have the space to name these experiences as violating, to respond to them with humour and agency, and to eventually learn from them and build community in response to them. With some similarity to the complex depictions of consent explored in the previous chapter's discussion of *I May Destroy You* (2020), *Sex Education*'s characters are often able to process difficult sexual (and non-sexual) experiences through talk and peer support, in implicit recognition that neither legal avenues nor the official teachings of sex and relationships curricula are alone able to provide knowledge, solace, or meaningful resolution.

Very differently, *Euphoria*'s teenagers often appear isolated in their experiences of violence and pain. When McKay is subjected to a violent hazing ritual in his first year at college as an American football player, he first cries, struggling to deal with an experience akin to an assault. However, he then goes on to pretend that everything is fine and gets aggressive with Cassie in turn – as if he needs to assert his power with her to mitigate the powerlessness he himself feels. These kinds of negative experiences are interspersed with more positive ones in the show's storylines, but even then the characters' responses to them frequently betray a different perspective, as in Cassie's statement: 'I feel like love is super dark and no one ever talks about it.' Likewise, Maddy first remarks on Kat and Ethan's relationship being 'non-toxic', but then continues: 'I will never find that kind of love . . . There's just no darkness. It's just sweet . . . I don't know if that would ever be enough for me.' Unbeknownst to Maddy, Kat continues to fantasize about rough, aggressive sexual encounters throughout her 'non-toxic' relationship with Ethan, as well as hiding her *Only Fans* career from him, eventually admitting to Maddy that she is bored with Ethan. Perhaps again in an echo of Fleabag's desire for the Priest to take sexual control, discussed in Chapter 1, Kat's lack of desire for the kind and considerate Ethan, and concomitant fantasies about rough and tough hyper-masculine men, could be read as a romantic and erotic attachment 'to an unequal gender binary' (Ward 2020: 22).

The two shows thus offer very different depictions of teenage sexuality: one dark, reckless, and largely humourless, one light, reflective and joyful. Both have, however, been heralded for bringing in a new era of sexual representation. The frankness and openness of both the sex depicted on the shows, and the discussions about sex they feature, have received praise particularly in their contrast to earlier representational tropes of teenage sexuality (see e.g. Horeck 2021). Relatedly, both shows have been commended for perfectly capturing the teenage experience: David Levesley in *GQ* labels *Sex Education* 'the best portrayal of the chaotic neutrality of teenagers you'll ever see' (2019), and Rebecca Nicholson in *The Guardian* argues that *Euphoria* 'understands perfectly' the experience of adolescence as 'horribly cruel, and sweetly naïve, in ever-shifting combinations' (2019a). Further, much of the commentary has related its praise of the two shows directly to Generation Z, with both shows commonly framed as accurately and truthfully representing the experiences of the generation (Li 2022; Qobrtay 2021; Toomer 2019; Young 2024). In this reading, the 'Generation Z experience' is either a bleak and dystopian journey of drugs, sex, and violence or a sweet and empowering adventure towards adult sexual desire – but in either case sex is ubiquitous, and Gen Z teenagers, while anxious and wary, are keen to both have it and talk about it.

Learning about sex

The very different affective tones described above also carry over into the two shows' overall atmospheres and sexual pedagogies. While *Euphoria* is dark and glossy in its colour scheme (Figure 7.2), soundtrack, and storylines, *Sex Education* is colourful and quaint. The latter's twee, nostalgic feel is heightened by the show's setting in an unspecified time and place (Figure 7.1). While the filming took place in the UK and the characters' accents are British, the visual landscape is reminiscent of an American high school drama of the 1980s or 1990s: the characters wear varsity jackets (and not uniforms, common in most of the UK education system) and attend prom. Although most of the commentary has tended to assume that the show is both about and directed at Generation Z as we highlighted above, at the same time its nostalgic feel is strongly reminiscent of the high school dramas watched by earlier generations as teenagers. The viewing experience of millennial and older viewers may, indeed, be marked by not just feelings of nostalgia, but also of enviousness, as Emma Baty notes in the *Cosmopolitan*:

> I'm secretly a little bit jealous of the way these fictional high schoolers can express their individualism . . . The paralyzing fear of being even a little bit different is so high school, but the kids in the show don't grapple with that the same way I did. Maybe that's just the fiction of it all, or maybe teenagers now actually get to feel a bit more free. I hope for their sake it's the latter. (2023)

We, the book's millennial authors, similarly found great affective appeal in the show's representations, especially as queer viewers. Eric's narrative arc, in particular, allows for a reimagining of queer youth in a way that does not eradicate the frequently negative aspects of the experience, but at the same time gives Eric the chance to exercise agency and explore his queerness in the context of supportive friendships – something that many millennial and older queer viewers may have lacked in their own adolescence, as well as acting as a complex exploration of Black, queer femininity (Okundaye 2019). In season 1, Eric is regularly bullied at school, and after experiencing a violent homophobic incident, he tones down his self-expression and switches to plain clothes. He attends church, where the pastor speaks about self-love, and, inspired by the women at his church, he decides to attend a school dance in fabulous make-up and a Kente suit from Ghana. On the way to the dance, his father asks him, 'But why . . . do you have to be so much?', stating that he does not want Eric to get hurt. Eric responds: 'This is me . . . Look, I'll be hurt either way. Isn't it better to be who I am?' His father eventually counters with, 'Maybe . . . I am learning from my brave son', in a way that is considerate of Eric's struggle and bravery. The remaining seasons see Eric continuously negotiating his sexuality with his faith: in season 3, he attends a family wedding in Nigeria and goes to a local gay bar with a man he meets at the wedding; and in season 4, he meets other religious queer and trans people at his new school. He then hooks up with a man from his church in a nightclub toilet, who explains why he cannot leave the church: 'It's my community. My family. It's . . . my heart. I can't cut it out.' Eventually Eric decides not to get baptized, but does not leave his faith, determined to become a pastor.

Eric's storyline offers the kind of nuance that was sorely missing from the high school dramas of the 1990s and thus allows the audience to reimagine their own youths as just a little bit better, a little bit easier, and a little bit more accepting. Even Otis, the fumbling and anxious hero of the show gets an arc of personal growth and development: in season 3, he dates the most popular girl in school, Ruby, and by season 4, his long-term crush Maeve – perhaps providing comfort for any viewers who themselves were the 'awkward kid' in school. Aimee, after her sexual assault on the bus, breaks up with her boyfriend, and starts making feminist art and chronicling her orgasms in a journal she has titled 'My Healing Journey'. Apart from Eric, queer and trans representation is also everywhere on *Sex Education* – a transition storyline is depicted in the final season, as is sex between a trans girl and trans boy. Even the new school the main characters all attend in the final season is 'super queer', with gender-neutral toilets and a new cadre of cool queer friends for Eric. Some of the old characters struggle at the new school, however, with its smart screens, obsession with recycling and disability-inclusive language. The school even has its own, much cooler, sex therapist, O, who makes Otis' plan to set his own clinic up again at the new school difficult. He has been nervous about sending a nude photo to Maeve in response to hers, and ends up taking O's advice and reconnecting with Maeve via phone sex. Eventually Otis leans into his awkwardness and opens his clinic again.

At times, such storylines, where the *Sex Education* characters experience learning and gain important life lessons, can have the feel of a pedagogical show, however, with Otis educating both his classmates and the audience about enthusiastic consent and the fluidity of sexuality. One commentator notes that the show 'quite literally teaches its viewers the sex education our schooling failed to provide millions of students – including myself' (DeLallo 2021). The teenagers on the show also frequently offer guidance to adults, who also learn about self-acceptance, inclusivity, and even sexual expression – such as when Adam offers his father advice about performance anxiety, or when Eric's pastor shows up at a school dance wanting to make the church more 'inclusive'. In such moments, the young characters appear adultlike, offering sage advice and guidance in neatly packaged soundbites, with the sex and relationship issues raised often fixed within one episode's narrative arc. This can sometimes shift the show's affective tone from a teen drama to that of the somewhat didactic 1990s afterschool special, aimed at inexperienced teenagers. This tone is further enhanced by the fact that the show's adolescent characters are all played by adults – a choice that has been criticized by some for potentially contributing to body image issues and the sexualization of teenagers (Heritage 2021; Zhao 2020), but applauded by others for allowing the show to depict the 'diverse reality of sex' (DeLallo 2021).

The sexual pedagogy offered by the series, thus, presents an opportunity for redemption for older viewers, who might have lacked such education and guidance in their own youth, thereby also speaking 'to viewers' feelings of generational belonging' (Loock 2018: 8) in a somewhat similar vein to the reboot shows discussed in Chapter 5 of this book. At the same time, however, the show's focus on *verbal* communication as the solution to any problems one might face – sexual or otherwise – positions sex in the cognitive, rather than embodied, realm. In one episode, Otis even counsels a peer to 'establish a clear verbal intercourse' with a sexual partner (Figure 7.3). The final few episodes of the show are especially full of talk about sex, with Otis, O, and even a third 'student therapist' offering sex and relationship therapy at the college; Otis' mother Jean doing the same with listeners on her new radio show; and Eric extending his support to a classmate struggling to come to terms with their transness – leading in part to him deciding to be a pastor. Here the show's sex education works in a similar way to much of actual sex education aimed at young people: 'by appealing to their intellects – by asking them to deliberate, question and understand' (Srinivasan 2022: 63–4). At the centre of such an approach

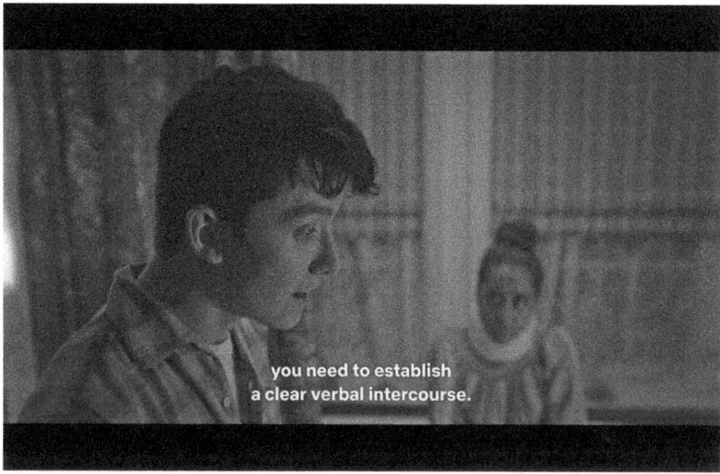

Figure 7.3 Sex in *Sex Education* is represented through a focus on talk and discourse – exemplified here by one of Otis' sex advice sessions in which he encourages his peers to establish 'verbal intercourse' first. *Sex Education* © Eleven Film/Netflix 2019–23.

is the assumption that one's desires can and should be fully *known* to oneself, and that the pleasure and enjoyment of sex are the result of uncovering and understanding these desires, and then acting on them.

However, as Katherine Angel points out, 'speech and truth-telling are not inherently emancipatory, and neither speech nor silence is inherently liberating or oppressive' (2021a: 18), because, she continues, 'we don't always begin with desire; it is not always there to be known' (2021a: 49). In *Sex Education*, sex and other kinds of physical intimacy are also shown – and plenty of it is also good sex, in contrast to some of the recent representational trends we have explored in previous chapters, portraying sex as almost exclusively in some way *bad*. Curiously, however, rarely do these encounters come across as *sexy*, at least within the normative representational conventions of 'sexiness'. Rather, sex itself tends to be portrayed as either sweet or comical – and conversely, as mostly devoid of passion and intensity, and perhaps most significantly, of uncertainty. The representation of sex as something to be cognitively learned, and desire as something to be discovered, fully formed, within ourselves, removes the aspect of sex that has perhaps the greatest potential to generate pleasure – its *unknowability*.[1] As Angel also suggests, via Leo Bersani, desire unfolds in interaction with others, and a key part of pleasure 'is the way it shatters . . . the boundary between ourself and the other' (2021a: 126), or in Oliver Davis and Tim Dean's words, 'sex disorders us' (2022: 20). This is certainly unsettling, but if we take seriously the claim that the joys and pleasures of sex derive at least in part from its unknowability, is it enough for sex education to just convey factual *information* about sex?

No future sex

While *Sex Education* represents many of the challenges and difficulties of sex and relationships, they tend to be resolved fairly quickly in the show's narratives through communication and self-discovery, as we have discussed above. But what about problems that cannot be solved by talking to a 'student therapist' in the disused school bathroom? Maeve offers perhaps the only major contrast to this type of representation, due to the character's poor and troubled upbringing with a drug-addicted mother, but even this is overcome with a narrative arc in the final season that illustrates to viewers that Maeve has a way out of her difficult circumstances: as a gifted writer, she gets a prestigious scholarship to attend a writing programme in the United States. In contrast, unsolvable problems and challenging, even brutal, circumstances are everywhere on *Euphoria*. Throughout the show's two seasons, main character and voice-over Rue descends further and further into her drug addiction – while she is clean at the end of the second season, it is not from any desire to get better, but because 'in some ways, it was just easier'. Cassie starts sleeping with and then gets into a relationship with her best friend Maddy's long-term on-and-off boyfriend Nate, severing the two girls' previously close friendship. Cal reveals his sexual exploits with men, trans women, and teenagers to his family, and eventually his son Nate calls the police on him. Cassie's sweet younger sister Lexi puts on a school play about her group of friends, leaving all the major relationships in the show in turmoil at the end of season 2.

On *Euphoria*, sex, drugs, and violence are ubiquitous. Rue's friend and dealer Fez is a regular attendee at parties, which frequently descend into dark montages of violent chaos (Figure 7.4) – in one particularly disturbing sequence, Fez beats Nate to a pulp shortly after exchanging sweet dialogue with Lexi. Rue stumbles through these parties, and everything else, in a drug-fuelled haze, while attempting a relationship with Jules. Various sexual scandals rock the school, usually following the release of an explicit video of one of the teenage characters on

Figure 7.4 Group party scenes in *Euphoria* are often depicted as dark and excessive. Here, Nate drinks and dances while his anger is normalized in Rue's voice-over. *Euphoria* © A24/HBO 2019– .

social media. Sex, and needing to appear to be having lots of it, is ever-present, but no one seems to be particularly enjoying it. In season 1, Rue details her 'super brief' sexual history: 'four hand jobs in eighth grade, two blow jobs in ninth, one of which I was emotionally coerced into.' Through all this, many of the characters appear disaffected and cool – there is a glamour and glossiness to them, even when they are going through horrific experiences that, in real life, teenagers are having fewer and fewer of.[2]

Similarly to *Sex Education*, the adolescent characters on *Euphoria* are played by adult actors, and claims about the show being really about older generations getting to relive their youths similarly abound in the commentary. Adrian Horton in *The Guardian* argues that the show 'is best understood as a millennial revisionist fantasy of their own proto-social media high school days, if the current digital hellscape was our teenage playground' (2022), and Delia Cai in *Vanity Fair* asks about the show's (and others' like it) intended audience: 'Is it for today's teens, or the sentimental adults in the room?' (2022). If *Sex Education*'s teenagers are too adultlike in their all-knowingness, then *Euphoria*'s 'teens are possessed with a preternatural confidence and swagger' (Esquire Editors 2022); and while *Sex Education* has the feel of the afterschool special, *Euphoria* evokes a landscape akin to the film *Kids* (1995), which similarly resulted in considerable moral panic upon its release. The former embraces the awkwardness of adolescence, teaching the show's young characters (and audiences) how to work through it; the latter erases it entirely, allowing viewers to reimagine their own youths as just a little more exciting and glamorous, or less mundane, than they really were. Both shows present a revisionist fantasy of high school, giving us the chance to return to those years, and either learn from them or live through them recklessly.

Earlier we suggested that at points *Sex Education*'s tone shifts into the didactic, coaxing and expecting us to learn to do both youth and sex better than we were able to as teenagers – in contrast, perhaps one of the draws of *Euphoria* is that it relieves us of the pressure to do so. In the *Euphoria* universe, bad sex and relationships are not just common but also all that any of us can expect. Kat finds the sex she is actually having boring and instead derives some pleasure (as well as money) from dominating submissive men online and fantasizes about dominant men in turn. Jules is almost compulsively drawn to hooking up with older men in at times dangerous situations, alongside or despite also experiencing her first queer love with Rue. Maddy and Nate's relationship follows a familiar pattern of abuse, bouncing from declarations of love to violence, and back again. When Nate starts a relationship with Cassie, he fantasizes about her being pregnant, and in a dreamlike sequence Cassie declares to him: 'I would love for you to fuck me, whenever and however you want. You can control what I wear, what I eat, who I talk to . . . And I will never complain because I trust you know what's best.' In the final episode of season 2, after angrily storming the stage and disrupting her sister's play, Cassie ends up in a fight with her friends. After the fight, she says to the other girls: 'You know what's funny? Nate broke up with me before I even went on that stage.' Maddy responds: 'Don't worry. This is just the beginning' – gesturing towards the cycle of abuse that likely now awaits Cassie.

Euphoria's characters lean into their worst experiences and the worst parts of themselves, and mostly wearily accept the chaos and destruction that follows from their choices. This could be read as a rejection of the futurity that marks *Sex Education*'s at times patronizing affect. The latter suggests to its viewers that a better future awaits us all, whether gay or straight, if we just take time to learn and talk about sex and ourselves. Contrastingly, *Euphoria* coaxes us to accept the inevitability of pain and violence, suggesting that no better future awaits us, perhaps in an echo of Lee Edelman's (2004) anti-social queer theory. Edelman polemically argues for a queer rejection of futurity, proposing 'accepting and embracing' (2004: 4) such negativity in place of a reproductive, heteronormative politics that underpins many political projects, including queer ones. He continues: 'we do not intend a new politics, a better society, a brighter tomorrow, since all of these fantasies reproduce the past, through displacement, in the form of the future' (2004: 30). *Euphoria*'s adolescents seem to do exactly this: they act in the present as if there is no future, no hope for a better world, embracing or at least accepting the pain and destruction ever-present in their lives. This reading is perhaps accentuated by a montage in the very first episode depicting school shootings and the September 11 attacks, with Rue's voice-over explaining: 'I was born 3 days after 9/11', illustrating the normalization of a state of crisis throughout the characters' lives. For them, a positive future is simply unimaginable, so why attach to a utopian hope for it?

This radical negativity presents a potentially different form of sexual pedagogy. Rejecting the optimistic and sometimes didactic sex advice of *Sex Education*, in *Euphoria* teenagers learn, or rather refuse to learn, through engaging in reckless sex in often brutal circumstances. Following Angel (2021a), Bersani and others, we could think of these experiences not just as full of pain, trauma, and detachment but also as opportunities for the exploration of new pleasures, for sexuality to shatter the certainty of the self. After all, arguably what makes *Euphoria* so successful is that, at least in comparison to the comedic yet earnest *Sex Education*, the show comes across to many as *sexy*. Through its dark, glossy, and at points nearly pornographic aesthetic, the show invites its audience to witness sexual recklessness and thereby to confront their own dark pleasures and sexual fantasies. In some ways, then, could we think of *Euphoria*'s sexual pedagogy as one of extreme experimentation, where the characters go to and experience the limits and extremes of sex for us? Could the constant repetition of scenes portraying sex as (at least borderline) violent and abusive be a way to get the viewer to explore such desires, while also imagining a different kind of sex – in a non-prescriptive way? In other words, by repeatedly showing the worst of sex (in relatable ways to some, strange and shocking to others), does the show challenge the viewer to imagine something else, not in an optimistic but also not in a purely pessimistic register?

Interestingly, the main contrast to the ubiquitous negativity of *Euphoria* can be found in the sweet and tentative relationship between Rue and Jules. Differently to much of the representation of heterosexual sex on the show, Rue and Jules' relationship is mostly devoid of sex: we see the couple hug and cuddle, but rarely, if ever, actually have sex. In season

2, Elliot teases the couple about whether they have had sex yet, and then kisses Jules after offering her advice about giving oral sex to Rue. This curious lack of queer sex on the show – apart from the power-imbued and sometimes straightforwardly abusive encounters of Cal – has the effect of positioning queer sex and relationality as something different from their straight counterparts. The characters also relate to these two modalities of sex differently: while the straight characters approach the mostly bad sex they are having with fatigue and detachment, there appears to be genuine joy, awkward nervousness, and tenderness in the encounters between Rue and Jules. These contrasting representations again evoke those found in *Fleabag* (2016, 2019) and discussed in Chapter 1, whereby she relates to her heterosexual encounters with flat and cynical detachment, while her relationship with best friend Boo is full of warm intimacy. If *Fleabag* evokes a heteropessimist sensibility, then *Euphoria* embraces it to its logical conclusion – a world where straight relationships can only ever exist as a power differential, and the possibility of pleasure is a distant dream.

Queerness here represents, in Ward's words, 'to the extent that it emphasizes authenticity in one's sexual relationships and fulfilment of personal desires . . . an affront to the celebration of heteroromantic hardship' (2020: 129). Rue and Jules seem less weighted down by societal expectation than their straight classmates do, at least initially avoiding the tediousness and repetitiveness of straight culture, which Ward argues can be 'traced back to the way gender itself is a repetition, a never-ending process of attempting to achieve normative, or at least legible, femininity or masculinity' (2020: 125). Violence and misogyny – both pervasive in the *Euphoria* universe – make it difficult to discover and express desire due to their predictability (Angel 2021a). It makes sense in this context, then, that one of few explicit, obvious female orgasms we witness in *Euphoria* arrives as a result of Cassie riding a carousel at the town fair – not of sex shared between characters. As Davis and Dean argue, 'there can be no orgasm without at least temporary loss of control' (2022: 69), and clearly Cassie is more able to lose control alone, high on MDMA, on a carousel, than she is with the boys she has sex with throughout the show. Thus, *Euphoria* and *Sex Education* present very different imaginaries of youth – whether that of today or as reimagined by older viewers. *Sex Education* represents sex as *knowable* and experienced through learning and verbal communication, arguably leaving little space for surprise or vulnerability to the unknown. *Euphoria*, in contrast, develops a radically negative sexual pedagogy where any conscious possibility of transformation is forestalled by an often-cynical detachment from the violences of heteronormativity, yet within this negativity it also hints at moments of potential unknowability and openness.

New sexual pedagogies

Jack Halberstam critiques Edelman's formulation of anti-social queer theory through an archive of almost exclusively gay male authors, 'bound by a particular range of affective responses[:] fatigue, ennui, boredom, indifference, ironic distancing, indirectness, arch dismissal, insincerity and camp' (2008: 152). Such affective responses signify one way of negatively countering the confines of heteronormativity, and indeed, they seem to no longer be directed at *hetero*normativity alone, as we have argued in earlier chapters. From Fleabag and the girls of *Euphoria*, to Mae, Abby and Josh of *Feel Good* (2020–21), *Work in Progress* (2019, 2021) and *Please Like Me* (2013–16), respectively, many of the characters in the current televisual landscape of sexual representation seem to mostly feel tired, bored, indifferent or distanced from sex and sexuality – whether their own or more generally. Sex is mostly bad, but even when it is good, everything else is probably bad – these shows seem to suggest, with a shrug. This leads us to propose that the primary affect both of on-screen sexual politics, and concomitantly of contemporary TV viewership, might indeed be weary pessimism, now expanded from the original heteropessimism to a range of queer pessimisms too.

As discussed in this chapter, a key counterpart to such pessimisms can be found in the relentless, nostalgically tinted, almost utopian optimism of *Sex Education*, which in turn perhaps echoes the melodramatic, utopian longings *Pose* (2018–21) and *It's a Sin* (2021) direct at the past, discussed in Chapter 4, or even the nostalgic returns to the good sex of the pioneering shows of the 1990s, staged by the various reboot shows, explored in Chapter 5. In these cases, sex is almost exclusively good, as to portray it as anything else would shatter the fantasy of return, along with our attachments to this fantasy. However, such optimism seems to only be possible in the contemporary representational landscape when imagined in relation to the past – whether the real (but reimagined) pasts of *It's a Sin* and *Pose*, the pasts represented by the original shows in the reboots, or one's own past imagined as just a little bit better in *Sex Education*. In contrast, the best we can seemingly hope for in the present are forms of *good enough* sex, discussed in our analysis of *Special* (2019, 2021) and *Please Like Me* in Chapter 3, sex that is all considered nurturing and satisfying. It is as if, in the broader contemporary context of ever-expanding neoliberalisms, environmental destruction, and a seemingly continuous state of political crisis, we can only imagine the past ending well – not the present. But this type of nostalgia-filled optimism leaves something to be desired too, in its replication of a progress narrative that hinges our hopes for both better sex and better representation of sex on something changing somewhere else, in some other time.

These two affective modalities of sexual politics – weary pessimism and relentless optimism – might be understood to reach their logical conclusions in shows such as *The Idol* (2023), *Euphoria* creator Sam Levinson's next venture that arguably takes *Euphoria*'s shock factor even further (into often unbearable territory); and *Heartstopper* (2022–), a pastel-coloured utopian dream of queer acceptance, but critiqued for its 'PG-rated purity, almost chastity' (Johnson 2023) – which we return to in the conclusion to this book. But are these the only ways of doing sexual politics or pedagogy? Halberstam continues their critique of Edelman by suggesting that he ignores another kind of archive of negativity, one drawing on Black feminist and queer theorizing, associated with affective states such as: 'rage, rudeness, anger, spite, impatience, intensity, mania, sincerity, earnestness, over-investment, incivility, brutal honesty and so on' (2008: 152). There are hints of these types of affective engagements with sexual politics in both shows under analysis here – Aimee is certainly angry about being sexually assaulted, and so are the disabled students who stage a sit-in in *Sex Education*'s final season, protesting the school lift repeatedly breaking down. *Euphoria*'s girls are frequently brutally honest, even rude. More obviously, we see Halberstam's alternative archive represented in some of the different endings offered by *I May Destroy You* as potential ways of living on after sexual assault, explored in Chapter 6. As we noted then, the multiple endings suggest that there are no prescriptive solutions to the issue of sexual violence, nor easy resolutions to the bad feelings that commonly accompany experiences of it. Instead, we might read the different endings as a kind of opening, or as multiple openings – and this in itself as a kind of resolution, or at least a good feeling.

For Halberstam, it is in the second archive that one might find 'the other possibilities, the other potential outcomes, the non-linear and noninevitable trajectories that fan out from any given event and lead to unpredictable futures' (2008: 153), and it is 'here that the promise of self-shattering, loss of mastery and meaning, unregulated speech and desire are unloosed' (2008: 152). There is a similarity to how Halberstam describes the sexual politics that might arise from this Black feminist and queer archive of negativity, and how Angel (and others) describes the pleasure that might arise from being open to uncertainty in sex: 'letting oneself go to places of intensity, to the hairsbreadth space between knowing and not knowing what you want, between controlling the action and letting the action take over' (2021a: 117); and 'all sex, in fact, involves play with power and relinquishing; with the ambiguous space between desire and uncertainty. In all sex, we are quintessentially vulnerable: unclothed, injurable, both physically and psychologically' (2021a: 118).

Thus, we wonder what this kind of affect and attitude of openness and uncertainty tells us about what we can learn about sex, on screen or elsewhere. If learning about sex is all there is to sex, as in the *Sex Education* universe; or conversely, if there is really nothing to learn about sex except through negativity, as it can only ever exist as a violent reflection of heteronormative power dynamics, then what space is there to do either sex itself or sexual politics differently? This difficulty might be partially an issue with the logic of the screen, as Amia Srinivasan also suggests: 'While filmed sex seemingly opens up a world of sexual possibility, all too often it shuts down the sexual imagination, making it weak, dependent, lazy, codified' (2021: 70). Given these technological and representational confines, *Sex Education* and *Euphoria* mostly play with the repertoires currently available for the representation of sex, suggesting affectively and pedagogically that both the pleasures of sex and the possibilities for sexual politics are finite and predictable, yet in their radically different sexual pedagogies they also push beyond the limits of bad sex – in our imaginations if not explicitly on our screens.

With Srinivasan, we suggest that in these sexual pedagogies we can find at least a gesturing towards a more expansive sex education that could 'endow young people not just with better "rote responses" but with an emboldened sexual imagination – the capacity to bring forth "new meanings, new forms"' (2021: 71). She argues that such an education would necessarily be a non-prescriptive education, reminding young people that rather than with authority figures, 'the authority on what sex is, and could become, lies with them . . . They can, if they choose, remain as generations before them have chosen: violent, selfish and unequal. Or sex can – if they choose – be something more joyful, more equal, freer' (2021: 71). Our analysis of *Sex Education* and *Euphoria* mirrors and extends Srinivasan's argument by highlighting that learning (about) sex might require both learning and critical reflection on bad sex, and an experiential openness to what remains unknowable about better sex in the future. With this in mind we turn to the conclusion, where we discuss another possible end to bad sex in the context of everchanging televisual representation – namely, the spectre of no sex on our screens.

CONCLUSION
NO SEX OR THE END OF BAD SEX?

Bad sex today

Is this the end of bad sex? We ask this question here in two ways: First, as a way to reflect on what we have learned from exploring the rich landscape of bad sex as a defining frame of sexual representation in contemporary English language TV from the mid-2010s to the 2020s. What kinds of attachments has our exploration of bad sex on the small screen made tangible, and what can these structures of feeling tell us about wider sexual politics and possible futures? Second, we raise this question to speculate on what might come after bad sex in a moment in which both representations and discussions about awkward, messy and difficult sex might be, at least partially, exhausted, and we can identify the formation of new cultures of sex on the horizon. As we finish writing this book, the proliferating representations of bad sex are met with an emerging discourse about sex in the 2020s – that of 'no sex'. Across think pieces, social media, and academic debates, the possibility of a future without sex is discussed fervently, that is, speculation that the future will be one that simply disinvests from and gives up on sex as a key object of attachment. How do we make sense of the spectre of 'no sex', and what can it tell us about the relevance and limits of the frame of bad sex?

Across this book, we have argued that it is precisely because a greater diversity of people is having sex on TV today that there is now more room to show and explore all the ways that sex isn't necessarily working for everyone. Through this, we have shown how sex operates as a dense focal point of affective attachment in which questions of domination and liberation, pleasure and pain are negotiated. Sex, even if it is increasingly bad and disappointing, remains a site of hopeful promise, necessity and attachment, particularly in the context of dwindling material possibilities, escalating inequalities and the intensification of gendered and racialized forms of violence. In fact, sex is often experienced as bad precisely because it is invested with the hope that it will resolve, or at least offer respite from, the tensions, contradictions, and problems of an increasingly precarious present. As such, the analysis of bad sex has given us a way to explore the wider affective attachments that are produced in the neoliberal (and increasingly authoritarian and nationalist) present. Bad sex on television then is interesting precisely for what it teaches us not just about sex, but also about the disappointments, hopes and attachments of getting (it) on in today's world.

In the first three chapters, we established the analytic of bad sex through shows that explore the question of sex for millennial figures in the *present*. Here, *Fleabag* (2016, 2019), *Feel Good* (2020–21), *Work in Progress* (2019, 2021), *Special* (2019, 2021) and *Please Like Me* (2013–16) acted as key sites to investigate bad sex on TV. Sex in these shows is 'bad' not just vis-à-vis Gayle Rubin's (1984) framing in that it counters the normative, reproductive, monogamous but also in that it is experienced as bad emotionally – that is, the people having it are not enjoying it, invest too much in it or simply can't get enough out of it in otherwise unfulfilling and difficult lives. In this, we argued that representations of bad sex produce and allow for complex attachments for both characters and audiences. Across these representations, sex becomes a cruel attachment and promise, loaded with the expectation that romance, love, and sex can resolve (or at least hold at bay) the troubles of inequality, precarity, mental health crisis, and sexual and social violence that typify contemporary neoliberal life. In other words, bad sex is bad (even when it feels good) precisely because it cannot live up to our expectations and attachments in these times – it can never rescue us from these unjust conditions.

In these shows, sex is something that we cannot help but seek despite, or because, it cannot fulfil what we want it to – an argument aligned with Lauren Berlant's (2011) notion of 'cruel optimism' as the attachment to an inherently disappointing object. This becomes most evident in our analysis of *Fleabag* expressing heteropessimism as a condition that plagues the lives of many straight women, for whom the attachment to heterosexual love-objects remains despite the simultaneously proliferating critiques of the shortcomings of patriarchal heteronormativity – and of straight men. For the lesbians, bisexuals, and non-binary queers of *Feel Good* and *Work in Progress*, sex initially offers a possible queer escape from heteronormativity and otherwise difficult lives of mental health and precarity. But here, while sex offers some respite, it cannot hold the emotional weight it is invested with either, given the lack of wider infrastructures of care, intimacy, and queer collectivity in the protagonists' lives. Similarly, for the gay men of *Please Like Me* and *Special*, good and even better sex is the promise that would set them free from the shame they experience as neurodivergent and disabled gay men in the hetero- and homonormative, as well as ableist, worlds they find themselves in. Unable to reach the idealized norms of great and fabulous sex of gay male cultures, they find at least 'good enough' sex that, all things considered, is nurturing and intimate. Yet, they likewise remain haunted by the shameful scene of bad sex that comes to fracture their relationships and precarious sense of self. Our examination of these shows highlights how for at least partially marginalized and precarious subjects, then, sex is more often an ongoing problem rather than a straightforward solution. Yet, conversely, this also means that sex can, if not resolve, be a key site in which some of the contradictions, disappointments and discontents of the political present can be amended, or at least articulated and negotiated.

In Chapters 4 and 5, we explored depictions of the past, where sex was represented as fulfilling, hopeful or even liberatory and glamorous. In the current cultural landscape of bad sex, we argued that these representations are sustained by contradictory nostalgic attachments to lost political and sexual worlds: on the one hand, the loss of and longing for the presumably more communal and political sexuality of the 1970s and 1980s that was liberatory and transgressive vis-à-vis the gendered, racial and homophobic violences of its time; and on the other hand, the post-political 1990s as a time of care-free simplicity when such violences were imagined to have been resolved or simply as no longer relevant. Here we asked what the memory and imagination of these times as times of good sex allows for in the present, particularly when this is only possible through an investment and nostalgic attachment to a time that has passed (and that maybe never really was, or could have been). Our key argument here suggests that representations of good sex in past times tell us more about our longings and attachments in the political present than they do about the actual sex of the past.

In *It's a Sin* (2021) and *Pose* (2018–21) it was uncovering stories of good sex in the context of the loss, isolation, and suffering of the AIDS epidemic and intersecting violences that offered ambivalent attachments in the present. Here we found progressive storytelling about the political violence of the 1980s for queer and trans subjects of today. These narratives work through complex and often contradictory nostalgic attachments to bad political times represented as times of rampant homo and transphobia, yet also of communal cohesion and transgressive and exciting sexuality. As such, these shows not just construct narratives of progress, showing how we have presumably moved on from these times, but also communicate a sense of loss from the individualized neoliberal political present. In other words, the political and intimate disappointments of bad sex in the contemporary moment produce a paradoxical nostalgia for the (imagined) times of queer joy, transgression and sexual liberation, despite, or exactly because of, the knowledge that these times were marked by death and homophobia. In a different vein, we considered a return to our favourite scenes of good (i.e. liberatory, exciting, uncontroversial and fun) sex and friendship through remakes of the postfeminist and post-queer 1990s cable shows *Sex and the City* (1998–2004), *Queer as Folk* (1999–2000; 2000–5) and *The L Word* (2004–9). Here, we argued that the reboots function through complex affective modes of suspicion, reparation, and return. In desiring good sex with a bad ex, attachments to the *politics* of that time are simultaneously disavowed and cultivated. While these shows are eager to show how they have progressed from the narrow and often exclusionary white, middle-class, and gender-normative representations of their originals, at the same time they re-enact a longing for a presumably simpler, less complicated sexual political past in which sex could still be imagined as good and glamorous – despite, or precisely because, it was unencumbered from the more complex political concerns of positionality and social justice.

After considering the present and the past of bad sex, the final two chapters turned to how the future of sex is imagined, asking what we can or should expect for and from the sex of tomorrow: Will it ever be better again? We considered what we might learn from representations of bad sex and what kinds of sexual futures might be possible as a result. In *I May Destroy You* (2020), we found a powerful engagement with trauma and recovery from sexual violence. Here, it was through an intersectional engagement with friendship, care, and community in the aftermath of sexual violence that a better future of sex and life itself could be found. We argued that it was, paradoxically, precisely through dwelling on the haunted scene of sexual violence, and in naming the racial, gendered, and classed dimensions of stolen consent, that a more hopeful promise of transformation and recovery could be formed. This promise was enacted through wider networks of care and friendship that supported all three main characters to live on and through trauma and pain. Differently, in Chapter 7 we explored how *Sex Education* (2019–23) and *Euphoria* (2019–) play with the repertoires of knowing, learning, and working through the uncertainties of sex, as well as submitting to their often predictable disappointments. We argued that, despite their remarkably different aesthetic and affective tones, both shows presented potential if limited sexual pedagogies for unlearning bad sex in the present. Contrasting the affective mode of relentless optimism in *Sex Education* to *Euphoria*'s cynical pessimism, we suggested that learning (about) sex might require both critical reflection on bad sex and an experiential openness to the unknowable in sex in the future.

Across the book, we have argued that representations of bad sex – as well as the frame of bad sex itself – can tell us something important about the affective attachments, disappointments and cruel optimism of contemporary life (which the imperative to good and even better sex tends to obscure). The bad sex we see on our screens is interesting precisely because it grapples with the ambivalent and always incomplete expectations of *any* kind of sex, when lived out by marginalized people in the context of prevailing inequalities. Bad sex as a frame makes it possible to consider the various forms of intimacy, care, and trauma that transgress straightforward interpretations of what a happy sex life, or indeed a happy life, looks like for most people. The representation of sex as messy rather than glossy, awkward, and conflicted rather than harmonious, emotionally tense rather than simply pleasurable, reveals sex as the site of dense power relations: a site where racial, gendered, and sexual domination is enacted and reproduced, but also negotiated and possibly undone. In this, we have suggested that queer community, friendship and care are, at least in part, what enables sex to be more than a disappointing object in the neoliberal context of inequality, precarity and isolation. While care, friendship, and community can certainly also disappoint, we have argued that it is here that some of the promise for a better future of sex lies.

No sex tomorrow?

Having laid out the key contributions of this book, we want to use the last sections of this conclusion to speculate on what might come *after* the representations of bad sex on the small screen over the last decade. If the late 2010s saw a confrontation with the more straightforwardly *bad* of sexual politics (e.g. via MeToo), as well as increasing televisual representation of sex as messy, awkward, and disappointing, as we have argued in this book, then the early 2020s have been to some extent marked by emerging discussion and concern that the future will have 'no sex' at all. The spectre of 'no sex' is raised in discussions about Gen Z's eagerness to reject sexual representation in the context of pornified social media, where 'almost half of Gen Z viewers want less sex' on screen (Horton 2023; see also BPAS 2024; Rivas-Lara et al. 2023) and where the representation of sex is powerful (and bad) enough to make you 'voluntarily celibate' (Ford, King and Tham 2023). This discussion speculates about the re-emergence of anti-sex attitudes via a renewed 'censorship debate' (Burton 2023), as well as considers how particularly younger people are navigating a social world defined by saturated sexual representation, on the one hand, and dwindling forms of intimate connection, on the other (Ball et al. 2023; Wignall et al. 2021). Related to this is the multitude of reporting reflecting on sexual practice more broadly, suggesting that real people are just having less sex, or are at least less interested in having it (Graham et al. 2017; Ueda et al. 2020; Wellings et al. 2019). This includes discussions about the apparent growth of abstinence and voluntary celibacy (Hagen 2024; Katsha 2023; Taylor 2023; Willingham 2022), women's sexual fatigue and dissatisfaction (Saner 2023; Scott 2019), the disconnection of dating apps (Chen 2023) and more radicalized forms of incel culture (Williams 2022). Some of these discussions reveal biopolitical anxieties about national futures in the context of declining birth rates (see e.g. Holzberg 2024; Siddiqui 2021), a discourse that must always be considered in relation to its transnational, racialized and classed dimensions, alongside recognition of the material, gendered and intersecting conditions which might be shaping a turn away from sex.

Readers might wonder if the conclusion to this debate (and indeed this book), is that after bad sex there is just no sex at all. After all, if sex has become bad, why would we (or anyone) still want it? Within this context, our final reflections briefly consider two different ways in which representations of 'no sex' are taking place on TV as we complete the book. Here we try to untangle the potential of this representational choice in television – suggesting that rather than a sexless future, such representations might point to the continuation of sex and sexualities as an important frame for analysing contemporary politics, attachments, as well as gendered and sexual practices – whether sex is explicitly, visibly 'had' on screen or not. The first strand can be seen in a new generation of high school teenage shows best encapsulated in the much-loved series *Heartstopper* (2022–), based on the graphic novels of Alice Oseman, who herself identifies as asexual and aromantic. *Heartstopper* tells the story of fourteen-year-old Charlie falling in love and striking a romantic relationship with the rugby boy Nick. Together they navigate the ups and downs of a teenage romance.

As Dan Glass discusses in *Open Democracy*, what makes the show stand out is how it 'shows LGBTIQ freedom as a normal part of school life' (2022), perhaps taking the representational dynamics of *Sex Education*, discussed in the previous chapter, even further. The queer and trans characters explore romance, friendship and the complex social dynamics of high school in the same ways that straight characters would have in the high school films and series of the 1990s – though generally now depicted as nicer and more supportive than high school students in the earlier shows. With its pastel colour palette, illustrated flourishes and careful depictions of teenage intimacy, the show has gained a huge following. *The Guardian* describes the show as a 'phenomenon that defines a generation' (2023), millennial commentators like Glass yearn 'if only my own school days had been like that' (2022), and Gen Z audiences celebrate its much-needed depiction of 'queer joy as a positive feeling we get from encountering signs of progress in gender equality and gender diversity' (Russon 2024: 1). To us, however, what makes the show stand out is that in its representation of queer joy it basically represents no sex. As Penni Russon suggests, the 'narrative engine runs on themes of love, identity, first times, self-discovery, friendship and allyship' (2024). Here, romance and friendship are foregrounded, and while sexual desire and exploration are part of the narrative, sex itself is never really shown, centred or explicitly discussed in any depth.

Instead, we witness the two main characters, Nick and Charlie, falling in love while making snow angels (Figure 8.1), as trans character Elle starts to realize that her best friend Tao might be more than just

Figure 8.1 In *Heartstopper*, the romance between 'rugby boy' Nick and Charlie is represented through the two making snow angels with illustrated flourishes. *Heartstopper* © See-Saw Films/Netflix 2022–.

a friend when painting him in a goldenly lit garden. 'Draw me like one of your French girls', Tao jokes in reference to the (in)famous scene of heterosexual romance in *Titanic* (1997). The queer embrace and humorous subversion of classic straight romance tropes is a key part of the show's aesthetic and appeal – based on the promise that us queers also deserve the sweet, sticky joys of romance. Yet, even the somewhat coy representational world of *Titanic* is full of (explicit and implicit) sexual desire. At the time, the film generated controversy for a scene in which Jack sketches Rose naked, as well as including the now-iconic shot of Rose's handprint on a steamy car window as evidence of the passionate and orgasmic sex present in her love affair with Jack. Much like the previous chapter's discussion of *Sex Education*'s focus on talking about rather than having sex, the *Heartstopper* characters also talk about sex and their sexual insecurities, yet remain largely void of the overwhelming sexual desire typically associated with being a teenager. In season 2 of *Heartstopper*, we get some fumbling exploration of sexuality but as Jack King argues in *GQ*, 'it's as wholesome as you'd expect' (2023). When Nick and Charlie find themselves in the same bed on a school trip to Paris, the two of them make out, kissing each other carefully on the mouth and then on the neck. After checking in with each other how they feel about this intimate, maybe even sexual, moment, Charlie says: 'I didn't think we'd do . . . *that* right now.' And rather than doing *that*, they talk about their sexual expectations and decide to wait: in the *Heartstopper* universe, no sex might be better than bad sex, after all.

In many ways, *Heartstopper* can be read as a direct response to the representational landscape of bad sex we have considered in this book, and in particular the presumably changing viewing patterns of younger television audiences. *The Guardian*, for instance, recently reported on a much-publicized study by Stephanie Rivas-Lara et al. (2023), which found that 'the majority of adolescents aged 13-24 (51.5%) wanted to see more content centred around friendships and platonic relationships, rather than romantic ones' (Horton 2023). Similarly, 'a near-majority (47.5%) said sex was not needed for the plot in most TV shows and movies, while . . . nearly 39% wanted to see more aromantic or asexual characters on screen' (Horton 2023). While the analytical power of generational analysis like this (as well as the media discourses it generates) needs to be treated with caution, *Heartstopper* might be understood to exist in relationship to this context and the bad sex shows of the 2010s we have discussed across our chapters.

Further, if shows like *Euphoria* depicted sexuality and sexual desire as leading into the abyss, more recent shows like *The Idol* (2023) (also created by Sam Levinson) take the representation of bad sex to a new extreme, with commentators like Lucy Ford in *GQ* arguing that *The Idol* provides us 'one the worst sex scenes in history' (2023). In a show replete with sometimes bizarre and frequently distressing representations of the young pop star Jocelyn contorting her body for cameras, in the scene Ford refers to Jocelyn is watched voyeuristically by another woman while she masturbates blindfolded, as her fully dressed male lover crouches at a distance from her, flatly narrating it. In contrast to *Euphoria*, *The Idol's* representation of sex and voyeurism has been nearly universally critiqued: While 'cringe-inducing' sex (D'Souza 2023) is everywhere (e.g. in many of the shows discussed in this book), this show goes too far, and we can no longer learn anything meaningful from it. Certainly, *Heartstopper* marks a significant departure from this often uncomfortable, icky, and affectively flat direction in the representation of bad sex. 'No sex' here promises to avoid such potential for violation – a world both less disappointing and more emotionally connected. That is, in such representational landscapes, there is no risk of encountering the sticky, painful messiness of bad sex, because there is no sex at all.

A different direction to *Heartstopper* is taken in the popular series *Killing Eve* (2018–22). As another potential example of 'no sex' television, *Killing Eve* follows Villanelle, a skilful assassin, and Eve, the MI5 agent trying to catch her. Across four seasons, Eve tries to foil (and encourage) Villanelle, just as Villanelle continues to seek out (but not kill) Eve. Their mutual erotic obsession with each other destroys Eve's marriage, sees the death of her close friend at Villanelle's hands, and ruins Villanelle's easy transnational life as an assassin hired by the powerful international agency The Twelve. While the two come together, fall apart, backstab each other, and work together again and again, nothing quells their desire. Although the show is not ostensibly *about* sex, it certainly amps up the tension of unfulfilled sexual desire. In this, the series seems to dwell on queer desire as the origin of envy, rage, identity merging and reluctant respect – which can also be attached to illegitimate, inappropriate, and unachievable objects (or people). As Natalie Adler argues in her critique of the show's shifting implications of queerness: 'What better way to achieve the lesbian urge to merge than to join eternally in death?' (2019) – as in not explicitly through any act of sex itself. Perhaps closer to the heteropessimist framework we explored in earlier chapters, Villanelle has access to forms of consumption she *appears* to want, but is emotionless in receiving, just as Eve is unsustained by markers of normative success, perturbed by 'missionary' sex and mocking of performances of passive femininity. Instead, Eve is excited by Villanelle's skills, high-femme attractiveness and global life, and only performatively disgusted by her callous willingness to inflict violence on others. In turn, Villanelle just wants the simple domesticated experience of Eve making her dinner and 'someone to watch movies with'. While both are willing to give their lives up for a mission that binds them together extra-legally, they never have sex.

As Lynn Fujiwara (2023) suggests, Eve and Villanelle are desiring of each other in ways that are both sexual and more complicated than sexual – they are impressed, fascinated, and intrigued, in an echo of Jane Ward's (2020) argument that queer desire involves the merging of objectifying and subjectifying desire for those who are desired. Perhaps it is precisely because Eve and Villanelle's lust is not just sexual, but also for each other's 'complexities and accomplishments, both corporeal and otherwise' (Ward 2020: 171), that they do not know what to do with each other whenever they actually meet – in an echo of our discussion of the uncertainty of desire in Chapters 3 and 7. At the close of season 1, Eve catches Villanelle in her Parisian apartment and embraces her – at first it seems they might (finally) have sex (Figure 8.2). But as Eve

Figure 8.2 Eve prepares to stab the unknowing (and more violent) Villanelle by hinting at her inexperience, perhaps in both sex and murder. *Killing Eve* © Sid Gentle Films/BBC America 2018–22.

plunges a knife into Villanelle's side, Villanelle is clearly shocked, but mostly excited that this is the ending to their first encounter (even later explicitly interpreting it as an act of romance).

By the end of the series, Villanelle and Eve admit their feelings for each other and kiss once, before Villanelle is brutally murdered in front of distraught Eve. In contrast to the overwhelmingly positive responses to *Heartstopper*, *Killing Eve* viewers, and particularly queer viewers, were disappointed in (or in some cases outraged at) the characters' failure to achieve a happy ending – or to at least have sex – bringing the 'bury your gays' trope back into the centre of queer representation (Heritage 2022). Like viewers of *Fleabag* (Chapter 1), we remained attached to the hope that these characters would live and have sex in more normative ways – despite the consistent representation of the impossibility of this attachment. To us, the series is queer and interesting within the frame of 'no sex' precisely because it seems more invested in the many other ways that desire, passion and pleasure figure through Eve and Villanelle's strange coupling. As Jill Gutowitz argues, there is maybe even something specifically lesbian and queer to a show that recognizes the meaning of 'glances, clandestine hand-holds, unspoken tensions' (2019) which are a frequently, albeit jokingly, analysed aspect of lesbian and queer dating cultures. 'No sex' in *Killing Eve* does not mean an avoidance of the complexities (and indeed, even violences) of sexual desire.

Lacking the explicitly queer subtext of *Killing Eve,* another popular series *Beef* (2023) similarly focuses on the unresolved tension between two main characters, who in this case hate, terrorize, and remain desiring of destroying each other – without ever having sex (Kumari Upadhyaya 2023). Originally meeting through a road rage incident, Amy Lau and Danny Cho are obsessed with enacting revenge on each other, and the whole series is palpable with a desire that neither Amy nor Danny can name and, so, continue to direct towards a relationship of mutual destruction. Unlike in *Killing Eve*, Amy and Danny's connection is not explicitly, or even especially, sexual – though flirtation, desire, recognition, envy, and disgust are at work here, too. In the first episode, Amy hides in the closet of her grand but minimalist Californian home, and frustrated with the absence of sexual desire within her tepid 'vanilla' marriage, masturbates with an unloaded gun – turned on by the road rage encounter with Danny. Their second encounter is mutually flirtatious, rather than scary, despite Danny having misrepresented himself as a handyman to get inside Amy's house while she is alone. When, in his first act of revenge for the road rage incident, Danny urinates across Amy's bathroom, he is elated and later boasts about it to friends as if recounting a sexual conquest (Figure 8.3). Like the butterflies of a 'meet cute' in romantic comedies, Amy and Danny's rage-filled beef becomes the thing that gets them out of bed and excitedly motivates their (terrible) decisions, transforming the impotent, repressed and depressed feelings brought out by the material, gendered and racialized conditions of their lives. While the series has less often been interpreted through the lens of gender or sexuality than *Killing Eve* – perhaps because it does not represent the cis and straight characters' obsession through typical heteronormative or gendered coding – some viewers (and the cast) did question if the series could be interpreted as a 'romance' (Bitran 2024).

Like *Killing Eve*, the series remains palpable with the thrill of obsession that neither Amy nor Danny can expel (least of all through sex). Even when Amy catfishes and then sleeps with Danny's younger brother Paul, and Danny (albeit unknowingly and self-loathingly) masturbates over images of Amy, their destructive obsession remains. At the end of the series, we find Amy and Danny having lost everything, alone together in a Californian desert, believing they will die. They speak caringly and honestly to and for each other, hallucinating that

Figure 8.3 Danny tells his friends about the 'gallons' he pissed on Amy's bathroom floor as if boasting about a recent sexual conquest. *Beef* © A24/ Netflix 2023.

they are the same person. In these ways, *Beef* is an example of what Sarah Lahm (2024) considers a new 'existential' wave of feminist storytelling in the mid-2020s. For Lahm, these series explore the feelings of neoliberal malaise like many of the shows we have discussed in this book, and yet give up on the possibilities of normative sexual relief and individualism as its resolutions. Instead, *Beef*

> rests upon the idea that two characters who are neither in a familial relationship nor romantic partners care about and save one another. Since neoliberal and neoliberal feminist discourses continue to perpetuate individualism and responsibility only towards oneself and one's (nuclear) family, the bonds that are formed and nurtured in programmes such as . . . *Beef* question and negotiate this neoliberal common sense. (2024: 9)

Thus, unlike both the heteropessimist and homopessimist queers of earlier chapters of this book, or even the more hopeful communal and explorative queers and friends of later ones, for the characters of *Killing Eve* and *Beef*, sex is largely off the table – and yet life is not flat, disappointing, or unexciting.

By considering these shows through the frame of 'no sex', they become interesting in that they take the feelings framed through and in relation to sex and intimacy in earlier chapters (disappointment, resignation, confusion and loneliness) (*Fleabag, Euphoria, Please Like Me, Feel Good*) and explore them through different forms of agency and relationality – from confused flirtation to obsession and destruction which remain outside of sanctioned heteronormative and homonormative forms. Both shows remain invested in questions of sexual, material, and emotional desire, but here the characters seemingly eschew sex (its promises, its distractions, its disappointments) as any kind of real antidote. And so, differently, and yet somehow similarly to *Heartstopper*, a world without sex (if not without tension, sexual and romantic desire) might make room to explore other, new, and possibly more satisfying forms of attachment. If sex is never actually had, it can also never disappoint.

The future of sex

We raise these two different affective directions of contemporary TV without sex as a final consideration in this book about sex, precisely to put them into conversation with the suggestion that the future of bad sex is 'no sex' at all. Across this book we have demonstrated that much of the significance of sexual representation in contemporary television lies within the wider affective attachments and meanings made tangible by the sexual representations – which, with Raymond Williams (1977), we have called 'structures of feeling'. Further, these structures are often more interesting than the amount, screen time or exact style of sex we see on screen. What we hope to demonstrate through these final reflections is that the future of sex, or what we learn from sex on screen, will remain generative. No sex – choosing not to represent sex, not to end the story with sex, or forms of relationality that extend beyond sex – does not necessitate an end to the importance of thinking through the promises and disappointments of desire, attachment, intimacy and care under neoliberalism (which, of course, will also remain structured by hopes for sex and sexuality). Quite the opposite, given that the absence of sex can only take place through the active negation and refusal of sex. What desires, attachments and imagined futures, then, are expressed in such a negation or refusal?

The renewed sex negativity of the affective register of 'no sex' might be understood in relation, yet also in clear distinction, to early forms of sex negativity in queer and feminist debates. Reflecting on teaching her university students about the sex wars of the 1970s and 1980s, Amia Srinivasan (2022) is surprised that her students do not react in angry shock or bored dismissal to the anti-sex positions of some radical second-wave feminism. Instead of finding 'the anti-porn position prudish and passé', her students 'were riveted' (2022: 40), relating radical feminist ideas to their own experiences of growing up in a world in which sex is ubiquitous, yet not necessarily always in a good way. In our own teaching, we have similarly observed young women in particular to be keen to explore sex as a potential problem and vexed object of attachment (at points leaving us confused about our own attachments to a tradition of more sex-enthusiastic queer scholarship). The renewed sex criticality or negativity expressed in the desire for 'no sex', however, we (like Srinivasan) believe should not be confused with a simplistic return to the often crude and exclusionary anti-sex positions of the earlier sex wars. Instead, we could understand these emergent structures of feeling as a longing for forms of connectivity *beyond* the often disappointing and troubling object of sex. What if we do not invest in sex either as a good, transgressive, pleasurable and liberatory or as a troubling, difficult and disappointing object of queer feminist analysis, but instead cast it aside for other objects altogether – friendship, queer romance, mutual obsession? Isn't this partly what Berlant (2011) had in mind when they called for 'new objects' of attachment able to resist the stale emotional pull of cruel optimism?

Just like bad sex can be understood as a reaction and response to the affective dynamics and social pressures of the good sex representations of the neoliberal can-do era of the late 1990s and early 2000s, 'no sex' then seems to emerge as a response to the bad sex years of the last decade. 'No sex' breaks both with attachments to good sex as part of individual achievement for white, middle-class subjects and with the more minoritarian focus on sex as bad, awkward and difficult, even laced with the danger of violence and abuse. The provocative question that the frame of 'no sex' raises is whether the problem is not good or bad sex but our over-investment in sex in the first place. If so, then the solution might be not to repair sex but to disinvest from sex as a primary site of attachment and look for other forms of pleasure, intimacy and connection instead. This more reparative reading of the desire for 'no sex' becomes significant when we consider that the public concern over a sexless future also often implicitly re-emphasizes heterosexual norms of reproduction and presupposes that sexuality remains attached to particular kinds of domesticated formations (Emens 2014). While minoritized within both queer and mainstream communities, a growing recognition of asexual subjectivities seems significant here (Milks and Cerankowski 2014), alongside the many forms of queer attachment (such as ethical non-monogamy) which lay bare the exclusions and presumptions of sexuality as it is organized through heteronormative (or homonormative) coupling and reproductive practices (Schippers 2019). Queering an understanding of the sexual, but also of the reproductive and monogamous, then, provides some hesitancy to wider panics about a future without sex.

Having said this, as queer feminist scholars attached to sex as a, at least potentially, radical force and analytic, we wrestle both with the present of bad sex and with the idea of a potential future without sex. A world without the many forms of desire, care, intimacy, community and utopian imaginations that come with sex – and perhaps most crucially of course, *sex* itself – is perhaps less attractive for queer audiences and perspectives, for whom sex on TV has often existed only in subtext, or has only just explicitly appeared. Representations of no sex might also not be the only future direction in the cultural landscape of sex. While the frame of 'no sex' seems to garner attention in televisual representations, it exists amongst a range of sexual representations, many of which continue in the style of bad sex. New hit shows like *Baby Reindeer* (2024) explore sex (and sexual violence) in nuanced, but also awkward, tense, dark and addictive ways, while other more heteroromantic shows like *One Day* (2024) demonstrate continued nostalgia for the 1980s and 1990s as a time when good, even sexy, sex was presumably still possible. In this, then, we remain positive that good and bad sex are here to stay, as well as curious about what we might learn from the changing representations of sex, or lack thereof.

Despite our hesitations about a sexless future, we hope to engender an open curiosity as to what the scene of 'no sex' might tell us about the political and social moment we find ourselves in. In our conclusions to Chapters 6 and 7, this is precisely what we suggested we might learn. Here we found that if talking about sex, detaching from sex, or knowing for certain when sex was (going to be) bad could not promise a good sexual future, then openness to the possibilities of not yet knowing everything about sex, not yet knowing what we might *not* know about sex, or not yet knowing what we *want* from sex might be a better place to begin from. All the affective modes of sex – bad sex, good sex in bad times, good enough sex, and no sex – we deal with in this book are interesting particularly for the ways in which they mediate and open up forms of attachment to other objects, politics and the future. As such, we do not see a simple future without sex. Rather, we find a continued complication of the objects of attachment that sexual desire will find, embodied or not, just as the characters of *Heartstopper*, *Killing Eve* and *Beef* all do, if differently from each other. Like the frame of bad sex, 'no sex' might present us with generative avenues to explore the emergent structures of feeling, disappointments and hopes for the future. Even if nobody will want to have sex anymore, the *possibilities* for thinking through and learning from sexual representation – good, bad, good enough, or indeed, missing – remain not just central to the screen but also to the kitchen table, to be discussed and collectively explored.

NOTES

Introduction

1 Here we follow Aura Lehtonen (2023) in understanding neoliberalism as a market-driven economic logic which mingles with the political and cultural logics of sexuality, gender, race and class, and is marked by both narratives of individual responsibility and co-produced patterns of state withdrawal and coercive intervention. Following Lauren Berlant (2011), we are particularly drawn to the affective, cultural and political logics of neoliberalism, as they are figured through frames of intimacy and domesticity.

2 In many ways, this contrasts with a mainstream cinematic landscape where sex was frequently presented as dangerous and violent, particularly for trans and queer people. With the exception of New Queer Cinema (see e.g. Rich 2013), this tended to translate into narratives in which trans and queer people learnt lessons about ever-pending threat and danger (e.g. *Philadelphia, Boys Don't Cry, Brokeback Mountain*), while straight women mostly learnt about the relative banality of sex within heteronormative romance (e.g. *Bridget Jones' Diary, Notting Hill*).

3 See Woodard (2022) for a more detailed discussion of the problematic implications of some of this debate, and also for the need to investigate the term 'grey rape' further.

4 Some of the shows discussed here, including *Transparent* (2014–19), *Master of None, And Just Like That . . .* and *Beef* (2023) have also been subject to scandals related to sexual exploitation, harassment or inappropriate conduct on the production side. To counteract these dynamics, the use of intimacy coordinators has become increasingly common on TV and film sets and arguably been key to the success of shows like *I May Destroy You* and *Sex Education*. While these discussions are important to understanding and improving the changing landscape of sex on screen (see e.g. Sørensen 2022), we do not engage with these debates in the book, focused as we are on the shows as representations.

5 Alongside these shifts in fictional televisual representation, we note a concomitant and growing diversification of the field of sex and relationship reality TV, including both original queer-focused shows (*Couple to Throuple*; *I Kissed a Boy*; *I Kissed a Girl*; *Queer Eye*; *Ru Paul's Drag Race*; *The Real L Word*) and queer inclusion on or remakes of traditionally heterosexual shows (*Are You the One?*; *The Ultimatum: Queer Love*). While we do not explore these trends in reality TV in this book, some of the affective and political dynamics we chart here are arguably also evident in the world of reality TV. See Lovelock (2019) for a discussion of sexuality on reality TV.

6 Indeed, the first chapter of this book arose from discussions we had about the show *Fleabag*, taking its first form as an article by two of us in *Feminist Media Studies* (Holzberg and Lehtonen 2021) – and thus acting as a catalyst for the rest of the book.
7 It is interesting to note that the kitchen table also features in many of the shows we discuss here as a site of sharing intimacy, discussion and connection, including *It's a Sin* and *Pose*, as well as some of the written work we cite (see e.g. Smith and Smith 1981).

Chapter 1

1 For analyses of *Insecure*, see Havas and Sulimma (2020) and Dobson and Kanai (2019).

Chapter 2

1 As Kohnen argues of the Australian series *Please Like Me* (2013–16), which we discuss in the next chapter: 'whiteness anchors complex explorations of sexual identity and mental health: in rendering these topics highly visible, it asks viewers to think of white racial identities as invisible even though the stories told about struggles with queerness, depression, suicide, and aging are rooted in a specific white' experience (2022: 560).
2 See an alternative reading of this character as a 'bad' object of attachment by Cáel M. Keegan (2022).

Chapter 3

1 The 'even better' framing of gay male sex is also reflected within the heteropessimist framework for straight women we discussed in Chapter 1. Across representations of straight women's desires, a frequent lament is the *loss* of attractive, muscly and kind men to gayness in the common refrain that 'all the good ones are gay', or in the incorporation of the notion that gay men are free from straight romantic, gendered and social norms in makeover or 'sex-pert' focused media for straight and cis audiences. We will examine some of these relationships alongside the dynamics of shame, pride and learning in Chapter 5 in relation to the reboot of *Queer as Folk* (see also Munt 2000).
2 We draw here on literature in critical disability, neuroqueer and neurodiversity studies, aiming in this chapter to consider how ideas of dis/ability and neurotypical expectations converge with normative imaginations

of sex and sexuality. Thus, we make efforts to consider these ideas together, rather than emphasizing their theoretical tensions and differences (Egner 2019; Goodley and Runswick-Cole 2015; Runswick-Cole 2014).

3 This is also reflected in Josh Thomas' decision to later write a show about autism where he discussed his own experiences (Barasch 2021; McHenry 2020).
4 This representation of sex between a presumably non-disabled person and a disabled person is notable for how it contrasts with a scene in *Sex Education* (2019–23) (discussed in Chapter 7), in which sex between a non-disabled woman and disabled man who uses a wheelchair is enjoyed and made better for them through an explicit conversation about what each person can feel/enjoy/do.
5 Interestingly, the normatively attractive men who act as assistants and are presented for the delight of viewers on *Ru Paul's Drag Race*, are referred to as 'trade' on the show.
6 See Karen Soldatic (2017) for an analysis of the regulation of settler colonial masculinities in relation to disability and sexual politics in Australia.
7 Aileen Moreton-Robinson tracks these performances as part of the incommensurability between Aboriginal women and white Australian feminists where 'anti-racist practice, as an intellectual engagement is evidence of their compassion, but racism is not experienced as part of their interiority' (2000: 149).
8 Indeed, the series opens with Ryan aggressively providing the medical definition of CP to a child who has tried to innocently assist him when he falls on the street, and it is comically at this point, when confronted with a barrage of medical terminology about the 'thing' CP and childbirth, that the child screams.

Chapter 4

1 Our use of this term to refer to the 1980s should not be taken to suggest that the devastating impacts and the global, social, political and medical inequalities of the HIV/AIDS crisis do not continue today.
2 The space of the club as one of joy and ghosts is discussed by Jafari Allen through a quote by performance artist Kevin Aviance, who sees 'all my girlfriends who had died' at the disco ball: 'I can feel them, I can talk to them, they wave to me. I know this sounds really crazy – but that's the only time I can see those people again, and it's really amazing' (2022: 3).
3 This is somewhat similar to the magical realism present at the end of the original UK series of *Queer as Folk* (1999–2000) (see e.g. Munt 2000).

Chapter 5

1 See, for example, Achouche (2017) and Loock (2018) for discussions of the different types of reboots and adaptations that proliferate in the current landscape of cinematic and televisual representation.
2 While not discussed in this book, we are conscious of the not-quite reboot of *Queer as Folk*, *Cucumber* (2015). In the show, the *Queer as Folk* generation was revisited in their late forties. Here too they were out of place – failing to meet the norms of the exciting sex younger queer men have and haunted by the pains of coming of age during the AIDS epidemic.
3 Of particular interest is the sex scene between Brodie's disabled brother Julian and – unbeknownst to Julian – a sex worker who Brodie has hired in *Queer as Folk*. Julian is upset about having read the sex worker's interest in him as genuine, and the deception eventually drives Julian and Brodie's sibling relationship to a breaking point. This depiction of sex with a sex worker stands in significant contrast to the scene between disabled Ryan (played by the same actor who plays Julian, Ryan O'Connell) and a sex worker in *Special* (2019, 2021), discussed in Chapter 3, which Ryan finds empowering.
4 See Cáel M. Keegan (2022) for an exploration of the representational field of transness in the 'tipping point era'.
5 See also Hunting's (2012) discussion of the opposite dynamic, where some fan fiction of the original US *Queer as Folk* reimagines the show's depiction of a non-monogamous relationship as traditional, homonormative and monogamous.

Chapter 6

1 We note that we discuss a similar 'kitchen table' moment in our introduction about an episode of *Girls* (2012–17). In reading Onyekweli's discussion, we wonder how the *Girls* kitchen table discussion might have been framed by the exclusions we discuss in this chapter – as in, the impossibility of universalized frames of vulnerability when experienced at the intersections of race, sexuality and class.
2 These questions are visited by Woodard (2022) through a specific engagement with the term bad sex.
3 See also Rebecca Stringer, who argues that a 'victim-bad/agent-good' (2014: 59) formulation fails to consider that agency is a category mobilized in transnational and neoliberal discourses of gendered violence.
4 Here we are thinking with the implications of Imogen Tyler's (2008) discussion of the classed and sexual disgust levelled at young, working-class women across the UK's austerity era and beyond.

5 See also Sara Ahmed for a discussion of the work that universalizing accounts of 'women's pain' do in authenticating 'an ontological distinction between legitimate and illegitimate feminism' (2004: 173).

Chapter 7

1 One key exception to this framing of sex via talk is when Maeve and Isaac hook up. Here, in a context where disabled Isaac cannot feel parts of his body, explicitly and verbally stating what he wants is entirely necessary – here talk about sex facilitates sex, rather than substituting it.

2 In a major contrast to what we witness on screen in *Euphoria*, and as we discuss in the Conclusion, Generation Z famously engages in fewer risk-taking behaviours than earlier generations, whether in relation to sex, drugs or crime, leading, for instance, to a significant decrease in teenage pregnancies at least in the UK (Ball et al. 2023; BPAS 2018).

BIBLIOGRAPHY

Achouche, Mehdi. 2017. 'TV Remakes, Revivals, Updates, and Continuations: Making Sense of the Reboot on Television'. *Représentations Dans Le Monde Anglophone*: 59–78.

Adler, Natalie. 2019. 'Season 2 Of "Killing Eve" Killed The Queer Subtext, And All The Fun Along With It'. *Buzzfeed News*, 24 May. Accessed 6 May 2024. https://www.buzzfeednews.com/article/natalieadler/killing-eve-season-2-sandra-oh-jodie-comer-queer-subtext

Ahmed, Sara. 2004. *The Cultural Politics of Emotion*. Edinburgh: Edinburgh University Press.

Ahmed, Sara. 2006. 'The Nonperformativity of Antiracism'. *Meridians*, 7(1): 104–26.

Ahmed, Sara. 2010. *The Promise of Happiness*. Durham: Duke University Press.

Ahmed, Sara. 2012. *On Being Included*. Durham: Duke University Press.

Ahmed, Sara. 2014. 'Feminist Complaint'. *Feminist Killjoys Blog*, 5 December. Accessed 14 March 2024. https://feministkilljoys.com/2014/12/05/complaint/.

Ahmed, Sara. 2021. *Complaint*! Durham: Duke University Press.

Alexander, Ella. 2021. '*Sex and the City*: What it Got Right vs What it Really Didn't'. *Harper's Bazaar*, 12 January. Accessed 16 November 2023. https://www.harpersbazaar.com/uk/culture/a21093577/sex-and-the-city-what-it-got-right-vs-what-it-really-didnt/.

Allen, Jafari S. 2022. *There is a Disco Ball Between Us: A Theory of Black Gay Life*. Durham: Duke University Press.

Allen, Robert Clyde and Hill, Annette. 2004. *The Television Studies Reader*. New York: Psychology Press.

Anderson, John. 2019. "Work in Progress' Review: Laughing Through the Pain'. *The Wall Street Journal*, 5 December. Accessed 3 December 2022. https://www.wsj.com/articles/work-in-progress-review-laughing-through-the-pain-1157557706.

Angel, Katherine. 2021a. *Tomorrow Sex Will be Good Again*. London: Verso.

Angel, Katherine. 2021b. 'Why We Need To Take Bad Sex More Seriously'. *The Guardian*, 11 March. Accessed 15 March 2024. https://www.theguardian.com/news/2021/mar/11/why-we-need-to-take-bad-sex-more-seriously-metoo.

Aronowitz, Nona Willis. 2022. *Bad Sex: Truth, Pleasure and an Unfinished Revolution*. New York: Plume.

Aurthur, Kate. 2022. 'Cynthia Nixon Thinks Miranda Was Always Queer on "Sex and the City": She Had "Lesbianic Qualities"'. *Variety*, 1 June.

Accessed 16 November 2023. https://variety.com/2022/tv/news/cynthia-nixon-miranda-sex-and-the-city-queer-lesbian-1235281614/.

Bahr, Robyn. 2019. '"The L Word: Generation Q": TV Review'. *The Hollywood Reporter*, 5 December. Accessed 16 November 2023. https://www.hollywoodreporter.com/tv/tv-reviews/l-word-generation-q-review-1259503/.

Bailey, Marlon M. 2011. 'Gender/Racial Realness: Theorizing the Gender System in Ballroom Culture'. *Feminist Studies*, 37(2): 365–86.

Bailey, Marlon M. 2013. *Butch Queens up in Pumps: Gender, Performance, and Ballroom Culture in Detroit*. Ann Arbor: University of Michigan Press.

Ball, Jude et al. 2023. 'The Great Decline in Adolescent Risk Behaviours: Unitary Trend, Separate Trends, or Bascade?'. *Social Science & Medicine*, 317: 115616.

Barasch, Alex. 2021. 'Josh Thomas's Comedy of Self-Diagnosis'. *The New Yorker*, 5 April. Accessed 15 March 2024. https://www.newyorker.com/magazine/2021/04/12/josh-thomas-comedy-of-self-diagnosis.

Barker, Meg-John. 2013. 'Consent is a Grey Area? A Comparison of Understandings of Consent in *Fifty Shades of Grey* and on the BDSM Blogosphere'. *Sexualities*, 16(8): 896–914.

Barker, Meg-John, Gill, Rosalind and Harvey, Laura. 2018. *Mediated Intimacy: Sex Advice in Media Culture*. London: Polity.

Baty, Emma. 2023. 'Okay, So When Does "Sex Education" Really Take Place? No, Really?'. *Cosmopolitan*, 24 September. Accessed 1 March 2024. https://www.cosmopolitan.com/entertainment/tv/a45249635/when-does-sex-education-take-place/.

BBC. 2019. '*Fleabag* Star Speaks About her Fear of Being a "Bad Feminist"'. *BBC*, 10 March. Accessed 30 June 2020. https://www.bbc.co.uk/news/entertainment-arts-47515753.

Benson-Allott, Caetlin. 2020. 'How I May Destroy You Reinvents Rape Television'. *Film Quarterly*, 74(2): 100–5.

Berlant, Lauren. 2011. *Cruel Optimism*. Durham: Duke University Press.

Berlant, Lauren and Edelman, Lee. 2014. *Sex, or the Unbearable*. Durham: Duke University Press.

Bernard, Riese. 2009. 'A Letter to Ilene Chaiken From Trans Computer Search Champion Max Sweeney'. *Autostraddle*, 1 March. Accessed 16 November 2023. https://www.autostraddle.com/a-letter-to-mama-chaiken-from-ftm-computer-search-champion-mighty-max-sweeney/.

Bernard, Riese. 2023. 'The L Word Generation Q Episode 310 Recap: Looking Full Steam Ahead I Guess'. *Autostraddle*, 20 January. Accessed 16 November 2023. https://www.autostraddle.com/the-l-word-generation-q-recap-episode-310-finale/2/.

Bitran, Tara. 2024. 'The *BEEF* Ending Has "A Little Glimmer of Hope"'. *Tudum*, 14 May. Accessed 14 June 2024. https://www.netflix.com/tudum/articles/beef-ending-danny-and-amy.

Blay, Zeba. 2017. 'A Black Woman's Reflection On (White) "Girls"'. *Huffington Post*, 14 April. Accessed 15 March 2024. https://www.huffingtonpost.co.uk/entry/a-black-womans-reflection-on-white-girls_n_58f109a6e4b0da2ff8605f4f.

Bollas, Angelos. 2022. 'Viral Representations in Pose (2018–2021)'. *Journal of Popular Film and Television*, 50(3): 112–29.

Bradbury-Rance, Clara. 2019. *Lesbian Cinema After Queer Theory*. Edinburgh: Edinburgh University Press.

Bradbury-Rance, Clara. 2024. 'Ambivalent Masculinities in Contemporary Film and TV: On Lesbian and Trans Representability'. *Film Quarterly*, 77(3): 35–43.

British Pregnancy Advisory Service (BPAS). 2018. 'Social Media, SRE, and Sensible Drinking: Understanding the Dramatic Decline in Teenage Pregnancy'. *BPAS*. Accessed 1 March 2024. https://www.bpas.org/media/wsefjwh2/bpas-teenage-pregnancy-report.pdf.

Brown, Tom. 2013. *Breaking the Fourth Wall: Direct Address in the Cinema*. Edinburgh: Edinburgh University Press.

Brownmiller, Susan. 1975. *Against our Will: Men, Women and Rape*. New York: Simon & Schuster.

Burton, Jamie. 2023. 'Gen Z's Distaste for Sex Scenes Sparks Hollywood Censorship Debate'. *Newsweek*, 20 February. Accessed 3 March 2024. https://www.newsweek.com/gen-z-distate-hollywood-sex-scenes-sparks-censorship-debate-1782040.

Butler, Judith. 1993. 'Imitation and Gender Insubordination'. In Abelove, Henry, Aina Barale, Michelle and Halperin, David (eds), *The Lesbian and Gay Studies Reader*. New York: Routledge, 307–20.

Butler, Judith. 1995. 'Melancholy Gender – Refused Identification'. *Psychoanalytic Dialogues*, 5(2): 165–80.

Butler, Judith. 1999. 'Gender is Burning: Questions of Appropriation and Subversion'. In Sue Thornham (ed.), *Feminist Film Theory: A Reader*. Edinburgh: Edinburgh University Press, 336–52.

Byrd Jr, Robert D. 2019. 'Qauring Queer Eye: Millennials, Moral Licensing, Cleansing and the Queer Eye Reboot'. In Colman, Loren Saxton and Campbell, Christopher (eds), *Media, Myth, and Millennials: Critical Perspectives on Race and Culture*. Lanham, Boulder, New York and London: Lexington Books, 63–80.

Cai, Delia. 2022. 'High School Forever'. *Vanity Fair*, 25 February. Accessed 1 March 2024. https://www.vanityfair.com/style/2022/02/high-school-forever.

Case, Sue-Ellen. 1996. *The Domain-Matrix: Performing Lesbian at the End of Print Culture*. Bloomington: Indiana University Press.

Casey, Baroness. 2023. 'Final Report: An independent Review into the Standards of Behaviour and Internal Culture of the Metropolitan Police Service'. *Met Police*. Accessed 13 March. https://www.met.police.uk/SysSiteAssets/media/downloads/met/about-us/baroness-casey-review/update-march-2023/baroness-casey-review-march-2023a.pdf.

Cerankowski, Karli June and Milks, Megan. 2020. 'New Orientations: Asexuality and its Implications for Theory and Practice'. *Feminist Studies,* 36(3): 650–64.

Chen, Eva. 2013. 'Neoliberalism and Popular Women's Culture: Rethinking Choice, Freedom and Agency'. *European Journal of Cultural Studies,* 16(4): 440–52.

Chen, Nathan. 2023. '9 Reasons Why Grindr Is Ruining Your Life'. *Medium,* 8 April. Accessed 4 March 2024. https://medium.com/@thenathanchen/9-reasons-why-grindr-is-ruining-your-life-9663254151ec.

Chu, Andrea Long. 2019. 'The Impossibility of Feminism'. *Differences: A Journal of Feminist Cultural Studies,* 30(1): 63–81.

Chung, Gabrielle. 2023. 'Kim Cattrall Returning to *And Just Like That* Amid Years of Feud Rumors'. *E! Online*, 31 May. Accessed 16 November 2023. https://www.eonline.com/news/1376010/kim-cattrall-returning-to-and-just-like-that-amid-years-of-feud-rumors.

Cohen, Cathy. 1997. 'Punks, Bulldaggers, and Welfare Queens: The RadicalPotential of Queer Politics?' *GLQ: A Journal of Gay and Lesbian Politics*, 3(4): 437–65.

Coleman, Loren and Campbell, Christopher (eds). 2019. *Media, Myth, and Millennials: Critical Perspectives on Race and Culture.* Lanham, Boulder, New York and London: Lexington Books.

Cookney, Franki. 2022. 'Ever had bad sex? You're Not Alone – and the Effects Can Last For Years'. *The Independent*, 22 February. Accessed 4 March 2024. https://www.independent.co.uk/voices/sex-bad-experiences-health-trauma-b2020377.html.

Coontz, Stephanie. 2020. 'How to Make Your Marriage Gayer?'. *New York Times*, 13 February. Accessed 30 June 2020. https://www.nytimes.com/2020/02/13/opinion/sunday/marriage-housework-gender-happiness.html.

Corbett, Holly, 2022. '#MeToo Five Years Later: How The Movement Started And What Needs To Change'. *Forbes*, 27 October. Accessed 4 March 2024. https://www.forbes.com/sites/hollycorbett/2022/10/27/metoo-five-years-later-how-the-movement-started-and-what-needs-to-change/.

Crenshaw, Kimberlé. 1991. 'Mapping the Margins: Intersectionality, Identity Politics, and Violence against Women of Color'. *Stanford Law Review*, 43(6): 1241–99.

Cvetkovich, Ann. 2003. *Archive of Feelings: Trauma, Sexuality and Lesbian Public Cultures.* Durham: Duke University Press.

Cvetkovich, Ann. 2012. *Depression: A Public Feeling*. Durham: Duke University Press.

D, Ricky. 2022. '*Queer as Folk* - A Cultural Milestone'. *Tilt Magazine*, 9 June. Accessed 16 November 2023. https://tilt.goombastomp.com/tv/queer-folk-cultural-milestone/.

D'Souza, Shaad. 2023. 'Tedious, Pointless, Cringe-inducing: Why The Idol was a Failure from Start to Finish'. *The Guardian*, 4 July. Accessed 31 May 2024.

https://www.theguardian.com/tv-and-radio/2023/jul/04/tedious-pointless-cringe-inducing-why-the-idol-was-a-failure-from-start-to-finish.

Darling, Orlaith. 2020. '"The Moment You Realise Someone Wants Your Body": Neoliberalism, Mindfulness and Female Embodiment in *Fleabag*'. *Feminist Media Studies*, 22(1): 132–47.

Davies, Adam, et al. 2021. 'A Critical Examination of the Intersection of Sexuality and Disability in Special, a Netflix Series'. In Jeffress, Michael S. (ed.), *Disability Representation in Film, TV, and Print Media*. London: Routledge, 44–64.

Davis, Angela Y. 1983. *Women, Race & Class*. New York: Vintage.

Davis, Angela Y. 2000. 'The Color of Violence Against Women'. *Colorlines*, 3(3): 4.

Davis, Angela Y., Dent, Gina, Meiners, Erica R. and Richie, Beth E. 2022. *Abolition. Feminism. Now.* Chicago: Haymarket Books.

Davis, Oliver and Dean, Tim. 2022. *Hatred of Sex*. Lincoln: University of Nebraska Press.

DeClue, Jennifer. 2020. 'Theorize for What? Reading Black Queer Film and Popular Culture'. *Palimpsest: A Journal on Women, Gender, and the Black International*, 9(2): 43–54.

DeLallo, Grace. 2021. 'Entertainment Needs to Stop Sexualizing Teenagers — Except For "Sex Education"'. *The Pitt News*, 8 October. Accessed 1 March 2024. https://pittnews.com/article/167651/opinions/columns/opinion-entertainment-needs-to-stop-sexualizing-teenagers-except-for-sex-education/.

Delany, Samuel R. 1999. *Times Square Red, Times Square Blue*. New York: New York University Press.

Dhaenens, Frederik, Van Bauwel, Sofie and Biltereyst, Daniel. 2008. 'Slashing the Fiction of Queer Theory: Slash Fiction, Queer Reading, and Transgressing the Boundaries of Screen Studies, Representations, and Audiences'. *Journal of Communication Inquiry*, 32(4): 335–47.

Divalentino, Ariana. 2022. 'Miranda Hobbes Has Always Been Gay. And Also, She Hasn't'. *Cosmopolitan*, 20 January. Accessed 16 November 2023. https://www.cosmopolitan.com/entertainment/tv/a38817843/miranda-hobbes-cynthia-nixon-sexuality-essay/.

Dobson, Amy Shields and Kanai, Akane. 2019. 'From "can-do" girls to insecure and angry: affective dissonances in young women's post-recessional media'. *Feminist Media Studies*, 19(6): 771–86.

Dove-Viebahn, Aviva. 2007. 'Fashionably Femme: Lesbian Visibility, Style, and Politics in The L Word'. In Peele, Thomas (ed.), *Queer Popular Culture: Literature, Media, Film, and Television*. New York: Palgrave Macmillan, 71–84.

Dry, Jude. 2022. '"The L Word" Star Daniel Sea on the "Reparative Gesture" of Max's Return'. *IndieWire*, 14 December. Accessed 16 November 2023. https://www.indiewire.com/features/general/the-l-word-max-daniel-sea-interview-1234792321/.

Duckels, Gabriel. 2022. 'AIDS Melodrama Now: Queer Tears in It's a Sin and Pose'. *European Journal of Cultural Studies*, 21(1): 122–8.
Duggan, Lisa. 2004. *The Twilight of Equality?: Neoliberalism, Cultural politics, and the Attack on Democracy*. New York: Beacon Press.
Dworkin, Andrea. 1987. *Intercourse*. New York: Free Press.
Edelman, Lee. 2004. *No Future: Queer Theory and the Death Drive*. Durham: Duke University Press.
Egner, Justine E. 2019. '"The Disability Rights Community was Never Mine": Neuroqueer Disidentification'. *Gender & Society*, 33(1): 123–47.
Eloit, Ilana and Hemmings, Clare. 2019. 'Lesbian Ghosts Feminism: An Introduction'. *Feminist Theory*, 20(4): 351–60.
Emens, Elizabeth F. 2014. 'Compulsory Sexuality'. *Stanford Law Review*, 66: 303–86.
Esquire Editors. 2022. '"Euphoria" Isn't About Gen Z. It's a Fantasy Revision of High School for Millennials'. *Esquire*, 20 January. Accessed 1 March 2024. https://www.esquire.com/uk/culture/tv/a38799020/euphoria-high-memes-gen-z-sex-scenes-season-2/.
Eyewitness News. 2020. 'Josh Thomas Apologizes for Race Comments'. *Eyewitness News*, 16 June. Accessed 15 March 2024. https://abc7.com/josh-thomas-freeform-everythings-gonna-be-okay-casting/6250477/.
Factora, James. 2021. '*And Just Like That…* Fans Get Mediocre Nonbinary Representation'. *Them*, 13 December. Accessed 16 November 2023. https://www.them.us/story/and-just-like-that-mediocre-nonbinary-representation.
Felski, Rita. 2015. *The Limits of Critique*. Chicago: The University of Chicago Press.
Flint, Emma. 2022. 'And Just Like That... Fails Che Diaz with a Clichéd Take on Non-binary Representation'. *Digital Spy*, 13 January. Accessed 16 November 2023. https://www.digitalspy.com/tv/ustv/a38745991/and-just-like-that-che-diaz-non-binary/.
Floegel, Diana. 2020, '"Write the Story You Want to Read": World-Queering through Slash Fanfiction Creation'. *Journal of Documentation*, 76(4): 785–805.
Ford, Jessica. 2019. 'Women's Indie Television: The Intimate Feminism of Women-centric Dramedies'. *Feminist Media Studies*, 19(7): 928–43,
Ford, Lucy. 2023. 'The Idol Just Gave us the Worst Sex Scene in History'. *GQ*, 12 June. Accessed 15 March 2024. https://www.gq-magazine.co.uk/article/the-idol-episode-2-sex-scene.
Ford, Lucy, King, Jack and Tham, Xuanlin. 2023. '10 Sex Scenes that will Make you Voluntarily Celibate'. *GQ*, 7 July. Accessed 31 May 2024. https://www.gq-magazine.co.uk/article/worst-sex-scenes-film-tv.
Frye, Marilyn. 1978. 'Some Reflections on Separatism and Power'. *Sinister Wisdom*, 6: 30–9.
Fujiwara, Lynn. 2023. 'Intersectional Feminist Pleasure and the Bind of Heteronormativity in Killing Eve'. In Nash, Jennifer C. and Pinto, Samantha

(eds), *The Routledge Companion to Intersectionalities*. London: Routledge, 459–70.

Fuss, Diane. 1994. *Essentially Speaking*. New York: Routledge.

Garofalo Geymonat, Giulia. 2019. 'Disability Rights Meet Sex Workers' Rights: the Making of Sexual Assistance in Europe'. *Sexuality Research and Social Policy*, 16: 214–26.

Gavey, Nicola. 1999. '"I Wasn't Raped, but . . ." Revisiting Definitional Problems in Sexual Victimization'. In Lamb, Sharon (ed.), *New Versions of Victims: Feminists Struggle with the Concept*. New York: New York University Press, 57–81.

Gerhard, Jane. 2005. 'Sex and the City'. *Feminist Media Studies*, 5(1): 37–49.

Giampaolo, Federica. 2023. 'The Spiritual Death of Miranda Hobbes: When a Queer-coded Feminist Icon Becomes the Punchline'. *Screen Queens*, 17 October. Accessed 16 November 2023. https://screen-queens.com/2023/10/17/the-spiritual-death-of-miranda-hobbes-when-a-queer-coded-feminist-icon-becomes-the-punchline/.

Gibbs, Jacqueline and Lehtonen, Aura. 2019. 'I, Daniel Blake (2016): Vulnerability, Care and Citizenship in Austerity Politics'. *Feminist Review*, 122(1): 49–63.

Gill, Rosalind. 2007. 'Postfeminist Media Culture'. *European Journal of Cultural Studies*, 10(2): 147–66.

Gill, Rosalind. 2008. 'Culture and Subjectivity in Neoliberal and Postfeminist Times'. *Subjectivity*, 25(1): 432–45.

Gill, Rosalind. 2012. 'Media, Empowerment and the "Sexualization of Culture" Debates'. *Sex Roles*, 66: 736–45.

Gill, Rosalind. 2017a. 'Afterword: *Girls*: Notes on Authenticity, Ambivalence and Imperfection'. In Nash, Meredith and Wheelhan, Imelda (eds), *Reading Lena Dunham's Girls: Feminism, Postfeminism, Authenticity and Gendered Performance in Contemporary Television*. London: Palgrave Macmillan, 225–42.

Gill, Rosalind. 2017b. 'The Affective, Cultural and Psychic Life of Postfeminism: 10 Years On'. *European Journal of Cultural Studies*, 20(6): 606–26.

Gilmore, Ruth Wilson. 2022. *Abolition Geography: Essays Towards Liberation*. London: Verso Books.

Giorgis, Hannah. 2022. '*And Just Like That...* Addresses Its Che Diaz Problem'. *The Atlantic*, 14 July. Accessed 16 November 2023. https://www.theatlantic.com/culture/archive/2023/07/and-just-like-that-che-diaz-character/674703/.

Glass, Dan. 2022. 'I was a child of Section 28. "Heartstopper" Helps Heal the Pain'. *Open Democracy*, 7 May. Accessed 15 March 2024. https://www.opendemocracy.net/en/5050/heartstopper-netflix-lgbt-drama-series/.

Glock, Allison. 2005. 'She Likes to Watch'. *New York Times*, 6 February. Accessed 16 November 2023. https://www.nytimes.com/2005/02/06/arts/television/she-likes-to-watch.html.

Gonsalez, Marcos. 2020. 'Paris Doesn't Always Have to be Burning'. *Public Books*, 14 September. Accessed 12 March 2024. https://www.publicbooks.org/paris-doesnt-always-have-to-be-burning/.

Goodley, Dan and Runswick-Cole, Katherine. 2015. 'Big Society? Disabled People with the Label of Learning Disabilities and the Queer(y)ing of Civil Society'. *Scandinavian Journal of Disability Research*, 17(1): 1–13.

Gould, Deborah B. 2009. *Moving Politics: Emotion and ACT UP's Fight Against AIDS*. Chicago: University of Chicago Press.

Graham, Cynthia A. et al. 2017. 'What Factors are Associated with Reporting Lacking Interest in Sex and How Do These Vary by Gender? Findings from the Third British National Survey of Sexual Attitudes and Lifestyles'. *BMJ Open*, 7: e016942.

Gregory, Drew Burnett. 2020a. '"The L Word": Generation Q' Should Change Its Mind About Trans Actresses Playing Cis Characters'. *Autostraddle*, 20 January. Accessed 16 November 2023. https://www.autostraddle.com/the-l-word-generation-q-should-change-its-mind-about-trans-actresses-playing-cis-characters/.

Gregory, Drew Burnett. 2020b. '"Work in Progress" Is Too Much and So Am I'. *Autostraddle*, 30 January. Accessed 15 March 2024. https://www.autostraddle.com/work-in-progress-is-too-much-and-so-am-i/.

Griffin, F. Hollis (ed.). 2023. *Television Studies in Queer Times*. London: Routledge.

Gutowitz, Jill. 2019. 'Why Do I Want Villanelle and Eve to Hook Up So Badly?'. *Them*, 13 May. Accessed 6 May 2024. https://www.them.us/story/killing-eve-sexual-tension.

Hagen, Sofie. 2024. *Will I Ever Have Sex Again?*. London: Blink Publishing.

Hakim, Jamie. 2019a. *Work That Body: Male Bodies in Digital Culture*. London: Rowman and Littlefield.

Hakim, Jamie. 2019b. 'The Rise of Chemsex: Queering Collective Intimacy in Neoliberal London'. *Cultural Studies*, 33(2): 249–75.

Halberstam, Jack. 2005. 'Shame and White Gay Masculinity'. *Social Text*, 23(3–4): 219–33.

Halberstam, Jack. 2008. 'The Anti-Social Turn in Queer Studies'. *Graduate Journal of Social Science*, 5(2): 140–56.

Halberstam, Jack. 2020. *The Queer Art of Failure*. Durham: Duke University Press.

Halperin, David M. and Valerie Traub (eds). 2009. *Gay Shame*. Chicago: University of Chicago Press.

Hammelsbeck, Rebekka. 2016. 'Self-Care as Activism: Negotiating Feminism in Neoliberal Times'. *London Conference in Critical Thought*, 25 June. Accessed 15 March 2024. https://static1.squarespace.com/static/64468fe2aea4fc6800606b62/t/652d7e424377eb5c1afcf3f6/1697480259355/LCCT-Long-Programme-2016-140620.pdf.

Harrison, Rebecca. 2023. 'Telephone Networks and Transactional Motherhood in Channel 4's It's A Sin'. *European Journal of Cultural Studies*, 26(1): 85–94.

Havas, Julia and Sulimma, Maria. 2020. 'Through the Gaps of my Fingers: Genre, Femininity, and Cringe Aesthetics in Dramedy Television'. *Television & New Media*, 21(1): 75–94.

Hemmings, Clare. 2011. *Why Stories Matter: The Political Grammar of Feminist Theory*. Durham: Duke University Press.

Heritage, Stuart. 2021. 'Arrested Development: Why are Adults Still Playing High-Schoolers on Screen?'. *The Guardian*, 21 September. Accessed 1 March 2024. https://www.theguardian.com/culture/2021/sep/21/arrested-development-why-are-adults-still-playing-high-schoolers-on-screen.

Heritage, Stuart. 2022. 'An Unrepentant eff You: Why I Loved the Audacious Killing Eve Ending'. *The Guardian*, 23 April. Accessed 6 May 2024. https://www.theguardian.com/tv-and-radio/2022/apr/23/killing-eve-finale-series-bbc.

Hirschman, Allegra. 2022. 'Miranda Was Always Already Queer'. *Medium*, 29 January. Accessed 16 November 2023. https://medium.com/@allegrahirschman/miranda-was-always-already-queer-5708e198aee0.

Hogan, Michael. 2020. 'Interview with Vicky Jones: "*Fleabag* Felt like a Tipping Point for Feminism"'. *The Guardian*, 12 April. Accessed 30 June 2020. https://www.theguardian.com/tv-and-radio/2020/apr/12/vicky-jones-fleabag-felt-like-a-tipping-point-for-feminism.

Hohl, Katrin. 2022. 'New Scorecards Show Under 1% of Reported Rapes Lead to Conviction'. *The Conversation*, 1 April. Accessed 13 March 2024. https://theconversation.com/new-scorecards-show-under-1-of-reported-rapes-lead-to-conviction-criminologist-explains-why-englands-justice-system-continues-to-fail-180345.

Holmes, Anna. 2012. 'White "Girls"'. *The New Yorker*, 23 April. Accessed 15 March 2024. http://www.newyorker.com/culture/culture-desk/white-girls.

Holmes, Martin. 2022. 'Chris Noth Scenes Cut From "And Just Like That" Following Sexual Assault Allegations'. *TV Insider*, 6 January. Accessed 16 November 2023. https://www.tvinsider.com/1027798/chris-noth-scenes-cut-from-and-just-like-that-following-sexual-assault-allegations/.

Holzberg, Billy. 2024. 'The Great Replacement Ideology as Anti-Gender Politics: Affect, White Terror and Reproductive Racism in Germany and Beyond'. In Holvikivi, Aiko, Ojeda, Tomás, Holzberg, Billy (eds), *Transnational Anti-Gender Politics: Feminist Solidarity in Times of Global Attacks*. London: Palgrave Macmillan.

Holzberg, Billy and Lehtonen, Aura. 2021. 'The Affective Life of Heterosexuality: Heteropessimism and Postfeminism in Fleabag'. *Feminist Media Studies*, 22(8): 1902–17.

Hong, Grace Kyungwon. 2015. *Death beyond Disavowal: The Impossible Politics of Difference*. Minneapolis: University of Minnesota Press.

hooks, bell. 2000. *Feminist Theory: From Margin to Center*. London: Pluto Press.

hooks, bell. 2009. *Reel to Real: Race, Class and Sex at the Movies*. New York: Routledge.

Horeck, Tanya. 2021. 'Better Worlds: Queer Pedagogy and Utopia in Sex Education and Schitt's Creek'. *Jump Cut,* 60. Accessed 5 August 2024. https://www.ejumpcut.org/archive/jc60.2021/Horek-utopianTV/index.html.

Horton, Adrian. 2022. 'How did Euphoria Become the Most Loved and Hated Show on TV?'. *The Guardian*, 2 March. Accessed 1 March 2024. https://www.theguardian.com/tv-and-radio/2022/mar/02/euphoria-most-loved-hated-tv-show.

Horton, Adrian. 2023. 'Almost Half of Gen Z Viewers Want Less Sex on Screen, Study Finds'. *The Guardian*, 25 October. Accessed 3 March 2024. https://www.theguardian.com/culture/2023/oct/25/gen-z-less-sex-tv-movie-trend.

Horvat, Anamarija. 2022. *Screening Queer Memory: LGBTQ Pasts in Contemporary Film and Television*. London: Bloomsbury.

Hunting, Kyra. 2012. '"Queer as Folk" and the Trouble with Slash'. *Transformative Works and Cultures*, 11. Accessed 5 August 2024. https://scholars.uky.edu/en/publications/queer-as-folk-and-the-trouble-with-slash.

Illouz, Eva. 2012. *Why Love Hurts: A Sociological Explanation*. Cambridge: Polity.

Johnson, Allyson. 2023. 'Teen Sexuality 101: "Sex Education", "Heartstopper", and "Euphoria"'. *Pajiba*, 27 September. Accessed 1 March 2024. https://www.pajiba.com/tv_reviews/teen-sexuality-101-methods-and-explorations-in-sex-education-heartstopper-and-euphoria-.php.

Jones, Owen. 2019. 'Queer As Folk was a Joyful Revelation for LGBT Viewers Like Me'. *The Guardian*, 28 February. Accessed 16 November 2023. https://www.theguardian.com/commentisfree/2019/feb/28/queer-as-folk-lgbt-channel-4.

Jones, Sandra C. 2022. 'Hey Look, I'm (Not) on TV: Autistic People Reflect on Autism Portrayals in Entertainment Media'. *Disability & Society,* 39(2), 1–18.

Kafer, Alison. 2013. *Feminist, Queer, Crip*. Indianapolis: Indiana University Press.

Katsha, Habiba. 2023. 'Celibacy Is On The Rise, Should You Consider Trying It?'. *Huffington Post*, 26 January. Accessed 3 March 2024. https://www.huffingtonpost.co.uk/entry/celibacy-is-on-the-rise-should-you-consider-trying-it_uk_63d25bc3e4b0c2b49ada9810.

Keating, Shannon. 2019a. 'Let's Talk About that Confession Scene in *Fleabag*'. *Buzzfeed,* 20 May. Accessed 30 June 2020. https://www.buzzfeednews.com/article/shannonkeating/fleabag-season-2-phoebe-waller-bridge-hot-priest.

Keating, Shannon. 2019b. 'The Year in Heteropessimism'. *Buzzfeed,* 30 December. Accessed 30 June 2020. https://www.buzzfeednews.com/article/shannonkeating/straight-romance-heteropessimism-marriage-story.

Keegan, Cáel M. 2022. 'On the Necessity of Bad Trans Objects'. *Film Quarterly*, 75(3): 26–37.

Keeling, Kara. 2019. *Queer Times, Black Futures*. New York: New York University Press.

Kessler, Sarah. 2021. 'Are You Being Sirred? Work in Progress, Nanette, Douglas, and the New Butch Middlebrow'. *Film Quarterly,* 74(3): 46–55.

King, Jack. 2023. '*Heartstopper* Season 2 Handles the Awkward First Fumbles of Gay Sex with Grace. August 2023'. Accessed 14 June 2024. https://www.gq-magazine.co.uk/article/heartstopper-season-2-sex.

Klein, Melanie. 2002. *Love, Guilt and Reparation: And Other Works 1921-1945.* New York: Simon and Schuster.

Kohnen, Melanie E.S. 2022. 'Distributing Whiteness: Please Like Me and Global Television Circulation'. *Television & New Media,* 23(6): 555–74.

Kumari Upadhyaya, Kayla. 2023. 'Netflix's Beef Is Very Stressful — It's Also an Incredible Work of Art'. *Autostraddle*, 11 April. Accessed 4 March 2024. https://www.autostraddle.com/beef-on-netflix/#comments.

Lahm, Sarah. 2024. 'They were Too Fragile': Questioning Feminist Resilience in Russian Doll'. *Journal of Gender Studies,* 11: 1–10.

Lane, Nikki. 2019. *The Black Queer Work of Ratchet: Race, Gender, Sexuality, and the (Anti) Politics of Respectability*. Washington, DC: Palgrave Macmillan

Lee, Sangwon, Lee, Seonmi, Joo, Hyemin and Nam, Yoonjae. 2021. 'Examining Factors Influencing Early Paid Over-The-Top Video Streaming Market Growth: A Cross-Country Empirical Study'. *Sustainability,* 13(10): 5702.

Lehtonen, Aura. 2023. *The Sexual Logics of Neoliberalism in Britain: Sexual Politics in Exceptional Times*. London: Routledge.

Lennon, Kathleen and Alsop, Rachel. 2020. *Gender Theory in Troubled Times.* Cambridge: Polity Press.

Levesley, David. 2019. 'Sex Education on Netflix is the Best Portrayal of Sex, and Teenagers, Out There'. *GQ Magazine*, 10 January. Accessed 1 March 2024. https://www.gq-magazine.co.uk/article/netflix-sex-education-review.

Lewis, Isobel. 2023. 'From the Extremes of Euphoria to the Funny Fumblings of Sex Education – How to Get Sex in Teen Dramas Right'. *Everand*, 21 September. Accessed 1 March 2024. https://www.everand.com/article/672668640/From-The-Extremes-Of-Euphoria-To-The-Funny-Fumblings-Of-Sex-Education-How-To-Get-Sex-In-Teen-Dramas-Right.

Leyda, Julia and Negra, Diane. 2023. 'Gender, Family, and Therapeutic Regionalism in *One Mississippi*'. In Lyons, James and Yannis Tzioumakis (eds), *Indie TV: Industry, Aesthetics and Medium Specificity.* Oxon and New York: Routledge.

Li, Shirley. 2022. 'The Gen-Z Drama That Launched a Million Memes'. *The Atlantic*, 3 March. Accessed 1 March 2024. https://www.theatlantic.com/culture/archive/2022/03/euphoria-hbo-season-2-review/624173/.

Liu, Rebecca. 2019. 'The Making of a Millennial Woman'. *Another Gaze,* 20 June. Accessed 30 June 2020. https://www.anothergaze.com/making-millennial-woman-feminist-capitalist-fleabag-girls-sally-rooney-lena-dunham-unlikeable-female-character-relatable/.

Loock, Kathleen. 2018. 'American TV Series Revivals: Introduction'. *Television & New Media*, 19(4): 299–309.

López, Quispe. 2022. 'Max Is Back: The L Word's Daniel Sea and Leo Sheng Discuss the Infamous Trans Character's Return'. *Them*, 9 December. Accessed 16 November 2023. https://www.them.us/story/daniel-sea-leo-sheng-the-l-word-generation-q-interview-max-return.

Lorde, Audre. 1984. *Sister Outsider*. Berkley: Crossing Press.

Lorde, Audre. 1988. *A Burst of Light: And Other Essays*. New York: Ixia Press.

Lotz, Amanda. 2014. *The Television Will be Revolutionised*. New York: New York University Press.

Love, Heather. 2009. *Feeling Backward: Loss and the Politics of Queer History*. Boston: Harvard University Press.

Lovelock, Michael. 2019. *Reality TV and Queer Identities: Sexuality, Authenticity, Celebrity*. Cham: Palgrave Macmillan.

Lyons, James and Tzioumakis, Yannis (eds). 2023. *Indie TV: Industry, Aesthetics and Medium Specificity*. New York: Routledge.

Lyons, Margaret. 2013. 'On Girls, Adam, Rape, and Consent'. *Vulture*, 12 March Accessed 4 March 2023. https://www.vulture.com/2013/03/on-girls-adam-rape-and-consent.html.

Mackinnon, Catharine. 1997. 'Rape: On Coercion and Consent'. In Conboy, Katie, Medina, Nadia and Stanbury, Sarah (eds), *Writing On the Body: Female Embodiment and Feminist Theory*. New York: Columbia University Press, 42–58.

Macpherson, William. 1999. *The Stephen Lawrence Inquiry*. London: Stationery Office. Accessed 9 March 2024. https://assets.publishing.service.gov.uk/media/5a7c2af540f0b645ba3c7202/4262.pdf.

Maple, Taylor. 2019. 'This "Special" Moment Will Resonate With Anyone Who's Had to Work Overtime Just to Fit in'. *Bustle*, 12 April. Accessed 15 March 2024. https://www.bustle.com/p/kims-speech-in-netflixs-special-will-resonate-with-anyone-whos-felt-like-they-had-to-work-overtime-to-fit-in-17028811.

Marcus, Sharon. 1992. 'Fighting Bodies, Fighting Words: A Theory and Politics of Rape Prevention'. In Butler Judith and Scott, Joan W. (eds), *Feminists Theorize the Political*. New York: Routledge, 385–403.

Marquez, Yvonne. 2014. 'Latin Lovers and Spicy Bombshells: What "The L Word" Got Wrong About Latinas'. *Autostraddle*, 3 February. Accessed 16 November 2023. https://www.autostraddle.com/latin-lovers-and-spicy-bombshells-what-the-l-word-got-wrong-about-latinas-218800/.

McHenry, Jackson. 2020. 'Josh Thomas Isn't Afraid of America After Please Like Me'. *Vulture*, 11 February. Accessed 15 March 2024. https://www.vulture.com/2020/02/josh-thomas-everythings-gonna-be-okay.html.

McNicholas Smith, Kate. 2020. *Lesbians on Television: New Queer Visibility and the Lesbian Normal*. Bristol: Intellect.

McRobbie, Angela. 2004. 'Notes on Postfeminism and Popular Culture: Bridget Jones and the New Gender Regime'. In Harris, Anita (ed.), *All About the Girl: Culture, Power and Identity*. London: Routledge, 29–40.

McRuer, Robert. 2010. 'Compulsory Able-Bodiedness and Queer/Disabled Existence'. In Davis, Lennard J. (ed.), *The Disability Studies Reader, 3*. New York: Routledge, 383–92.

Meyer, Doug. 2022. 'Racializing Emasculation: An Intersectional Analysis of Queer Men's Evaluations of Sexual Assault'. *Social Problems*, 69(1): 39–57.

Milks, Megan and Cerankowski, Karli, June. 2014. *Asexuality: Feminist and Queer Perspectives*. New York: Routledge.

Mittell, Jason and Thompson, Ethan. 2020. *How to Watch Television*. New York: New York University Press.

Montgomery, Hugh. 2019. 'Queer as Folk at 20: How Russell T Davies' Gay Drama Changed the Landscape of TV'. *iNews*, 19 February. Accessed 16 November 2023. https://inews.co.uk/culture/television/20-years-queer-folk-russell-t-davies-changed-television-259715.

Moreton-Robinson, Aileen. 2000. 'Troubling Business: Difference and Whiteness within Feminism'. *Australian Feminist Studies*, 15(33): 343–52.

Moreton-Robinson, Aileen. 2015. *The White Possessive: Property, Power, and Indigenous Sovereignty*. Ann Arbor: University of Minnesota Press.

Mulholland, Claudia. 2019. '*Fleabag* is the Bad Feminist We All Need'. *Kettle Mag*, 20 June. Accessed 30 June 2020. https://kettlemag.co.uk/fleabag-is-the-bad-feminist-that-we-all-need/.

Muñoz, José Esteban. 1996. 'Ephemera as Evidence: Introductory Notes to Queer Acts'. *Women & Performance: A Journal of Feminist Theory*, 8(2): 5–16.

Muñoz, José Esteban. 2019. *Cruising Utopia: The Then and There of Queer Futurity*. New York: New York University Press.

Munt, Sally R. 2000. 'Shame/Pride Dichotomies in Queer As Folk'. T*extual Practice*, 14(3): 531–46.

Murphy, Ann V. 2012. *Violence and the Philosophical Imaginary*. Albany: State University of New York Press.

Nadasen, Premilla. 2017. 'Rethinking Care: Arlie Hochschild and the Global Care Chain'. *Women's Studies Quarterly*, 45(3/4): 124–8.

Nash, Meredith and Grant, Ruby. 2015. 'Twenty-something *Girls* v. Thirty-something *Sex And The City* Women: Paving the Way for "Post? Feminism"'. *Feminist Media Studies*, 15(6): 976–91.

Nelson, Elizabeth. 2023. 'The Trouble With Reboot TV'. *New York Times*, 8 February. Accessed 16 November 2023. https://www.nytimes.com/2023/02/08/magazine/night-court-velma-that-90s-show-reboots.html.

Ngai, Sianne. 2004. *Ugly Feelings*. Boston: Harvard University Press.

Nicholson, Rebecca. 2019a. 'Euphoria Review – So Explicit it Makes Skins Look Positively Victorian'. *The Guardian*, 6 August. Accessed 1 March 2024. https://www.theguardian.com/tv-and-radio/2019/aug/06/euphoria-review-zendaya-rue-sex-drugs-teen-drama-skins.

Nicholson, Rebecca. 2019b. 'The Return of The L Word: The Groundbreaking Lesbian Show is Back'. *The Guardian*, 2 December. Accessed 16 November

2023. https://www.theguardian.com/tv-and-radio/2019/dec/02/return-of-the-l-word-lesbian-show.

Nicholson, Rebecca. 2023. '"71 seconds of Regal Poise": Kim Cattrall's Short, Sweet Return to the Sex and the City Universe'. *The Guardian*, 24 August. Accessed 16 November 2023. https://www.theguardian.com/tv-and-radio/2023/aug/24/kim-cattrall-samantha-and-just-like-that-sex-and-the-city.

Nussbaum, Emily. 2016. '*Fleabag*, an Original Bad-Girl Comedy'. *The New Yorker,* 19 September. Accessed 30 June 2020. https://www.newyorker.com/magazine/2016/09/26/fleabag-an-original-bad-girl-comedy.

Nussbaum, Emily. 2018. 'The Home-Cooked Pleasures of "Please Like Me"'. *The New Yorker,* 19 November. Accessed 15 March 2024. https://www.newyorker.com/magazine/2018/11/26/the-home-cooked-pleasures-of-please-like-me.

Odets, Wats. 2019. *Out of the Shadows: The Psychology of Gay Men's Lives.* London: Penguin UK.

Okundaye, Jason. 2019. 'Sex Education's Vital, Complex Portrayal of Black Queer Teenhood'. *Dazed,* 22 January. Accessed 14 June 2024. https://www.dazeddigital.com/film-tv/article/43014/1/sex-education-eric-netflix-black-queer-teens-ncuti-gatwa.

Olufemi, Lola. 2020. *Feminism, Interrupted: Disrupting Power.* London: Pluto Press.

Onyekweli, Nonny. 2020. 'I May Destroy You Changed the Way My Friends and I Talk About Consent'. *Slate,* 4 September. Accessed 13 March 2024. https://slate.com/culture/2020/09/i-may-destroy-you-consent-metoo.html.

Oppliger, Patrice. 2022. *Transmasculinity on Television.* New York: Routledge.

Ortega, Teresa. 2008. 'Latina Characters on "The L Word"'. *AfterEllen*, 9 March. Accessed 16 November 2023. https://afterellen.com/latina-characters-on-the-l-word/.

Pattillo, Alice. 2022. 'Rediscovering Queer As Folk: The Groundbreaking UK Series Years Ahead of Its Time'. *Den of Geek*, 19 August. Accessed 16 November 2023. https://www.denofgeek.com/tv/rediscovering-queer-as-folk/.

Pearl, Monica B. 2023. 'Tell the Story of a Virus'. *European Journal of Cultural Studies*, 26(1): 110–14.

Pensis, Eva. 2019. '"Running Up That Hill" On Love, Sex, and Work in *Pose*'. *Journal of Popular Music Studies,* 31(2): 15–24.

Petter, Olivia. 2021. 'And Just Like That's Shocking Twist Betrayed Everything Sex and the City Was About'. *The Independent*, 11 December. Accessed 16 November 2023. https://www.independent.co.uk/arts-entertainment/tv/features/and-just-like-that-sex-and-the-city-betrayal-big-death-b1973512.html.

Phipps, Alison. 2020. *Me, Not You: The Trouble With Mainstream Feminism.* Manchester: Manchester University Press.

Price, Devon. 2022. *Unmasking Autism: The Power of Embracing Our Hidden Neurodiversity.* New York: Hachette.

Probyn, Elspeth. 2005. *Blush: Faces of Shame*. Minneapolis and London: University of Minnesota Press.

Puar, Jasbir. 2007. *Terrorist Assemblages: Homonationalism in Queer Times*. Durham: Duke University Press.

Qobrtay, Ameena. 2021. 'Move over "Euphoria", "Sex Education" is Generation Z's Staple Show'. *The Daily Targum*, 30 September. Accessed 1 March 2024. https://dailytargum.com/article/2021/09/move-over-euphoria-sex-education-is-generation-zs-staple-show.

Raghavan, Priya. 2023. 'Resisting the Binary: Reconciling Victimhood and Agency in Discourses of Sexual Violence'. *Feminist Theory*, online first.

Rajan, Rajeswari Sunder. 1993. *Real and Imagined Women: Gender, Culture and Postcolonialism*. London and New York: Routledge.

Rao, Rahul. 2015. 'Global Homocapitalism'. *Radical Philosophy*, 194 (Nov/Dec): 38–49.

Rao, Rahul. 2020. *Out of Time: The Queer Politics of Postcoloniality*. New York: Oxford University Press.

Rich, Adrienne. 1980. 'Compulsory Heterosexuality and Lesbian Existence'. *Signs: Journal of Women in Culture and Society*, 5(4): 631–60.

Rich, B. Ruby. 2013. *New Queer Cinema: The Director's Cut*. Durham: Duke University Press.

Riggs, Damien W. 2006. 'Priscilla, (White) Queen of the Desert: Queer Politics and Representation in a "Postcolonising" Nation'. *Gender Forum: An Internet Journal for Gender Studies*, 14: 38–55.

Ringrose, Jessica and Walkerdine, Valerie. 2008. 'Regulating the Abject: The TV Make-Over as Site of Neo-Liberal Reinvention toward Bourgeois Femininity'. *Feminist Media Studies*, 8(3): 227–46.

Rivas-Lara, Stephanie, Kotecha, Hiral, Pham, Becky and Yalda, T. Uhls. 2023. *CSS Teens & Screens 2023: Romance or Nomance*. Los Angeles: Center for Scholars & Storytellers. https://www.scholarsandstorytellers.com/css-teens-and-screens-2023-report.

Rottenberg, Catherine. 2014. 'The Rise of Neoliberal Feminism'. *Cultural Studies*, 28(3): 418–37.

Rubin, Gayle. 1984. 'Thinking Sex: Notes for a Radical Theory of the Politics of Sexuality'. In Carol S. Vance (ed.), *Pleasure and Danger: Exploring Female Sexuality*. New York: Routledge.

Rudy, Kathy. 2001. 'Radical Feminism, Lesbian Separatism, and Queer Theory'. *Feminist Studies*, 27(1): 191–222.

Runswick-Cole, Katherine. 2014. '"Us' and 'Them": The Limits and Possibilities of a "Politics of Neurodiversity" in Neoliberal Times'. *Disability & Society*, 29(7): 1117–29.

Russon, Penni. 2024. 'Why Heartstopper is Gen Z's Defining Publishing Phenomenon'. *The Conversation*, 6 February. Accessed 15 March 2024. https://theconversation.com/why-heartstopper-is-gen-zs-defining-publishing-phenomenon-221726.

Salam, Maya. 2021. 'Mae Martin Embraces Ambiguity in "Feel Good", and in Life'. *New York Times*, 24 May. Accessed 18 November 2022. https://www.nytimes.com/2021/05/24/arts/television/mae-martin-feel-good-netflix.html.

Samutina, Natalia. 2016. 'Fan Fiction as World-Building: Transformative Reception in Crossover Writing'. *Continuum*, 30(4): 433–50.

Saner, Emine. 2023. 'The Rise of Voluntary Celibacy: "Most of the Sex I've Had, I Wish I Hadn't Bothered"'. *The Guardian*, 26 April. Accessed 4 March 2024. https://www.theguardian.com/lifeandstyle/2023/apr/26/the-rise-of-voluntary-celibacy-most-of-the-sex-ive-had-i-wish-i-hadnt-bothered.

Scharff, Christina. 2016. *Repudiating Feminism: Young Women in a Neoliberal World*. London: Routledge.

Schippers, Mimi. 2019. *Polyamory, Monogamy, and American Dreams: The Stories We Tell About Poly Lives and the Cultural Production of Inequality*. London and New York: Routledge.

Schulman, Sarah. 2016. *Conflict is Not Abuse: Overstating Harm, Community Responsibility, and the Duty of Repair*. Vancouver: Arsenal Pulp Press.

Schulman, Sarah. 2021. *Let The Record Show: A Political History of ACT UP New York, 1987-1993*. New York: Farrar, Straus and Giroux.

Scott, Kellie. 2019. 'When Bad Sex Isn't Just a One-Off, But Your Life'. *ABC*, 23 April. Accessed 4 March 2024. https://www.abc.net.au/everyday/when-bad-sex-isnt-just-a-one-off-but-your-life/11004236.

Sedgwick, Eve Kosofsky. 2003. *Touching Feeling: Affect, Pedagogy, Performativity*. Durham: Duke University Press.

Sedgwick, Eve Kosofsky and Frank, Adam. 1995. 'Shame in the Cybernetic Fold: Reading Silvan Tomkins'. *Critical Inquiry*, 21(2): 496–522.

Seresin, Asa. 2019. 'On Heteropessimism'. *The New Inquiry*, 9 October. Accessed 30 July 2024. https://thenewinquiry.com/on-heteropessimism/.

Sexton, Jared. 2017. *Black Masculinity and the Cinema of Policing*. New York: Palgrave Macmillan.

Sharpe, Christina. 2016. *In the Wake: On Blackness and Being*. Durham: Duke University Press.

Siddiqui, Sophia. 2021. 'Racing the Nation: Towards a Theory of Reproductive Racism'. *Race & Class*, 63(2): 3–20.

Silverman, Gillian and Hagelin, Sarah. 2018. 'Shame TV: Feminist Anti Aspirationalism in HBO's *Girls*'. *Signs: Journal of Women in Culture and Society*, 43(4): 877–904.

Skeggs, Beverley. 1997. *Formations of Class and Gender: Becoming Respectable*. London: Sage.

Smith, Barbara and Smith, Beverly. 1981. 'Across the Kitchen Table: A Sister-to-Sister Dialogue'. In Moraga, Cherríe and Gloria Anzaldúa (eds), *This Bridge Called My Back: Writings by Radical Women of Color*. New York: Kitchen Table, Women of Colour Press, 113–27.

Sobande, Francesca. 2019a. 'Awkward Black Girls and Post-Feminist Possibilities: Representing Millennial Black Women on Television in *Chewing Gum* and *Insecure*'. *Critical Studies in Television*, 14(4): 435–50.

Sobande, Francesca. 2019b. 'Woke-Washing: "Intersectional" Femvertising and Branding "Woke" Bravery'. *European Journal of Marketing*, 54(11): 2723–45.

Soldatic, Karen. 2017. 'Postcolonial Reproductions: Disability, Indigeneity and the Formation of the White Masculine Settler State of Australia'. In Soldatic, Karen and Sean Grech (eds), *Disability and Colonialism: (Dis)encounters and Anxious Intersectionalities*. London and New York: Routledge, 63–78.

Sørensen, Inge E. 2022. 'Sex and Safety on Set: Intimacy Coordinators in Television Drama and Film in the VOD and post-Weinstein Era'. *Feminist Media Studies*, 22(6): 1395–410.

Srinivasan, Amia. 2022. *The Right to Sex*. London: Bloomsbury Publishing.

St James, Emily. 2013. 'The Golden Age of TV is Dead; Long Live the Golden Age of TV'. *AV Club*, 20 September. Accessed 4 March 2024. https://www.avclub.com/the-golden-age-of-tv-is-dead-long-live-the-golden-age-1798240704.

Stamm, Laura. 2020. 'Pose and HIV/AIDS: The Creation of a Trans-of-Color Past'. *TSQ: Transgender Studies Quarterly*, 7(4): 615–24.

Staples, Louis. 2019a. 'I'm Glad There's an Online Thirst-Fest over Andrew Scott's *Fleabag* Character'. *The Independent*, 31 March. Accessed 30 June 2020. https://www.independent.co.uk/voices/fleabag-andrew-scott-hot-priest-gay-man-lgbt-heart-throb-season-two-phoebe-wallerbridge-a8848031.html.

Staples, Louis. 2019b. 'Twenty Years on, Queer as Folk Remains a More Radical and Fearless Tribute to Gay Life Than Many LGBT+ Shows Today'. *The Independent*, 23 February. Accessed 16 November 2023. https://www.independent.co.uk/voices/queer-as-folk-stuart-vince-nathan-russell-t-davies-lgbtq-discrimination-tv-culture-20th-anniversary-a8793316.html.

Steiner, Emil and Xu, Kun. 2020. 'Binge-Watching Motivates Change: Uses and Gratifications of Streaming Video Viewers Challenge Traditional TV Research'. *Convergence*, 26(1): 82–101.

Stockton, Kathryn Bond. 2006. *Beautiful Bottom, Beautiful Shame: Where "Black" Meets "Queer"*. Durham: Duke University Press.

Stringer, Rebecca. 2014. *Knowing Victims: Feminism, Agency and Victim Politics in Neo-Liberal Times*. London and New York: Routledge.

Sulimma, Maria. 2022. *Gender and Seriality: Practices and Politics of Contemporary US Television*. Edinburgh: Edinburgh University Press.

Taylor, Magdalene. 2023. 'Have More Sex, Please!'. *The New York Times*, 13 February. Accessed 4 March 2023. https://www.nytimes.com/2023/02/13/opinion/have-more-sex-please.html?smid=nytcore-ios-share&referringSource=articleShare.

The Guardian. 2019. '"Mouthful by Mouthful": The 2019 Bad Sex Award in Quotes'. *The Guardian*, 27 November. Accessed 4 March 2023. https://www.theguardian.com/books/2019/nov/27/mouthful-by-mouthful-the-2019-bad-sex-award-in-quotes.

The Guardian. 2023. 'The Guardian View on Heartstopper: A Phenomenon that Defines a Generation'. Accessed 14 June 2024. https://www.theguardian.com/commentisfree/2023/aug/03/the-guardian-view-on-heartstopper-a-phenomenon-that-defines-a-generation.

Toomer, Jessica. 2019. 'How "Sex Education" Is a Series Tailored for the Gen Z Crowd'. *The Hollywood Reporter*, 1 February. Accessed 1 March 2024. https://www.hollywoodreporter.com/tv/tv-news/how-sex-education-is-a-series-tailored-gen-z-crowd-1181844/.

Trimmel, Theresa. 2018. 'TV's New Sexual Narratives? Unconventional Sex and Intimacy in *Transparent* and *Broad* City'. *MAI: Feminism & Visual Culture*, 2. Accessed 5 August 2024. https://maifeminism.com/tvs-new-sexual-narratives-unconventional-sex-and-intimacy-in-transparent-and-broad-city/.

Tyler, Imogen. 2008. 'Chav Mum Chav Scum: Class Disgust in Contemporary Britain'. *Feminist Media Studies*, 8(1): 17–34.

Ueda, Peter, Mercer, Catherine H., Ghaznavi, Cyrus and Herbenick, Debby. 2020. 'Trends in Frequency of Sexual Activity and Number of Sexual Partners Among Adults Aged 18 to 44 years in the US, 2000-2018'. *JAMA Network Open*, 3(6): e203833–e203833.

Upton, Mike. 2023. '"They Won't Wear Condoms, so Why Would we Expect them to Wear Masks?": Social Media, "Circuit Queens" and the "Gay Civil War" during COVID-19'. *Sexualities*, 1–20.

Van Esler, Mike. 2020. 'Reproducing Television Canons: Streaming Services and the Legacy of Linear TV'. *Journal of Popular Culture*, 53(4): 946–66.

Waggoner, Erin B. 2018. 'Bury Your Gays and Social Media Fan Response: Television, LGBTQ Representation, and Communitarian Ethics'. *Journal of Homosexuality*, 65(13): 1877–91.

Wahlquist, Calla. 2016. 'Actor Jack Charles Calls for Training for Taxi Drivers after Being Refused Service'. *The Guardian*, 14 April. Accessed 15 March 2024. https://www.theguardian.com/australia-news/2016/apr/14/indigenous-actor-jack-charles-to-take-on-taxi-drivers-for-racial-profiling.

Wanzo, Rebecca. 2016. 'Precarious-Girl Comedy: Issa Rae, Lena Dunham, and Abjection Aesthetics'. *Camera Obscura*, 31(2): 27–59.

Ward, Jane. 2020. *The Tragedy of Heterosexuality*. New York: New York University Press.

Warner, Michael. 2000. *The Trouble with Normal: Sex, Politics and the Ethics of Queer Life*. Cambridge: Harvard University Press.

Waters, Terri. 2021. 'How Sex and the City Changed the Narrative around Female Sexuality'. *The Unedit*, 15 January. Accessed 16 November 2023. https://www.the-unedit.com/posts/2021/1/15/how-sex-and-the-city-changed-the-narrative-around-female-sexuality.

Wearing, Sadie. 2013. 'Dementia and the Biopolitics of the Biopic: From *Iris* to the *Iron Lady*'. *Dementia*. 12(3): 315–25.

Wellings Kaye, Palmer Melissa J., Machiyama, Kazuyo and Slaymaker, Emma. 2019. 'Changes in, and Factors Associated with, Frequency of Sex in

Britain: Evidence from Three National Surveys of Sexual Attitudes and Lifestyles (Natsal)'. *BMJ*, 365: l1525.

Wignall, Liam, et al. 2021. 'Changes in Sexual Desire and Behaviors among UK Young Adults During Social Lockdown Due to COVID-19'. *The Journal of Sex Research*, 58(8): 976–85.

Williams, Apryl and Gonlin, Vanessa. 2017. 'I Got All My Sisters With Me (on Black Twitter): Second Screening of *How to Get Away with Murder* as a Discourse on Black Womanhood'. *Information, Communication & Society*, 20(7): 984–1004.

Williams, Raymond. 1977. *Marxism and Literature*. Oxford and New York: Oxford University Press.

Williams, Zoe. 2017. 'Too Closure for Comfort: the Death of Definitive TV Endings'. *The Guardian*, 24 April. Accessed 16 November 2023. https://www.theguardian.com/tv-and-radio/2017/apr/24/tv-endings-breaking-bad-walking-dead-big-little-lies.

Williams, Zoe. 2022. 'Involuntary Celibacy is a Genuine Problem, But a 'Right to Sex' is Not the Answer'. *The Guardian*, 20 October. Accessed 4 March 2024. https://www.theguardian.com/commentisfree/2022/oct/20/involuntary-celibacy-incels-problem-right-to-sex-not-the-answer.

Williams, Zoe. 2023. 'Why Do So Many people Still Love Friends? Because it Reminds Them of a Time When Life Was Still Fun'. *The Guardian*, 30 October. Accessed 16 November 2023. https://www.theguardian.com/commentisfree/2023/oct/30/why-do-so-many-people-still-love-friends-because-it-reminds-them-of-a-time-when-life-was-still-fun.

Willingham, Emily. 2022. 'People Have Been Having Less Sex—whether They're Teenagers or 40-Somethings'. *Scientific American*, 3 January. Accessed 3 March 2024. https://www.scientificamerican.com/article/people-have-been-having-less-sex-whether-theyre-teenagers-or-40-somethings/.

Winnicott, Donald W. 2016. *The Collected Works of DW Winnicott*. Oxford: Oxford University Press.

Wiseman, Eva. 2022. 'A Friend Told Me She Had "Bad Sex" With A Mutual Acquaintance While Drunk. Should I Call Him Out On It?'. *British Vogue*, 21 October. Accessed 15 March 2024. https://www.vogue.co.uk/arts-and-lifestyle/article/bad-drunken-sex.

Wittig, Monique. 1992. *The Straight Mind: And Other Essays*. Boston: Beacon Press.

Woodard, Elise. 2022. 'Bad Sex and Consent'. In Boonin, David (ed.), *The Palgrave Handbook of Sexual Ethics*. Cham: Palgrave Macmillan, 301–39.

Woods, Faye. 2019. 'Too Close for Comfort: Direct Address and the Affective Pull of the Confessional Comic Woman in *Chewing Gum* and *Fleabag*'. *Communication, Culture & Critique*, 12: 194–212.

Yagoda, Maria. 2023. 'Why Everyone Is Having Bad Sex (Especially Young People)'. *Time*, 31 May. Accessed 4 March 2024, https://time.com/6283422/bad-sex-young-people/.

Young, Chanté-Marie. 2024. 'Euphoria is Gen Z's Most Honest Portrayal of Teen Life Yet'. *Yes Gurl*, no date. Accessed 1 March 2024. https://yesgurl.co.uk/euphoria-is-gen-zs/.

Young, Stella. 2014. 'I'm Not Your Inspiration, Thank You Very Much'. *TedxSydney*, April. Accessed 15 March 2024. https://www.ted.com/talks/stella_young_i_m_not_your_inspiration_thank_you_very_much/transcript.

Żerebecki Bartosz G., Opree Susanna J., Hofhuis, Joep and Janssen, Susanne. 2021. 'Can TV Shows Promote Acceptance of Sexual and Ethnic Minorities? A Literature Review of Television Effects on Diversity Attitudes'. *Sociology Compass*, 15(8): e12906.

Zhao, Valerie. 2020. 'Opinion: Showing Teenagers in Sexually Explicit Scenes Has Detrimental Effects'. *Through Teen Lenses*, 29 August. Accessed 1 March 2024. https://www.throughteenlenses.com/post/opinion-showing-teenagers-in-sexually-explicit-scenes-has-detrimental-effects.

TV SHOW AND FILM BIBLIOGRAPHY

A League of Their Own. 2022. Television Series. Season 1. US: Amazon Prime.
And Just Like That . . .. 2021–. Television Series. Season 1. US: HBO Max.
Angels in America. 2003. Television Series. Season 1. US: HBO.
Are You the One? 2019. Reality Television Show. Season 8. US: MTV.
Baby Reindeer. 2024. Television Series. Season 1. UK: Netflix.
Banana. 2015. Television Series. Season 1. UK: Channel 4.
Basic Instinct. 1992. Film. US: Tristar Pictures.
Beef. 2023. Television Series. Season 1. US: Netflix
Better Things. 2016–22. Television Series. Seasons 1–5. US: FX.
Big Little Lies. 2017, 2019. Television Series. Seasons 1–2. US: HBO.
Blue is the Warmest Colour. 2013. Film. France: Wildbunch.
Boys Don't Cry. 1999. Film. US: Independent Film Channel Productions.
Breaking Bad. 2008–13. Television Series. Seasons 1–4. US: AMC.
Bridget Jones's Diary. 2001. Film. UK: Universal Picture.
Broad City. 2014–19. Television Series. Seasons 1–5. US: Comedy Central.
Catastrophe. 2015–19. Television Series. Seasons 1–4. UK: Channel 4.
Chewing Gum. 2015, 2017. Television Series. Seasons 1–2. UK: E4.
Couple to Throuple. 2024. Reality Television Show. Season 1. US: Peacock.
Cucumber. 2015. Television Series. Season 1. UK: Channel 4.
Ellen. 1994–98. Television Series. Seasons 1–5. US: ABC.
Euphoria. 2019–. Television Series. Seasons 1–2. US: HBO.
Everything Now. 2023. Television Series. Season 1. UK: Netflix.
Feel Good. 2020–21.Television Series. Seasons 1–2. UK: Channel 4.
Fifty Shades of Grey. 2015. Film. US: Focus Features.
Fleabag. 2016, 2019. Television Series. Seasons 1–2. UK: BBC.
Fresh Prince of Bel-Air. 1990–96. Television Series. Seasons 1–6. US: NBC.
Friends. 1994–2004. Television Series. Seasons 1–10. US: NBC.
Full House. 1987–95. Television Series. Seasons 1–8. US: ABC.
Girls. 2012–17.Television Series. Seasons 1–6. US: HBO.
Glow. 2017–19. Television Series. Seasons 1–3. US: Netflix.
Gossip Girl. 2021–23. Television Series. Seasons 1–2. US: HBO.
Heartbreak High. 2022–. Television Series. Season 1. Australia: Netflix.
Heartstopper. 2022–. Television Series. Seasons 1–2. US: Netflix.
How I Met Your Mother. 2005–14. Television Series. Seasons 1–9. US: CBS.
I Kissed a Boy. 2023–. Reality Television Show. UK: BBC.
I Kissed a Girl. 2024–. Reality Television Show. UK: BBC.
I Love Dick. 2016–17. Television Series. Season 1. US: Amazon Prime.
I May Destroy You. 2020. Television Series. Season 1. UK: BBC.
Insecure. 2016–21. Television Series. Season 1–5. US: HBO.

It's a Sin. 2021. Television Series. Season 1. UK: Channel 4.
Juice. 2023. Television Series. Season 1. UK: BBC.
Kids. 1995. Film. US: Independent Pictures.
Killing Eve. 2018–22. Television Series. UK: BBC.
Looking. 2014–15. Television Series. Seasons 1–2. US: HBO.
Mad Men. 2007–15. Television Series. Seasons 1–7. US: AMC.
Master of None. 2015–21. Television Series. Seasons 1--3. US: Netflix.
Never Have I Ever. 2020–23. Television Series. Seasons 1–4. US: Netflix.
Normal People. 2020. Television Series. Season 1. UK: BBC3, RTE One, Hulu.
Notting Hill. 1999. Film. UK: PolyGram Film Entertainment.
One Day. 2024. Television Series. Season 1. UK: Netflix.
Paris is Burning. Film. US: Miramax.
Peep Show. 2003–15. Television Series. Seasons 1–9. UK: Channel 4.
Philadelphia. 1993. Film. US: Tristar Pictures.
Please Like Me. 2013–16. Television Series. Seasons 1–4. Australia: Netflix.
Pose. 2018–21. Television Series. Seasons 1–3. US: FX.
Pretty Woman. 1990. Film. US: Touchstone Pictures.
Pride. 2014. Film. UK: Pathé.
Queer as Folk. 1999–2000. Television Series. Seasons 1–2. UK: Channel 4.
Queer as Folk. 2000–05. Television Series. Seasons 1–5. US: Showtime.
Queer as Folk. 2022. Television Series. Season 1. US: Peacock.
Queer Eye. 2018–. Reality Television Show. US: Netflix.
Roseanne. 1988–97. Television Series. Seasons 1–10. US: ABC.
Ru Paul's Drag Race. 2009–. Reality Television Show. US: Logot TV, VH1, MTV.
Sex and the City. 1998–2004. Television Series. Seasons 1–6. US: HBO.
Sex and the City. 2008. Film. US: New Line Cinema, HBO.
Sex Education. 2019–23. Television Series. Seasons 1–4. UK: Netflix.
Sexify. 2021. Television Series. Season 1. Poland: Netflix.
Sharp Objects. 2018. Television Series. Seasons 1. US: HBO.
Shrill. 2019–21. Television Series. Seasons 1–3. US: Hulu.
Sort Of. 2021–23. Television Series. Season 1–3. Canada: CBC.
Special. 2019, 2021. Television Series. Seasons 1–2. US: Netflix.
St Elmo's Fire. 1985. Film. US: Channel-Lauren Shuler.
Starstruck. 2021–. Television Series. Seasons 1–3. UK: BBC.
The Adventures of Priscilla, Queen of the Desert. 1994. Film. Australia: PolyGram Filmed Entertainment.
The Big Bang Theory. 2007–19. Television Series. Seasons 1–12. US: CBS.
The Bisexual. 2018. Television Series. Season 1. UK and US: Channel 4 and Hulu.
The Idol. 2023. Television Series. Season 1. US: HBO.
The Inbetweeners. 2012. Television Series. Season 1. US: MTV.
The L Word. 2004–9. Television Series. Seasons 1–6. US: Showtime.
The L Word: Generation Q. 2019–23. Television Series. Seasons 1–3. US: Showtime.

The Real L Word. 2010–12. Reality Television Show. US: Showtime.
The Sopranos. 1999–2007. Television Series. Seasons 1–6. US: HBO.
The Ultimatum: Queer Love. 2023. Reality Television Show. Season 1. US: Netflix.
The Wire. 2002–08. Television Series. Seasons 1–5. US: HBO.
This Way Up. 2019–21. Television Series. Seasons 1–2. UK: Channel 4.
Transparent. 2014–19. Television Series. Seasons 1–5. US: Amazon Prime.
Twenties. 2020–21. Television Series. Seasons 1–2. US: BET.
Vida. 2018–20. Television Series. Seasons 1–3. US: Starz.
Wall Street. 1987. Film. US: American Entertainment Partners.
Will & Grace. 1998–2006; 2017–20. Television Series. Season 1–11. US: NBC.
Work In Progress. 2019, 2021. Television Series. Seasons 1–2. US: Showtime.
Working Girl. 1988. Film. US: 20th Century Fox.

INDEX